Ireland encastellated, AD *950–1550*

Ireland encastellated, AD 950–1550

Insular castle-building in its European context

Tadhg O'Keeffe

FOUR COURTS PRESS

Set in 10.5pt on 12.5pt Bembo by
Carrigboy Typesetting Services for
FOUR COURTS PRESS LTD
7 Malpas Street, Dublin 8, Ireland
www.fourcourtspress.ie
and in North America by
FOUR COURTS PRESS
c/o IPG, 814 N Franklin St, Chicago, IL 60610.

A catalogue record for this title
is available from the British Library.

ISBN 978–1–84682–863–8

Frontispiece: Tullowmacjames Castle (Tipperary)

Printed in England,
by CPI Antony Rowe, Chippenham, Wilts.

For beautiful Anne-Elise

*may you always remember the fun we had when
we explored castles together*

Contents

Illustrations

A NOTE ON ILLUSTRATIONS

Plans and sections are redrawn from many sources, sometimes with small modifications. The sources should be apparent from the accompanying text.

Abbreviations

AC	*Annála Connacht: the Annals of Connacht,* AD 1224–1544, ed. A.M. Freeman (Dublin, 1944)
AClon.	*The Annals of Clonmacnoise,* ed. and trans. Denis Murphy (Dublin, 1896)
AFM	*Annals of the kingdom of Ireland by the Four Masters,* ed. and trans. J. O'Donovan, 7 vols (Dublin, 1851)
AI	*Archaeology Ireland*
AIn.	*The Annals of Inisfallen,* ed. and trans. S. Mac Airt (Dublin, 1951)
AJ	*The Archaeological Journal*
ALC	*The Annals of Lough Cé,* ed. W.M. Hennessy, 2 vols (London, 1871)
AM	*Archéologie médiévale*
AT	'The Annals of Tigernach', ed. and trans. W. Stokes, *Revue Celtique,* 16 (1895), 374–419
AU	*Annála Uladh, Annals of Ulster,* ed. W.M. Hennessy and B. MacCarthy, 4 vols (Dublin, 1887–1901)
BM	*Bulletin Monumental*
CCM	*Cahiers de Civilisation Médiévale*
CDI	*Calendar of documents relating to Ireland,* ed. H.S. Sweetman, 5 vols (London, 1875–86)
CELT	Corpus of Electronic Texts [www.ucc.ie/celt]
CG	*Château Gaillard: études de castellologie médiévale*
CS	*Chronicon Scotorum,* ed. W.M. Hennessy (London, 1866)
CSGJ	*The Castle Studies Group Journal*
DIB online	*Dictionary of Irish biography* [https://dib.cambridge.org]
DMLBS	*Dictionary of medieval Latin from British sources* (London: British Academy, 1975–2013) [https://logeion.uchicago.edu]
eDIL	*Electronic dictionary of the Irish language,* eds Gregory Toner, Máire Ní Mhaonaigh, Sharon Arbuthnot, Marie-Luise Theuerkauf and Dagmar Wodtko (www.dil.ie 2019)
JBAA	*Journal of the British Archaeological Association*
JCHAS	*Journal of the Cork Historical and Archaeological Society*
JGAHS	*Journal of the Galway Archaeological and Historical Society*
JIA	*Journal of Irish Archaeology*
JMH	*Journal of Medieval History*
JRSAI	*Journal of the Royal Society of Antiquaries of Ireland*
MA	*Medieval Archaeology*
MGH	*Monumenta Germaniae Historica* (1826+)
MIA	*Miscellaneous Irish Annals,* AD 1114–1437, ed. S. Ó hInnse (Dublin, 1947)
NLI	National Library of Ireland
NMAJ	*North Munster Antiquarian Journal*
PRIA	*Proceedings of the Irish Academy*
UJA	*Ulster Journal of Archaeology*

A note on placenames

To eliminate repetition, county, shire or département names are given for sites when they are first mentioned in the text but not thereafter. They are also given in the index. In certain cases (the names of cities, or of places that have the same names as their counties/shires) such extra geographical information is deemed unnecessary. For England, Wales and Scotland, the pre-1974 county divisions are used.

Map 1

Map 1. Sites in Ireland mentioned in the text

Map 2 15

Map 2. Sites in Britain mentioned in the text

Map 3. Sites in France mentioned in the text

CHAPTER I

Introduction

At the edge of the village of Bruree (Limerick), in the townland of Lotteragh Upper, stands a single late medieval tower of relatively little architectural distinction. It is the only substantial remnant of a multi-period enclosure castle which was intact a century ago. The tower is an insert into an older wall of demonstrable pre-Norman date, very short stretches of which survive (Fig. 1). That original wall is all that remains of *Dún Eochair Maige*, constructed by the king of Munster, Brian Bóraime (*c*.941–1014), at the very start of the eleventh century.[1]

The documentary source which gives us its date and patron, *Cogadh Gáedhel re Gallaibh*, a propaganda piece commissioned in the early twelfth century by King Muirchertach Ua Briain (reigned 1086–1114) to glorify Brian, conveys the impression of a fortress with a solely strategic *raison d'être*. But the architectural evidence suggests that *Dún Eochair Maige* was intended to be much more than a garrisoned marker of territory. The effort that went into its construction was too great. The wall, of which that small fragment survives, was originally about 5m high, over 2m thick at the base and over 1m thick at the top, and it ran in an oval loop for a total length of approximately 175m. The stones quarried for it were cut into square or rectangular blocks and dressed with flat faces, which would have involved a significant additional and, from a practical perspective, unnecessary investment of time, and a substantial volume of lime mortar was mixed as a bonding agent. Its builders had know-how: the laying of the stones in regular horizontal courses imitated the practice in contemporary church-building – one imagines the comparison was intended to register among those who saw the fortress – and the consistent batter on the wall suggests careful attention to its structural stability.

Were there no record of its construction, one would still conclude that the pre-Norman enclosure in Lotteragh Upper was, first, a product of coercive lordship, and second, a monument informed in its design and structure to some degree by knowledge of architecture outside Ireland. On the former point, one cannot conceive reasonably of a monument like this being erected unless a substantial labour force was directed to work on it by a seigneurial power with both control of the requisite resources and a desire to impress. On the latter point, it was not – insofar as the evidence to date permits the claim – a monument in a tradition attested to archaeologically in Ireland in the first millennium AD; while the oval plan was unusual but not unique, earlier stone forts did not have such high and thin walls, stones cut to

1 O'Keeffe and MacCotter 2020.

1 A view of the castle in Lotteragh Upper from inside the former enclosure. The coursed walling on the right-hand side survives from *Dún Eochair Maige* (see also Fig. 39). A lot of its mortar has been washed out. Some walling also survives on the other side of the late medieval tower. Ground level inside the former enclosure is higher today than it was in the Middle Ages.

2 Two enclosures of *c.*1000: the *castrum* of Andone, and *Dún Eochair Maige* (as recorded in the mid-nineteenth century). The structures inside the Andone enclosure are contemporary with it; those in the north-east corner were a large hall or ceremonial room (above a service room) and two adjacent chambers, while those in the south-west corner include a stable and a forge.

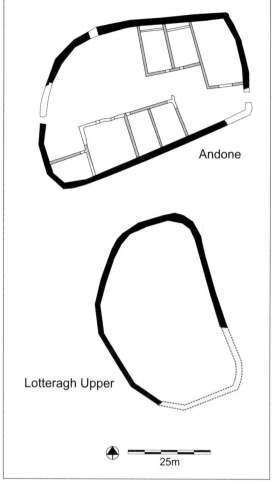

Andone

Lotteragh Upper

25m

size, or mortar. The best parallel for the Lotteragh Upper enclosure in terms of ground plan happens to be in France and to be of the same approximate date: it is the *castrum* of Andone (Charente), established in the 970s and abandoned before 1030 (Fig. 2).[2]

The identification of the enclosure in Lotteragh Upper as Brian Bóraime's *Dún Eochair Maige* makes contextual sense: royal patronage best explains its character within the pre-Norman context in Ireland, and the militarist species of overlordship exercised by Brian, according to *Cogadh Gáedhel re Gallaibh*, compares not unfavourably in principle with that of contemporary magnates in Capetian France, such as Fulk Nerra, count of Anjou (*c.*970–1040).[3] I have no doubt that a French scholar reviewing Brian's career in Ireland in the late tenth and early eleventh centuries would have little difficulty imagining him as a 'feudal' castle-builder, and would probably expect the fortress outside Bruree to be described in the sources as a *castrum* or *castellum*. Although

2 Bourgeois 2009.   **3** O'Keeffe 2019a. For Brian Bóraime see Ní Mhaonaigh 2007; for Fulk Nerra see Bachrach 1993.

very primitive indeed by the extraordinary standard of Fulk Nerra's work, its date of *c.*1000 would not be problematic from an architectural-historical perspective, as the Andone parallel reveals. The only query might be in respect of its geographical location: Ireland?

A EUROPEAN DEBATE

For most of the second half of the twentieth century, a period of animated debate on the early history of encastellation in Europe, scholars almost everywhere subscribed to the view that castles originated in France in the context of the late tenth-century collapse, following a century of decline, of Carolingian hegemony, and the subsequent, if not causative, emergence of feudalism.[4] Indeed, Michel de Boüard, the father of French medieval archaeology, confidently insisted in 1980 that the birthplace of the castle was specifically north-central France, between the middle Loire valley and the Rhineland.[5] His opinion was informed to no small degree by his discovery through excavation that a motte at Doué-la-Fontaine (Maine-et-Loire) concealed an unfortified residential building of tenth-century date.[6] De Boüard made no reference to then-current thinking on feudalism in his report on Doué-la-Fontaine, but the association of castle-building with feudalism was by then already firmly established in the minds of historians.[7] Michel Bur boldly proclaimed in 1982 that the motte, as a specific type of castle, was 'a weapon' by which early Capetian lords imposed feudal order.[8] At the time, few would have described differently the motte's role in the transformation of England after 1066 by the Normans, or of Ireland after 1169 by the Anglo-Normans.

Castellologists (castle scholars, after the French *castellologie*, the study of castles) today would not challenge the central importance of the pre-millennium Loire Valley or, beyond it to the north-east, the Île-de-France, in the story of European castle-origins. But, inferring from the literature, and from its silences more than from its explicit assertions, it would seem that many scholars doubt that a pan-European phenomenon as complex as 'the castle' could have had a single moment of birth in a single region, even one as politically dynamic as north-central France. Such caution as has developed over the past quarter-century might be regarded as evidence of a push-back against the role of French historical scholarship in shaping the narrative of medieval *European* history; in such history, Timothy Reuter wryly noted, 'everything starts in France, from administration history, architecture and Arthurian romances, through chivalry, crusades and castles, to universities and water-mills'.[9] And it is probably part of the push-back against the historical veracity of feudalism itself,[10] or at least against the theory that feudalism had a 'big bang' birth in France shortly before AD 1000.[11] But this caution might also reflect a realization that a definition of 'castle' is actually irretrievable from medieval sources. No specific definition has passed down from the Middle Ages; even the authors of the famous *Consuetudines et iusticie*

---

4 See, for example, Durand 1999, 5.   5 De Boüard 1981, 9.   6 De Boüard 1973.   7 For example, Brown 1977.   8 Bur 1982.   9 Reuter 1997, 187–8.   10 Brown 1974; Reynolds 1994; Barthélemy 1997.   11 For that push-back see Barthelémy 2009. 'Big bang' is my phrase.

Normanniae (1091), which set out, among other things, the rights of Norman barons to build castles, 'found it difficult to define a castle'.[12] The absence of a definition, combined with the recent critiques of feudalism, has left castellologists with no real basis for continuing to privilege the middle Loire Valley over other erstwhile imperial regions in determining possible places of origin for the entire European stock of castles.

So, what other parts of Europe should be considered alongside northern France in discussing castle-origins? One is Italy, where a process of encastellation, *incastellamento*, is documented with unambiguous clarity as early as the start of the tenth century.[13] The 'castles' in question there were essentially fortified settlements within which lease-holding peasants lived. The communal nature of these fortifications might explain why castellologists, long believing castles to be 'private' fortifications, have paid little attention to the Italian evidence, but Charles Coulson's demonstration that medieval castles were not 'private', at least in the narrow modern sense of that word,[14] should provoke a rethink. Another region is east of the Rhine, where, in Nordrhein-Westphalia alone, near-square towers were built in the tenth century at Düren, Soest and Xanten.[15] While recent discoveries pertaining to the early history of donjons or keeps[16] have secured the pivotal importance of most of northern France, including Normandy, in the narrative of castle development in north-west Europe, the possibility of formative influence from Westphalia and Lower Saxony, located to the east again and formerly part of the Ottonian empire of tenth-century east Francia, cannot be dismissed.[17]

Ireland has barely featured in the pan-European conversation on the matter of castle-origins (a state of affairs not helped by, but certainly not to be blamed on, the fact that no attention was paid to the remarkable monument in Lotteragh Upper townland before its near-complete destruction in the past half-century). One can understand why that is the case. The earliest use in Ireland of a word which translates without controversy as castle – *caistél* – dates from the early twelfth century, which is very late by western European standards. Of course, the island's location at the edge of the Continent is also a factor. Omitted from the expansionist ambitions of the

---

12 Pounds 1990, 27. **13** See Miller 2009. For a detailed discussion of *incastellamento*, including its impact of settlement patterns, see Toubert 1973, *passim*, and Francovich 1998. See also p. 59 below. **14** They were, paradoxically, as he notes, 'private' because they were places of 'individual, familial, and dynastic' ownership, but they were 'at the same time institutionally (and, with varying capacity, also structurally) public places' (Coulson 2003, 182). **15** Fehring 1987, 110–11. **16** Donjon (from Old French; *dungun* in Anglo-Norman; see DMLBS) is used hereafter in this book; other versions used in the twelfth century include *dunjo* (see p. 44), *dungeo* and *dangio* (Latham 1965, 159); donjon seems to have connoted a great tower from the early thirteenth century (Trotter 2001). David Sweetman incorrectly asserted that donjon and keep refer conventionally to different things, the former being a strong tower and the latter a tower which contained 'long-term domestic quarters' (1999, 63). The term *tour maîtresse* was popularized in the French literature by Jean Mesqui (1991) but its translation – 'master tower' – has not been adopted in English-language literature. **17** De Boüard was familiar with the two episcopal towers, Soest and Xanten (1973, 88). The towers then featured in Herman Hinz's small book (1981). To this day, however, the Westphalian towers remain to be integrated into the narrative of the development of the donjon.

Roman empire-builders, and located at the periphery of the zones of influence of the great medieval *imperia*, of which the Carolingian was the most important, its geographical location has almost certainly encouraged the *prima facie* verdict that, viewed on the great European canvas, it was more likely to have been a place of imitation than of innovation. If its greatest post-1169 castles can occupy no more than (undeservedly) marginal places in the European narrative on castle-building culture, one can understand the indifference of European castellologists to the island's tiny corpus of poorly documented pre-1169 'castles'.

Oliver Creighton, recognizing that the first appearance of the term 'castle' does not necessarily mark the first appearance of the phenomenon that it customarily described, has been a lone advocate until now for the importance within European castle studies of the evidence for high-status fortified residences among the native, pre-1169, Irish.[18] Although he did not draw specific conclusions about the Irish evidence, he was absolutely right for three reasons to draw Ireland to the attention of international scholars interested in castle-origins.

First, as Luc Bourgeois has emphasized, knowledge of the forms and layouts of 'pre-castle' tenth-century (and earlier) sites of elite residence is so variable across western Europe that archaeologists have felt unable systematically to evaluate continuity and change between sites documented as 'castles' and the other (archaeologically-defined) types of elite site of the later first millennium.[19] Ireland is one of the few places in Europe where there is a good archaeological record, and a good record of archaeological investigation, from those critical centuries.[20]

Second, as Edward Impey has noted, the tradition of building donjons in France and England can be traced back to tenth-century northern and eastern France, but 'we cannot be … certain that the tradition itself had its origins in this area: towers are part of the common currency of architecture the world over, and were going up, certainly in an ecclesiastical context, in other areas of France and western Europe from at least the mid-ninth century'.[21] The importance of church towers, at least conceptually, in the developmental history of the donjon has not been explored much in the literature. This is surprising. Ecclesiastical fortifications are well documented from before the turn of the millennium.[22] Carolingian and Ottonian *Westwerken* were donjon-like in scale and, to a degree, in detailing and layout, and they commonly had upper chapels dedicated to St Michael, the saint associated with military endeavours.[23] Michael Shapland's exploration of the place of the Anglo-Saxon 'tower-nave' in the development of the donjon in England might now help to pave the way for a fresh appraisal.[24] The Irish Round Tower, which first appeared in the earlier tenth century (probably about the time that the first multi-floored donjons were being developed in

18 Creighton 2012, 41, 104, 106–7.   **19** Bourgeois 2006.   **20** By contrast, note, as has Peter Ettel, the need for more detailed work on the *Ungarnburgen* of southern Germany, reputedly erected in the late ninth and the first half of the tenth century to protect against Hungarian invasion (Ettel 2012a; 2012b).   **21** Impey 2008, 227.   **22** Bonde 1994, esp. 11–15.   **23** The dedication was not confined to structures which were fortified in appearance; chapels dedicated to St Michael were often in the porches and towers at the west ends of churches, thus allowing those spaces to be identified as conceptually protected. See Vallery-Radot 1929; Bonde 1994, *passim*.   **24** Shapland 2019.

3 The truncated early twelfth-century Round Tower at Dromiskin (Louth), which stood about 30m to the west of the medieval church, its doorway originally facing that of the church. The upper windows and conical roof date from the late Middle Ages.

northern France), really deserves to be considered within such an appraisal. It is conventionally associated with insular monasticism and regarded as a service building, its function being assumed to be that of an unconsecrated bell-tower. But I have argued at length that this is a misunderstanding that does a disservice to the European importance and interest of the type, including for castellologists.[25] There is evidence that the Round Tower was an actual form of church building (with a chapel at its summit), and was therefore in the tradition of the tall towers of later first millennium western Christendom. There is also evidence that it was a royal type, at least originally, and might have signified royal authority. That is noteworthy considering the royal, ducal or comital authorship of most of the earliest castle-towers in France. There is also reason to think that, because they were not needed for structural stability, the elevated doorways of the Irish Round Towers, especially those with sculptural elaboration, were 'display doorways', and were therefore in the tradition of the upper doorways in later donjons (Fig. 3).[26] This is not to say that the Irish towers were known about outside Ireland, and it is certainly not to claim that they were influential in any

25 O'Keeffe 2004a; 2009, 204. **26** For display doorways see Renn 1993; Marshall 2012.

way in the development of castle architecture. It is merely to draw attention to the fact that Ireland was not so peripheral to Continental Europe that it had no insular tradition of experimentation with the types of church tower which might well have contributed to the development of the donjon.

Third, that critique of feudalism and its beginnings which was spearheaded by Dominique Barthelémy in the 1990s allows the whole of the tenth century and the closing decades of the ninth to be enfolded more fully now into the problem of the birth of the medieval castle, thus moving the needle away from the late tenth century, the period suggested by Georges Duby in his influential work in the 1950s.[27] One does not need to accept the Barthelémy-led position on feudalism in its entirety to take from it a recognition that the social and political roles of fortifications and elite residences at the close of the tenth century cannot be understood without a lingering glance back in time to the age of Viking activity in the Carolingian empire, or to the creation of Normandy. Once the impact of the Vikings is invoked in the conversation on castle-origins, which contemporary documentation suggests is necessary, Ireland enters the frame, as does *Dún Eochair Maige*, the work of a later Viking-age native king in the Limerick region.

TOWARDS A NEW STUDY OF ENCASTELLATED IRELAND

The idea of writing this book originated in my realization that historical and archaeological evidence indicates clearly that Ireland does indeed, as Creighton wrote, merit inclusion in discussions about the early history of castle-building in Europe. Parts of a case were made in a paper that I published in 2019 (before the identification of *Dún Eochair Maige* as an actual early castle).[28] I argued there that concepts and practices of power in late first millennium Ireland compare with 'feudal' lordship in contemporary France, allowing one to conceive *in principle* of pre-Norman encastellation in Ireland. But I also cautioned that, any affirmative comparisons notwithstanding, the invocation of the concept of feudalism when analysing systems of power and the phenomenon of castle-building is actually unhelpful from the perspective of pre-1169 Ireland. This is because it privileges the French model of predatory lordship, itself now contested,[29] within an insular setting where there was never a declining hegemony – the Carolingian in the case of France – to begin with.

Rethinking Ireland's pre-1169 castles within their European context led me to ask some comparable questions of the post-1169 castles. How would I, were I an archaeologist or architectural historian based in some other part of north-western Europe, perceive Ireland's post-invasion castles? To elaborate, what structures in Ireland would appear to me to be typical of their periods? Would any of them seem to me to be innovative or radical by contemporary English or French standards? Would I interpret any divergence from the familiar as illustrative of the heterogeneity of

27 The point was made in Bourgeois 2011, 463. Duby 1953; Barthelémy 1992; 1997; 2009. **28** O'Keeffe 2019a. **29** For a critique of the concept of lordship itself, including in its supposed feudal guise, see Crouch 2012.

medieval architectural culture across the wide spatial domain of north-west Europe at any one moment in time, or would I regard it as evidence of the essential insularity of architectural culture in Ireland? And what inferences about Ireland's place in medieval Europe more broadly would I draw from the evidence of its castles and their forms?

The perspective from which I attempt in this book to answer such questions about pre- and post-1169 castles in Ireland could be described as outside-in in terms of geography and inside-out in terms of politics. In respect of the former, I look *in* at Ireland from beyond its shores; my principal vantage points are modern Britain and France, the parts of Europe demonstrably most relevant to my subject, and each of the chapters begins with and then pivots around some discussion of monuments in the key medieval polities – Capetian, Norman, Angevin – within those modern geographical frames. In respect of the latter, I look *out* at Ireland from a notional Europe core, from part of what is generally understood to be the middle, not the edge, of 'Romanesque' and 'Gothic' Europe. Concepts of core and periphery are deeply problematic of course, but they serve a purpose as starting points for a fresh study of castle-building in Ireland. In a sense, this book is predicated on the theory that cores, if they are to be regarded as real, can only be understood from peripheries.

Rejecting Romanesque and Gothic as style-labels

I want to comment here on the eschewing of the labels 'Romanesque' and 'Gothic' in the chapters which follow. Both words, but especially the former, appear in the French and English castellological literature; the words rarely feature in the Irish literature on castles, so we can leave Ireland to one side for the present.

One of the recurring features of the historiography of Romanesque architecture as a pan-European style between the tenth and twelfth centuries is the manner in which castles and related secular building-types are embedded in the narrative. They are treated not as participants in the creation of the supposed style in the first instance, nor even as important agents in its diffusion, but, rather, as passive recipients of structural and decorative forms developed in and for ecclesiastical contexts.[30] That the style should first have been identified (in the early nineteenth century) in church buildings, and then remain associated primarily with such buildings in the scholarly imagination, reflects two simple truths. First, the medieval church itself was the Roman church, so it was already in the institutional lineage. Second, and more importantly, churches everywhere in the medieval world conformed to one of two basic plan-forms which had originated in Roman architecture: the common rectangular (basilica) plan, or the less common circular (centralized) plan. The origin of Romanesque (*roman* in French; *Romanisch* in German; *románico* in Spanish; *romanica* in Italian) as a shared construct of international scholarship from the earlier twentieth century resides, first, in the observation that stylistic changes in church architecture in different parts of Europe coalesced around forms and motifs of Roman ancestry, and, second, in the theory that such changes were synchronized within the context of a renaissance of Christianized

---

30 In Hans Erich Kubach's survey of Romanesque architecture domestic and military buildings are given eleven pages in 387 pages of text (Kubach 1975).

Classical culture. In other words, the narrative is driven by the ecclesiastical architecture. Castle architecture of the same period was more heterogeneous than church architecture because it was not bound by universal rules that rigidly tied space to performance, or structure to belief.

Many of the castle buildings of the period up to the end of the twelfth century which feature in this book would normally be described as Romanesque were a style-name requested for them. The problems inherent in the term and construct 'Romanesque' notwithstanding,[31] the use of that style-name for any of the castles should be rejected because it enfolds them into a narrative invented *without* the input of the evidence which they offer. 'Romanesque' is not their word; it was not invented with cognisance of their architecture. This might seem a pedantic point, but it serves the larger purpose of informing the debate on the legitimacy and value of style-labelling in an age when our understanding of the evidence which is bunched under those style-labels is immensely more sophisticated than it was when they were invented. Marginalizing castle architecture in the Romanesque narrative has arguably helped maintain the illusion of stylistic coherence across all of Europe between 1000 and 1200.

Marvin Trachtenberg's reimagining of the sequential stylistic phenomena of Romanesque and Gothic as manifestations of, respectively, *historicist* and *modernist* impulses in the Middle Ages, offers an escape route from traditional terminology.[32] The distinction is one which would not necessarily have grated with the original 'Gothic' practitioners of the Middle Ages. Consciousness of 'modern' as a counter-distinction to 'the past' is captured in the comment of Rhabanus Maurus, a Carolingian cleric, that he and his contemporaries lived in *tempore moderno*, as distinct from Antiquity.[33] An apparent irony here is that the Carolingians enjoyed a *renovatio Romanorum imperii*. However, Rhabanus Maurus was referring to time, not culture. Consciousness of temporal change is itself cultural, so cultural changes, like the 'invention' of 'Gothic', created a sense of temporal change. Thus, the 'Gothic cathedral' – a literary trope from the nineteenth century,[34] and possibly a cultural trope before that – signified a medieval *tempore moderno*.

Trachtenberg posits the historicist–modernist distinction in the context of ecclesiastical architecture, and so must negotiate the Romanesque–Gothic boundary as it has been constructed by historians of such architecture over more than two centuries. In the field of castellology, however, a distinction between historicism and modernism can be adopted and moulded to its own needs, with a chronology that does not need exact synchronization with that of churches. Before *c.*1200, castle architecture in these islands certainly shared with contemporary church architecture some forms and motifs rooted in, and revealing of an ideological link with, *Romanitas*, especially *Romanitas* as transformed in the Carolingian renaissance. Its glance was backwards, in other words, and its perspective on style (insofar as one can determine it) can be

---

31 O'Keeffe 2007a seems to be the only book-length critique of the 'Romanesque', but it is not the only critique.   32 Trachtenberg 2001. For an appreciation of Trachtenberg's scheme alongside a defence of traditional style-names see Fernie 2008.   33 Corfield 2007, 133.   34 Hollis 2009, 219–42.

described accordingly as historicist. The point at which one can detect a change in the strictness of the adherence of castle-builders to the Classical inheritance – or, one might say, a change in their attitudes towards that inheritance – does not align exactly with the change in ecclesiastical architecture, but the match is reasonably close. I suggest that among castle-builders a modernizing tendency, a state of being knowingly 'after *Romanitas*', began in the second quarter of the twelfth century in France with the first cylindrical donjons, but really took off later in the century after a post-*Romanitas* ('Gothic') sensibility had emerged in ecclesiastical architecture and made non-Roman forms fashionable. Yes, a Classical pedigree for cylindrical donjons can be traced: Lindy Grant has even argued that these cylindrical towers were intended to convey *Romanitas*, and more recently Jeremy Knight has pointed to Classical precedents for elements of the geometrically planned castles of the late twelfth and early thirteenth centuries.[35] But the key point I wish to make is that the cylindrical form, and its aesthetic potential, appealed to castle-builders in an age – the later twelfth century and beyond – in which the *explicit* referencing of Roman work had passed out of vogue among church-builders. Accordingly, in one chapter (Chapter 3) I discuss buildings conventionally regarded as Romanesque but do not use that word, and in the next chapter (Chapter 4) I discuss buildings which were modernist, in a medieval context, because they knowingly reflected the 'after *Romanitas*' spirit of their age, but I do not refer to them as 'Gothic'.

The scope of this book

Two parts of the main title of this book probably require some small qualification. First, the phrase 'encastellation' is likely to be understood by some readers in terms of the act of fortifying: the act of building structures for the prosecution of, or for defence against, land-grabbing. The expectation might be, therefore, that this book addresses primarily the military dimensions of castle architecture. But that would be too narrow a reading of its title. The phrase 'Ireland encastellated' is intended to connote the Ireland in which castles were the principal physical manifestations on the landscape of ideas of power, were agents of governance at multiple scales, and were places wherein elite identities were expressed and reinforced performatively. These concepts are explained in the chapters which follow, insofar as they need explanation, but suffice it to say here that 'encastellation' could almost be regarded as a metonym for the formation of the complex cultural configuration of a medieval world in which militarism was but a part, and sometimes not much more than a symbolic part at that.[36]

Second, the date-range in the book's title breaches the conventional chronological framework in Irish castle studies. The book's pre-millennium opening date will already have raised eyebrows. I hope that the brief discussion at the start of this chapter of the Lotteragh Upper monument, built *c.*1000, will have helped to lower them again. The specific date of 950 is aligned with how European evidence across a range of categories

35 Grant 1994; Knight 2018, 157. **36** Some of these matters are discussed in O'Keeffe 2001a.

is being viewed increasingly by archaeologists.[37] As this book is concerned primarily with explaining the architecture of *medieval* Irish castles through a comparative European lens, its natural end date is in the sixteenth century. From the fourteenth century on, it is harder to trace specific lines of influence from individual buildings outside Ireland to individual buildings inside Ireland. Despite belonging in a pan-European tradition of tower-building, and despite circumstantial evidence that its earliest development was probably shaped by overseas contacts, the Irish tower-house developed insular characteristics in the first fifty years of the fifteenth century. And so, for the purpose of this book, I portray the late medieval period as being the long tail of the period of European influence. New ideas of European Renaissance origin began to appear in the second half of the sixteenth century, so 1550 is chosen as the notional cut-off date.

The book's approach

This book is not a beginner's introduction to castles and castle-building culture in medieval Ireland. Some knowledge, even limited, of the field and its historiography is assumed. Accordingly, it does not aim to be comprehensive. Rather, it is a series of essays, conventionally analytical in some places and both ruminative and subjective in others. There are elisions in which are muted some of the castles which feature in the other literature, and there are also thematic gaps, the most obvious of which is a full discussion of Anglo-Norman earth-and-timber castles. This is not to say, however, that its content will be accessible only to those who can identify the gaps and elisions. On the contrary, I would like to think that readers who understand the character of the medieval period and know something of its history, but have no intimate knowledge of the physical character of its castles, will follow this book's occasionally (and necessarily) labyrinthine structure and the outlines of its arguments, and will recognize how, if some of those arguments are deemed valid, they add to our holistic understanding of medieval Ireland.

While Irish readers who do indeed know the material might find that this book complements one or both books on Irish castles published by Tom McNeill and David Sweetman over twenty years ago, that is not its intention. Nor is it intended to complement the two chapters on castles in my own survey of medieval Irish architecture, published six years ago.[38] Indeed, I specifically do not want it to be used that way. Readers will find that it compares with the McNeill and Sweetman books insofar as it is, like them, a book in a very traditional castellological mould, with an emphasis on castles as physical structures, and with a focus on chronology and formal contexts. But I would like this book to be read as an attempt to map a much less linear, less canon-hugging, route towards a new understanding of the morphologies of Irish castles, in the hope that it will, whatever its own failures, persuade the next generation of researchers in Ireland to explore other ways of conversing about that corpus.

---

37 See, for example, the pre- and post-950 division in Loveluck 2013, 215, 222.   **38** O'Keeffe 2015.

As an educator, I regard that next generation as this book's natural target readership. I am anxious that it impresses upon that next generation two needs. The first is the need to be *au fait* with evidence outside Ireland. I have long been struck by how infrequently most castellologists in Ireland, especially in the Republic, refer to castles outside the island for comparative purposes, even English ones. One cannot understand the Irish evidence without some knowledge of non-Irish evidence. The process of writing this book taught me that I did not know that material as well as I thought I did, and it has made me aware of how much there is still to know. The second need is for some critical thinking in respect of classification. Enamoured particularly of the approach used by Harold Leask in his *Irish castles and castellated houses* (1941) and later adopted by David Sweetman in his *Medieval castles of Ireland* (1999), many Irish castle-researchers today adhere to handed-down classifications of monuments without ever reflecting on whether the classifications make sense, or whether the act of classifying is even necessary. Too few query the validity or even the value of class labels such as 'ringwork' and 'hall-house', preferring to treat them as if they carry the imprimatur of the medieval castle-makers themselves, which they do not. I am aware that my own objections to the uncritical use of such terms, articulated often in lectures and publications over many years, have fallen on deaf ears within the Irish archaeological community, but I continue to insist that terminology *does* matter. Imprecise terminology can invalidate the discourse in which it is used.

CHAPTER 2

Beginnings: voices and words, rings and mounds

Books on castles often begin with a definition. If one could reduce the published definitions to one, it would almost certainly read as follows: the medieval castle was the fortified residence of a feudal lord. Medieval records are not quite so clear on the issue, however. 'Castle' is a modern word, an etymological descendent of the Latin cognates *castrum* and *castellum*. One cannot easily determine the criteria by which medieval writers and record-keepers decided to describe some structures or groups of structures as *castra* (the plural of *castrum*) and others as *castella* (the plural of *castellum*). Were those words synonymous in the Middle Ages? How did those words, or their obvious vernacular derivatives (most of them derivatives of *castellum*), relate to other words used in the Middle Ages to describe fortifications or fortified residences, such as *oppidum* or *munitio*? Did medieval writers and recorders, or indeed medieval patrons, even think in terms of criteria before they chose their words?

That such questions need to be asked at all reflects the ambiguities in how castles feature in medieval sources. 'Castle' referred most often (but not exclusively, it must be said) to a structure or group or structures, but the problem for the modern scholar is that the sources rarely reveal whether a structure was described as a 'castle' because of how it looked or how it functioned, or both, and whether the social or political context in which it functioned was a factor. One assumes that appearance, function and context were all important, but were all three always important simultaneously? The key point is that the popular definition of a castle as the fortified residence of a feudal lord did not actually originate in the Middle Ages. That is not to say that it is incorrect – although the adjective 'feudal' is perhaps too problematic to be allowed remain in the definition[1] – but it is a reminder to the reader that it is a retro-fitted modern view.

Although medieval sources convey less information than is desired, it is only right that the castellologist starts with those sources. 'Castle' is not an archaeological concept or construct. This is an important point. Were there no single word to describe the multiple archaeological or architectural forms captured by the word 'castle', no single word would be invented by modern scholars for that purpose. So, whatever were the original meanings of those words (in medieval Latin and other vernacular languages) which are now translated as 'castle', they have come down to us solely in medieval written sources, wherein they are in the authentic if inscrutable voice of the Middle Ages. Thus, in this chapter I am allowing those voices to be heard first.

1 O'Keeffe 2019a. For a critique see also Johnson 2007, 118–21.   2 White 1973; for perspectives on the Middle Ages see Spiegel 1990; Lett 2016; O'Keeffe 2018a.

In the intellectual culture of the western hemisphere, documentary sources are privileged over physical remains as the most exact actual records of places and events of the past. Some documentary references concerning the medieval past are written with such minimal ambiguity that they can be read as straightforward reportage. Others are ambiguous to us because they were not written with the care which we would like. But medieval documents are also objects of *literary* culture, or at least of the culture of literacy, and while they are rarely in narrative form themselves (although they might reflect orally transmitted narratives), they are brought to life through narrative devices.[2] That is not to suggest that such documents are fictive but, rather, to recognize that writing, whether it is by the medieval scribe or the modern historian, is an act of representation, not reproduction or replication. Things and events do not have natural linguistic correlatives. Rather, they require transformation into the medium of language, and that transformative process creates and informs a mode of discourse which always remains separate from the events themselves. The language of the discourse is always reductionist; it never captures the full complexity of that to which it purportedly refers. We would do well to remember, then, that 'castle', as it appears in a medieval source, might have been intended to represent a building, but it might sometimes have represented a jurisdiction, or it might have been used as a signifier of a species of authority or its practice (akin perhaps to *ecclesia*), or it might even have been an explicit literary device, such as a metaphor.[3]

More important still, perhaps, the modern translation as 'castle' of medieval Latin words or Latin-derived vernacular words is less a transposition of language than an act of *re*-representation, the taking of an original word which had representational purpose(s) in the Middle Ages and giving it a new representational purpose further removed from its own phenomenal reality. In so doing, it potentially intrudes into the scientific understanding of the primary language those ways in which 'castle', transformed and detached from its original documentary contexts, has been portrayed for purposes other than historical understanding. One immediately thinks here of the castles which appear in romantic literature (*Ivanhoe*, say) or, more recently, in celluloid fiction (*Braveheart*, for example). To put this another way, 'castle', with the historiographical baggage it now carries, imposes a new set of meanings on that medieval terminology, thus altering how that terminology can be used to interpret the Middle Ages. That is not to say that the meanings of the modern word do not rhyme with the meanings of original medieval words, but, rather, to highlight the need to monitor the interface between what *was* medieval and what *is* modern. Having made this point, I will drop hereafter the inverted commas that flank the word – 'castle' – except when necessary, but the reader should know that the word always requires some of the qualification which inverted commas bestow.

CASTRUM AND *CASTELLUM*

The two earliest medieval words translated today as 'castle' are the Latin *castrum* and *castellum*. They were first used in Antiquity to describe fortified places, and they clearly

3 Whitehead 2003; Wheatley 2004.

retained that meaning into the Middle Ages. Therein lies the origin of, and the justification for, the view that medieval castles were practical objects of military culture. And therein also is the source of the reluctance of researchers in many parts of Europe[4] to dispense with military determinism when attempting to explain castle forms and their complex evolution.

Castrum and *castellum* clearly signified in the Middle Ages places or monuments of elite, royal or seigneurial power; if they were not built by such agents, they were at least built – or were allowed be retained by their builders – with the assent of such agents.[5] Beyond that, though, any morphological, social or functional distinctions that *castrum* and *castellum* were intended to convey between types of fortified place are not always clear in Latin texts of the Middle Ages. St Jerome, translating the Bible into Latin around the year 400, the dawn of the medieval period, used *castellum* to describe a protected settlement like an enclosed village or small town, and *castrum* to describe a more compact military camp.[6] But there was no great consistency in the usage of the words thereafter, however, and how they were used in one source was often flatly contradicted by how they were used in another. Indeed, in some places one of the words was apparently chosen to capture a full range of fortification-types while the other word was not used at all: in medieval Latium (central Italy), for example, 'the word *castrum* covers different realities, from the small castle with various functions to the big *bourg castral*'.[7] Given the complexity of the record, few scholars are now bothered to discuss the matter of a rigid distinction, and some among them simply cite Jan Verbruggen's famous paper of 1950 in which he claimed that the evidence was 'sufficient to establish that *castrum* and *castellum* were practically synonyms from the end of the ninth to the thirteenth century'.[8]

It should be noted, though, that Verbruggen drew this conclusion from thirty-three texts of mainly Flemish provenance, so he really should not be cited as an authority on all parts of Europe. He was not entirely correct anyway. The two words were often interchanged, especially in the tenth and eleventh centuries, but that does not necessarily mean that they were regarded as synonyms. There is a difference. For example, in his early eleventh-century *Chronicon*, Adémar de Chabannes, from the area of Limoges (Haute-Vienne), used *castellum* to describe protective enclosures constructed around monastic settlements specifically, and *castrum* to describe more conventional, compact, fortifications capable of being constructed very quickly.[9] But the preference

4 One sees this occasionally still in papers in the proceedings of the biennial Château Gaillard colloquium, for example: *Château Gaillard. Études de castellologie médiévale* (1964+). **5** Note the regnal instruction of Charles the Bald in 864 that those *castella et firmitates et haias* which had been constructed without authorization, and to the inconvenience of those living near them, be destroyed (Edict of Pîtres, Supp. C. 1: see Nelson 1992, 207). **6** Wheatley 2004, 23–24; Kraus 2017, 546–7. **7** Hubert 2000, 598–9. **8** Verbruggen 1950, 151; see also Tock 1998, 14–15. Verbruggen is cited in, among many others, Samson 1987 and Wheatley 2004, 26–7. **9** Bachrach 1975, 560, 563–4; Debord 1979, 104, 105, 107. André Debord suggested that the *castra* mentioned by Adémar de Chabannes must have been 'light constructions of earth and wood'; of the 26 *castra* mentioned by Ademar, six were, or probably were, mounds. Note that in the *Chronicon* a *castrum* was smaller than a *castellum*. If *castellum* originated as a diminutive of *castrum*, from at least an early stage of the eleventh century, insofar as one can generalize, seems to have been for *castrum* to have been retained for a protected or fortified communal settlement, a *bourg*, rather than a castle as we would generally define one today, and so it was used to describe villages attached to citadels or seigneurial residences;[10] the town attached to the citadel at Guingamp (Côtes-d'Armor), for example, was described as *castrum* from the beginning of the twelfth century.[11] Conversely and simultaneously, *castellum* became attached to the fortress residence.[12] Significantly, derivatives of *castellum*, not *castrum*, then emerged in vernacular languages through the eleventh and twelfth centuries – *castel* in (Middle) English, *chastel* in (Middle) French, *castell* in Catalan, *castèl* in Occitan, *caistél* in Irish, and so on – to give us the etymological root of the modern 'castle'. Revealingly, early in the twelfth century in Ariége, located on the north side of the Pyrenees, both *castrum* and *castellum* were used to describe what we would regard as conventional castles, but with the former used to refer to older ones and the latter to newer ones.[13] In the mid-twelfth century the poet Wace, translating Geoffrey of Monmouth's *Historia regum Britannie*, written less than twenty years earlier, chose to substitute *castrum* in the original with *chastel*.[14] One is tempted to describe Wace's translation as a snap-shot of a process of elimination of that terminological ambiguity surrounding the words *castrum* and *castellum* that had survived into the period of Domesday Book and Orderic Vitalis's *Historia*.[15]

I suggest that, as an alternative to the still-popular Verbruggen thesis, a distinction needed to be made early in the Middle Ages between the *scales* and, by extension, the *functions* of fortified places, specifically between nucleated settlements on the one hand (which could be fortified through the building of enclosing ramparts) and compact fortifications on the other. I suggest that *castrum* and *castellum* were used, albeit inconsistently, to fill that role, until eventually *castellum* came to be attached more consistently to the compact fortification after the turn of the millennium, and especially in the twelfth century.[16] Put another way, the key point is that the two words met a need for a distinction to be made between two types of fortified place during the first millennium, and that, being close cognates, they were deployed differently from place to place and with unintentional contradictions.[17]

The documentary evidence that a distinction between the *castrum* and the 'castle' (*castellum*) was not made consistently until the eleventh century in north-western Europe finds some support in the archaeological record for fortifications in the

as Roman usage would suggest, one wonders whether the diminution was in respect of the extent or efficacy of the fortification, rather than the area of the fortification. **10** Bur 1993, 7. **11** Beuchet 2014. **12** See, for example, Laffont 2009 for the pattern between the Rhone valley and the Massif Central. For the use of *castrum* in respect of planned fortified towns see Barrett 2018. **13** Guillot 2014, 612. **14** Wheatley 2004, 31–3. **15** For evidence of that ambiguity see respectively Harfield 1991 and Chibnall 1989. **16** 'In the tenth century, the castle [of Coucy (Aisne)] is designated by six terms: *castrum, munitio, municipium, oppidum, arx* and *turris*. The term *castellum* only appears in the twelfth century' (Leblanc 2005, 145). **17** In offering this interpretation it is important to stress that, *pace* R. Allen Brown (1977), one could not claim that a distinction was ever intended between a 'public' fortification (which, in his view, did not constitute a castle) such as an enclosed town, and a 'private' fortification, owned by an individual lord (which he regarded as a 'true' castle). On this point see Coulson 2003, 182.

preceding century. Structures described by these two words in the tenth century were quite heterogeneous in morphology, almost as if some standardization of the morphology of the 'castle', evident perhaps in the emergence of the multi-storeyed donjon (see Chapter 4 below), was awaiting a standardization of terminology in the early eleventh century. A selection of tenth-century fortifications is shown here (Fig. 4) to illustrate the point about morphological heterogeneity paralleling the contemporary ambiguity in terminology. The earliest of the group selected, dating from the start of the tenth century, is Boves (Somme). It had a mound at the end of a ridge, and its summit had traces of timber structures.[18] Excavation in the 1950s of the complex earthwork known as Der Husterknupp (Nordrhein-Westfalen) revealed that an eleventh-century motte-and-bailey (labelled Phase III by the excavator) was formed out of a pair of mid- to late tenth-century enclosures (Phase II), one of them, the *Hauptburg*, described by the excavator as a *Kernmotte* (basically a 'transitional motte' or 'proto-motte'), only slightly more elevated than the other, the *Vorburg*.[19] Dating from the later tenth century is the stone-walled enclosure and tower of Niozelles (Alpes-de-Haute-Provence); the monument crowns a rocky outcrop described as a *rocca* (or *roque*, or *roche*), regarded by some scholars as a natural topographic equivalent of the motte.[20] Pineuilh (Gironde) is an example of what the French describe literally as a small circular enclosure, a *petite enceinte circulaire*; in German literature such monuments are called *Ringwälle* ('ringwalls'), and their equivalents in Ireland are 'ringforts' (when attributed to native, pre-invasion, contexts) and 'ringworks' (when attributed to Anglo-Norman contexts).[21] Pineuilh was part-constructed with wood from trees felled in 977 at the earliest.[22] Finally, the Belgian site known as the Burgknapp (Attert) started life during the tenth century as an exceptionally *petite* circular enclosure defined by a palisade (and with no outer fosse) within which was a wooden tower.[23] Alongside these sites, we might recall the stone-walled *castrum* of Andone built in the 970s, and its near-contemporary parallel in Ireland, *Dún Eochair Maige*, monuments of very different type again (Fig. 2).

The key question is whether such monuments should be called castles by modern scholars? Historians will differ in their responses: supporters of the 'big bang' theory of feudalism would (almost certainly) object; supporters of the Barthélemy-led revisionism will (almost certainly) not. As an archaeologist, I find it difficult to take sides and to support one interpretation over the other with any authority, since the evidence is not capable of archaeological testing by simple virtue of the fact that 'castle' is not an archaeological type. However, an important archaeological observation is that each of these sites is *at very least* in the lineage of some morphological type of the eleventh and twelfth centuries that historians and archaeologists will agree to describe

---

18 Racinet 2008.   **19** Herrnbrodt 1958.   **20** Mouton 1997, 182–4; for the *rocca* as a type see Debord 1988, 18.   **21** On the Continent such enclosures are mainly of the later ninth and the tenth centuries, although examples continued to be built into the twelfth century, albeit apparently in reduced numbers. See, for example, Brather 2004, 312–13. Irish archaeologists appear to be unaware of European 'ringforts' beyond the 'Celtic west' and have not explored, therefore, the implications of Irish ringforts having an earlier chronological spread than their European parallels.   **22** Prodéo et al. 2006.   **23** Dhaeze and Fairon 2014.

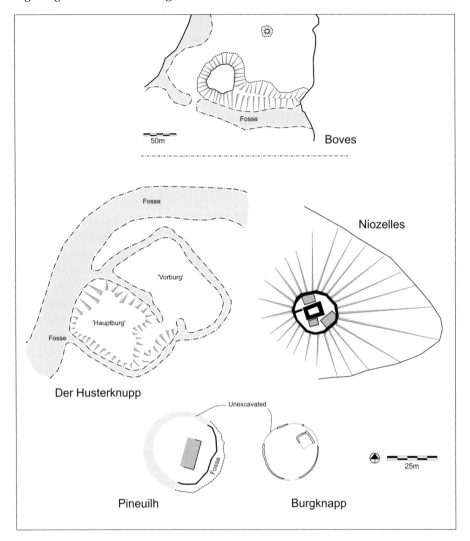

4 Comparative plans of five tenth-century fortifications.

as castles. Now, the archaeologist might be tempted, out of an abundance of caution, to regard these various sites as representing the castle in embryo, thus allowing them be part of the conversation on castle-origins while simultaneously disqualifying them as castles in their own right. But there is a fundamental problem with such a compromise: the concept of the embryonic castle (or 'proto-castle'?) presupposes that 'the castle' then had a moment of birth in the Middle Ages, followed by a life cycle as a form of monument bounded by universally agreed rules of social function, political rank and morphological character. But that was not the case: the archaeological evidence would certainly not support that interpretation, nor would Barthelémy's revisionist take on the historical evidence. So, if the monuments of the tenth century are demonstrably in the lineage of some morphological type of monument of the eleventh and twelfth centuries which historians and archaeologists would agree to describe without contestation as castles in the eleventh, a case has to be made to *exclude* them from the category of castle. I would not attempt to make the case.

CASTEL, CAISTÉL AND CAISLÉN

Castel/cæstel entered Old English (the language of Anglo-Saxon England) as a loan-word from *castellum*, and signified a village or small town, following the use of the Latin original in the Vulgate translation.[24] Although already in the language, it entered English again in the early 1050s as a new, independent, borrowing from the French *castel*.[25] According to its appearance in the Anglo-Saxon Chronicle, the re-entrant term was first used to refer not to fortified nucleated settlements but to a number of pre-conquest Norman-built fortresses, clearly castles in the conventional sense.[26] These castles, insofar as they can be identified, were almost certainly earth-and-timber constructions, and probably were (or had, from the outset, as elements within them) mottes.[27]

Before turning to Ireland, I want to comment briefly on England in the century or so before the first Normans settled there. The Anglo-Saxons had protected earth-and-timber settlements which, from an archaeological perspective, compare reasonably favourably with Norman fortifications in general scale, but they were not prominently mounded, nor did they have mounded elements.[28] But none of these compact Anglo-Saxon forts was described contemporaneously in English sources as a castle. Indeed, Orderic Vitalis famously remarked after the Norman invasion that '*munitiones* which the French call *castella* were scarcely known in the English provinces'.[29] The Anglo-Saxon sites were products of a society for which there is no evidence of the particular species of lordship – coercive, violent, *banal* – which is taken, rightly or wrongly, to represent feudalism in contemporary western Europe.[30] So, if function and context *together* determined what was regarded as a castle on the Continental mainland in the tenth and eleventh centuries, one can understand how, for somebody like Orderic, the

---

24 Cameron et al. 2007; Bosworth and Toller 2010.   **25** Durkin 2014, 282. Higham and Barker pointed out, however, that *c[h]astel* was not used in written French sources at the time, although they acknowledged that the word could have been in spoken usage (1992, 362–3). It might be relevant to note, though, that placenames in Old Breton (*c*.800–*c*.1100) use the suffix -*castel*. See Le Moing 1990, 238.   **26** Campbell 1971; Higham and Barker 1992, 362–3.   **27** The number is uncertain but there were at least three, and their sites are identified as Clavering (Essex), Ewyas Harold and Richard's Castle (Herefordshire) (Higham and Barker 1992, 43–5). See Davison 1967. **28** Blair 2018; see also Faith 1997, 163–4, 174–5.   **29** Chibnall 1968, 218–19. For the terminology in English sources see Williams 1986.   **30** O'Keeffe 2019a, 130–2; *banal* derives from *ban*, the right of the lord to coerce (see, for example, Brittain Bouchard 1998, 58–60). From the perspective of a Marxian understanding of feudalism, 'England before the Conquest seems … to have been a profoundly un-feudal society' (Faith 2020, 11). A similar conclusion can be drawn from the non-Marxian perspective on feudalism promoted by Susan Reynolds (1994), in which is emphasized the legal concept of land held 'in fee' from a lord: Tom Lambert has recently documented evidence of continuity, not change, in the Anglo-Saxon legal order through several centuries, at least into the reign of Cnut (†1035) (Lambert 2017).

5 Plan and sections of the pre-Norman *Caislen na Caillighe* (Hag's Castle).

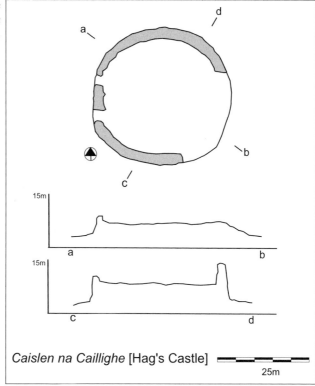

Caislen na Caillighe [Hag's Castle]

25m

Anglo-Saxon monuments did not merit the appellation *castellum*, or any derivative of it, notwithstanding any morphological similarities between them and European monuments. It is appropriate to mention here the perspective of Giraldus Cambrensis on Ireland, since it offers support for this interpretation of Orderic's testimony. Although he wrote that 'the Irish people possess no castles' (*gens Hibernica castellis carens*), Giraldus actually saw castles everywhere in Ireland. He identified Ireland's ringforts as abandoned castles, and even used the verb encastellation. He believed they were Viking castles, erected under Turgesius.[31] His error in attributing them to the Vikings is revealing. He recognized the ringforts as castle-like, even in their abandoned state, and assumed that they must have been erected by some military power. His notoriously ungenerous attitude to the Irish led him to conclude that they could not have been responsible, and so he turned to the Vikings, not coincidentally the ancestors of his own people. Giraldus, in other words, understood 'castle' to mean what Orderic understood it to mean. For both men, context was at least as important as morphology.

As in England, there was also a two-stage pattern of borrowing from *castellum* in medieval Ireland. However, unlike in England, each stage in Ireland gave the native language a different word.

The earlier borrowing, dating from the middle of the first millennium, yielded *caisel* (from which we get the early placename Cashel), and it appears into the twelfth

31 Dimock 1867, 137, 182–3; Forester 2000, 62, 83.

century in various sources and with variable spellings.[32] *Caislén*, which first appears in the annals in 1124 in Connacht (as will be shown below) and is now the root of the modern Irish word for 'castle', is also derived from *caisel*.[33] Circumstantial evidence suggests that the derivation dates from at least *c.*1100, and that *caislén* was therefore in the native language for a few decades before it is first seen in the annals. In 1195 the word was used for *Caislen na Caillighe*, Hag's Castle (Mayo), a mortared-stone enclosure on an island in Lough Corrib (Fig. 5).[34] Kieran O'Conor and Paul Naessens identified it as one of a number of western Irish lacustrine forts of demonstrably late eleventh- or early twelfth-century date.[35]

While it derived from a word with a long history of use in Ireland, the appearance of *caislén* was probably related to the second borrowing from the same Latin root: *caistél*. Also first attested to in 1124 in Connacht, this too is likely to have appeared for the first time in Ireland in the later eleventh century, even if it was not written down until the early twelfth. The second syllable (-*tél*) indicates that it was not a variation on the older *caisel* but was borrowed directly from Anglo-Norman, the variant of French spoken in Norman England,[36] so it could only have come to Ireland *as a word* after the mid-eleventh century.[37]

From annals to archaeology: introducing the eight documented pre-1169 castles

In 1124 three castles (*trí caisteoil*)[38] were built by the Connachtmen at the behest of Tairdelbach Ua Conchobair, the king of Connacht: Galway, Collooney (Sligo), and Ballinasloe (Galway). The first of these – Galway – is described in three annalistic collections as *caistél, caislén* and *Dún Gaillmhe*.[39] In 1132 it is referred to again in the three sources but with a slight change in terminology: *caislén, caislen* and *dún*.[40] That these references are to a compact castle rather than to a fortified settlement for a local population is indicated by the record that the *baile*, the settlement, of Galway was plundered and burned alongside the castle.[41] A final reference to the pre-invasion fortress of Galway in 1170 – the Anglo-Normans had not reached Galway by then, so the reference must be to the native castle – uses the word *caisdel*.[42] The castle of Ballinasloe is described in 1124 as *castél Dúin Leódha, caislén Dúin Leódha*, and *Dún Leoda*, mirroring the words used for Galway in those same sources.[43] The third castle, Collooney, is described in 1124 as *caistél* and *caislén*.[44]

---

32 McManus 1983, 65; eDIL s.v. Stone-walled circular forts in Ireland are commonly called 'cashels'. The chronology of these monuments is uncertain, and it is not known when the word 'cashel' was first attached to them.   **33** eDIL s.v. I previously suggested that the -*én* suffix of *caislén* might indicate that it was simply a diminutive of *caistél*, indicating in turn a physically smaller fortress (O'Keeffe 2014a, 32). Although I now think it unlikely, it is still possible: terms used in the Gascon vernacular, *casteg, casterot* and *casterasse*, appear to describe gradations in size (Berdoy 2014, 599).   **34** AFM 1195.9.   **35** O'Conor and Naessens 2012.   **36** Vendryes 1987, 23.   **37** Ingham 2010. It would have transferred to Ireland through cultural contacts at an elite level, English being spoken by lower ranks in Norman England (see Lucken 2015).   **38** AFM 1124.15.   **39** AT 1124.3; AFM 1124.15; CS 1124.277.   **40** Respectively AT 1132.6, AFM 1132.9, MIA 1132.21, and CS 1132.283.   **41** MIA 1132.21.   **42** AT 1170.7.   **43** Respectively AT 1124.3, AFM 1124.15, CS 1124.277; in the *Annals of Clonmacnoise* for 1131 it is described in a seventeenth-century translation as 'the castle of Donleo' (AClon., 191).   **44** AT 1124.3, AFM

Next in chronological sequence is the castle of Athlone (Westmeath), described at the time of its construction in 1129 by Tairdelbach Ua Conchobair as *caistél*, *caislén* and *caislén*.[45] In 1133 it is given as *caistiall*.[46] It is described as *daingen* in 1153,[47] and as *longport* in 1155.[48]

Neither of the next two castles in sequence is recorded as a *caistél*: in 1136 the castle on *Loch Cairrgin*, now Ardakillin Lough (Roscommon), is referred to as *caislen* and *caislén*,[49] while in 1155 the castle of *Cuilenntrach*, which can be identified as Cullentragh (Mayo), is described as *caislen* and *caislén*.[50]

The final documented 'castle' of the pre-invasion twelfth century in Connacht is that of Tuam (Galway), built by Ruaidrí Ua Conchobair (Tairdelbach's son) and identified as a *caislén ingantach*, a 'wonderful castle', in 1164. The Dominican Annals of Roscommon, compiled in the thirteenth century, describe the castle in Tuam – the same castle? – as *castrum* and attach no adjective.[51]

The final explicit reference to a castle before the invasion in Ireland is to that of Ferns (Wexford), described in 1166 as *caisteóil* and *caistiall*.[52] It was a royal castle. Its owner, Diarmait MacMurchada, was the native king who invited the Anglo-Normans to Ireland in 1169.

How do we make sense of these references? Harold Leask, the doyen of Irish castellology, acknowledged their existence but did not regard them as indicators of an established culture of castle-building in pre-Norman Ireland, even in Connacht.[53] Recent years have seen more attention paid to them.[54] The central issue now is whether *caistél* referred to an actual type of monument (which would mean, according to the analysis above, that the word was imported from the Anglo-Norman language alongside a morphological type and was then vernacularized) or was simply, as Tom McNeill put it economically, a 'fashionable' new word.[55] This debate – was *caistél* a new thing or a new word? – pertains to a bigger debate. Did Ireland see 'European-style' encastellation before 1169? And, if so, what was its scale?

Insofar as the literature communicates a consensus, it seems that most commentators are sceptical about pre-invasion encastellation beyond the embryonic stage suggested by the annals, mainly because of the infrequency of the term 'castle' in historical sources. The testimony of Giraldus Cambrensis – *gens Hibernica castellis carens* – is often cited too: 'a major reason for several scholars to doubt the existence of castles in pre-Norman Ireland lies in the writing of the greatest Anglo-Norman chronicler of the invasion, Giraldus Cambrensis (Gerald of Wales)'.[56] However, this contemporary testimony is repeatedly mis-read: as was noted above, Giraldus saw widespread evidence of what he understood to be an older phase of encastellation in Ireland, but

---

1124.15. **45** Respectively AU 1129.5, AFM 1129.11, ALC 1129.4. **46** AFM 1133.13. The bridge was rebuilt in wicker, so the castle was probably rebuilt also but there is no reference to this; the new bridge collapsed in 1146 (AT 1146.1). **47** AFM 1153.18; the event is dated 1162 in AClon., 205, wherein the castle is described as 'fort'. **48** AFM 1155.14. **49** AT 1136.9, AFM 1136.17. **50** AT 1155.8, and AFM 1155.15. For its identification as a townland in Mayo see O'Keeffe 2019a, 126–7. **51** AT 1164.2, *Annales Dominicani de Roscoman* s.a. 1163. **52** AFM 1166.14. **53** Leask 1941, 6–7. **54** Graham 1988; Flanagan 1996; Barry 2007; Valente 2015. **55** McNeill 1997, 10; I share McNeill's opinion (O'Keeffe 1998; 2014a; 2019a). **56** Barry 2007, 34.

did not believe that the native Irish had anything to do with it. Also, the archaeological evidence relevant to the matter has not been trusted to form the basis of a different narrative. Tom McNeill, for example, pointed to some sites which deserve to be discussed, but he pulled back from speculating on their implications, warning that 'there are not many swallows here to make a summer'.[57] The critically important archaeological work of Kieran O'Conor and Paul Naessens on pre-invasion mortared-stone enclosures in western Ireland[58] could now be cited in support of the argument that there was actually encastellation on a more extensive scale than the annalistic records suggest. Yet, I suggest, the power of that scepticism about terminology diverts even O'Conor and Naessens from that most natural conclusion. Addressing those annalistic references to pre-invasion *caisteoil* they write that

> It is clear from these entries that the chroniclers are aware that these buildings are an innovation and seem to be a departure from what has gone before. What is also apparent is that they are informed of the existence and probably the nature of the true 'castle' outside Ireland and are applying this epithet to the innovatory style of fortification that is appearing in the landscape of Connacht. Whether they actually considered these fortifications to be morphologically and functionally comparable to the Anglo-Norman and European castle is a moot point.[59]

This view is not unique to them so it seems invidious to single out this quotation, but every single line of its specific articulation here must, respectfully, be countered. It is not at all clear in the sources that these *caisteoil* were buildings (as distinct from monuments in which there were buildings). Nor is it clear from the references that, whatever they were, these *caisteoil* were innovative. It is not apparent from any texts that anybody in Ireland was 'informed' about castles outside Ireland, as distinct from having direct experience of them; indeed, it seems unlikely anyway that it was the chroniclers who were exclusively responsible for the terminology. The concept of a 'true' castle is also hugely problematic, and to assert that the Irish *caisteoil* were not 'true' is, first, to assume that there was a medieval distinction between 'real' and 'not-real' castles, and second, to gainsay the original Irish voices. Finally, 'the Anglo-Norman and European castle' – a pairing that suggests there was a distinction between them – had neither morphological nor functional consistency to begin with. Reversal of the scepticism that informs the O'Conor and Naessens quote, as well as much of

---

57 McNeill 1997, 14. The sites he mentioned are Duneight (Down), Downpatrick (Down), Limerick, and Dunamase (Laois). Duneight is discussed below (p. 52). The site at Downpatrick is *Dundáleathglais*, alias *Ráthceltchair* (Orpen 1907a, 137–8). McNeill suggested it might be the documented royal site of the eleventh and twelfth centuries. Note that its enclosure resembles in exact shape and topographical siting the 'egg-shaped' later tenth-century Anglo-Saxon ringworks at places like Fowlmere (Cambridgeshire) and Goltho (Lincolnshire) (see Blair 2018, 391). The excavated evidence McNeill cited in Limerick can now be excluded (see Wiggins 2016, 303–4). Full publication of the Dunamase excavations might clarify the significance of the remains found there.   58 O'Conor and Naessens 2012.   59 Ibid., 260.

the commentary on the same matter by others, requires two changes in mindset. First, the word 'castle' needs to have its magic-word status withdrawn from it; it should not be privileged as *the* word which, if it is not used explicitly, excludes sites and structures from consideration as *de facto* castles. Second, there needs to be a recognition that there is nothing intrinsically 'un-castle' about the mortared stone-walled enclosures on the western Irish lakes.

Examination of the (admittedly) meagre topographical and archaeological evidence permits a new reading of the 1124–62 references, and it encourages the view that those documented castles were not the only ones. Of the eight, two remain mysterious: Galway and Collooney.[60] But two were probably or possibly crannogs (*Loch Cairrgin* and *Cuilenntrach* respectively).[61] In these two cases, the label castle was applied by annalists at the time of destruction, not construction, so we cannot know how old they were by then and whether they were considered castles by those who occupied them. Another one of the eight was of stone (Ferns), and yet another (the 'wonderful castle' of Tuam) was probably of stone also.[62] That leaves two: Ballinasloe and Athlone, first mentioned when constructed in 1124 and 1129 respectively.

COULD BALLINASLOE AND ATHLONE HAVE HAD MOTTES IN 1124?

It has been suggested that the site of the 1124 castle in Ballinasloe might be the low-lying site occupied by the town's late medieval castle.[63] However, in April 1709 Samuel Molyneux saw and noted in the town of Ballinasloe 'a Danes-mount, with a large trench round it: 'tis so flat one might allmost take it for a fort'.[64] This was a motte. In the absence of a record of a castle at Ballinasloe after the invasion, this is most likely to have been the castle of 1124. All surface traces are gone, but there is evidence that it was located on the site now occupied by the church of St John the Evangelist in the centre of the town (Fig. 6): that church occupies the highest ground in the town, it appears from cartographic evidence to have been built on the site of a circular earthwork, and the name of the castle in the twelfth century is preserved in a street name beside the church.[65]

It has been suggested that the site of the native castle in Athlone is on the east bank of the river Shannon, directly opposite the Anglo-Norman castle.[66] This, too, is an incorrect identification. I have argued elsewhere that it was on the west bank, that it was a motte, and that the Anglo-Normans revetted it a decade into the thirteenth

60 A castle-site in the flood plain at the intersection of two rivers outside the town of Collooney has been suggested as the 1124 site (McGarry 1980, 5), but I think the original castle was on higher, drier, ground. **61** For both, see O'Keeffe 2019a, 126–7; the 'slave chain' discovered on *Loch Cairrgin* (Wood-Martin 1886, 237) could be reinterpreted as a chain for prisoners, in line with one of the imprisoning strategies of castle-owning society in the eleventh and twelfth centuries (see Dunbabin 2002, 32–4). **62** It is not inconceivable that these two castles had stone donjons: such donjons seem to have been used in native contexts in Scotland in the first half of the twelfth century, as at Roxburgh and Edinburgh (Oram 2008, 174). **63** Barry 2007, 38. **64** https://celt.ucc.ie//published/E700002–001/index.html: entry 5. **65** O'Keeffe 2019a, 122–3. **66** Murtagh 1994, 2–3.

6 The church of St John the Evangelist, Ballinasloe, which probably occupies the site of the 1124 castle. The open ground in front of the church has never been built upon and might therefore have originated as a place of assembly in front of the castle.

century.[67] In brief, given the identity of its builder, Tairdelbach Ua Conchobair, the pre-Norman castle must have been on the Connacht side of the river. Moreover, the annalistic references make clear that it and the bridge were paired, and the fact that it

67 See O'Keeffe 2019a, 123–6.

7 Athlone Castle from the Leinster side of the river Shannon. The pre-Norman bridge exited to the left of the thirteenth-century circular tower in the middle of the photograph. The polygonal tower (see Fig. 51) sits on a motte, now suggested as pre-Norman in origin.

was sometimes left undamaged when the bridge was attacked from Leinster is a sure sign that it was on the Connacht side of the river; the Leinster armies would not have gone around the castle to destroy the bridge. The site of the bridge is known: the motte overlooks where it reached the west bank of the river (Fig. 7).

The identification of a motte at pre-invasion Ballinasloe is fairly secure, then, and the case for one at pre-invasion Athlone is very strong. Tairdelbach Ua Conchobair was responsible for both. The other two castles of the 1120s, Galway and Collooney, were also works of Tairdelbach Ua Conchobair, so they too might have had mottes. In any case, the two strong identifications provide a context for a longer discussion of the phenomenon of the motte.

The term mota

Differentiating between the scales and functions of fortified places in the eleventh and twelfth centuries was perhaps sometimes achieved by medieval clerks and chroniclers by the deployment of words other than 'castle', such as *municipium, oppidum* and *fortalicium*. Alas, these words do not bring much clarity to the modern researcher as they are not obviously descriptive. A word like *turris*, tower, clearly referred to a part of (or an element within) a fortification, but, even then, one cannot always be sure that it was not a synecdoche for a whole structure, a whole *castrum* or *castellum*. Another word which referred to an element of a fortification but might also have been a synecdoche for a castle in its entirety is *mota* or *motta*, motte, now understood to refer simply to a mound.

Matching extant monuments or parts of monuments with the words used to describe them in the Middle Ages is obviously the best method by which one can understand what those words might have meant, but it can be done only in the contexts of individual sites. Given what has been observed above about interchangeability of words in medieval documentary contexts, it would be foolhardy to attempt to identify other examples of a named class or type, such as *castrum* or *castellum*, or even a *turris*, based on the morphology of a surviving example (assuming, of course, that the original documented fortification is the one that is seen at a site today). Yet, that is exactly what has happened with the *mota*.

Indications that this word most commonly referred to a castle-mound have distracted scholars from the possibility that it sometimes referred instead to non-military structures: toponymic evidence in France, for example, reveals that it could refer to the mound under a windmill or a gibbet.[68] Many sources even warn us away from assuming that *mota* always signified a castle-mound. Archaeological investigations have shown us that the first castle at Trim (Meath), for example, described in the late twelfth century as a *mot*, had at most a very low mound, regarded by Trim's excavators as too small in volume of soil to be described as a motte; the *mottam comitis* mentioned in 1123 at Guingamp was probably a not-dissimilar earthwork-enceinte.[69] Also, other words were used in the Middle Ages for mounds which would conventionally be regarded as mottes, indicating that the equation of word and object was not fixed. In the famous description by Lambert of Ardres (*c.*1181), the circular *domus* of the castle at Guines (Pas-de-Calais) was a multi-storeyed residential wooden structure on a mound, described as a *dunjo*.[70] Finally, when references to mottes post-date the main period of construction of castle-mounds (as evidenced archaeologically), one cannot be sure that the word was used in respect of an ancient mound. For example, in a relatively small district in the diocese of Bazas (Aquitaine), *mota* signified a conical mound when used in eleventh- and twelfth-century contexts, but in the thirteenth century, when mound-building had passed from fashion, it was used to describe what

68 Proust 1981.   **69** Mullaly 2002, line 3300. For the view that, contrary to the accepted opinion, the 'ringwork' visible at Trim is not the original earthwork, see O'Keeffe 2017a, 47–52; 2018b; for Guingamp see Beuchet 2014.   **70** Coulson 2003, 73; Shopkow 2010, 111.

is otherwise described in sources as a *maison forte*, a strong house.[71] Typifying the challenge of matching words and structures is thirteenth-century documentation from low-lying Zeeland in which the raised medieval settlement mound known in Dutch as a *werf* was translated into *motte* in French, and both were regarded as equivalent to *munitio* as used in twelfth-century Latin sources.[72]

The assumption that *mota* always connoted a castle-mound has led scholars to try to identify its morphological boundaries, as if motte-builders of the Middle Ages actually followed such rules. Thanks to the published proceedings of the Château Gaillard colloquium wherein his work has been widely cited for years, Michael Müller-Wille's suggestion that mounds less than 3m in height above ground level should not be regarded as mottes continues to reach a wide audience outside the German-speaking world.[73] It says much about the limitations of traditional archaeology that Michel de Boüard based his objection to Müller-Wille's suggestion of a height-criterion on the fact that mounds have eroded;[74] he did not, in other words, object to the principle of defining mottes according to morphology. Ideally, of course, we should not describe any castle-mounds as mottes unless authorized to do so by the use of *mota* or a cognate in a medieval historical source, but that has not been the way of scholarship; that horse has already bolted.

Archaeology

Michel de Boüard postulated that *mota* designated in the ninth century a piece of turf or sod, that it came to be applied to mounds or banks (built of layers of turves) in the tenth and eleventh centuries, and that it was only in the latter century, in France and England, that it was first used to designate a castle-mound.[75] That *mota* attained widespread use as a 'castle word' in the second millennium, mainly after 1100, is attested to in French sources. In western Gascony, for example, it appears with that very purpose in the early twelfth century (and was still in use into the later thirteenth century).[76] But the first appearance of the word does not signify the first appearance of the type of high earthwork monument to which the word is now most routinely attached. In the Breton charters, for example, the word first appears in the middle of the twelfth century,[77] yet the building of mottes started before the turn of the millennium.[78] The earliest actual evidence for extensive building of mottes is in France (the caveat being that France has seen the most excavation). Early sites which fall within the broad morphological definition would include Boves from *c.*900 and Montfélix (Marne) from *c.*950.[79] Mesqui has commented on the 'incredibly rapid diffusion' of the motte from the end of the tenth century,[80] but the relative speed of its diffusion – or, more accurately, of its acceptance as a form of castle – is not easily gauged. The number of new mottes in France certainly appears to have increased around AD1000, with a growth in numbers continuing through the following century, but there have

71 Faravel 2014. **72** Hoek 1981, 31; Mostert 2013. **73** Müller-Wille 1966, 7. **74** De Boüard 1981, 7. **75** Ibid., 18. **76** Boutoulle 2014, 604. **77** Jones 2001, 48. **78** Chédeville and Tonnerre 1987, 190. **79** Racinet 2008; Renoux 2018. **80** Mesqui 1991, 16.

been too few excavations for one to speak authoritatively about the exact chronology. The motte tradition seems to have lingered into the thirteenth century in places, as in Normandy, where the peasantry was expected to make or repair *motas* for their lords.[81]

On the whole, mottes appear to have been infrequent outside the general area of modern France before the middle of the eleventh century. In the British Isles, for example, mottes are conventionally regarded as an introduction of Normans (into England, after *c.*1050) and Anglo-Normans (into Ireland after 1169),[82] while in areas east of the Elbe, for example, mottes only started around 1200, and then lasted into the fifteenth century.[83] But mottes were not unknown outside France around 1000: for example, there is now some evidence of early examples in Flanders to the north, and in the Netherlands, further north again.[84]

From the known to the unknown: mottes in pre-Norman Ireland

Goddard Orpen argued more than a century ago that the motte as a type was introduced into Ireland by the Anglo-Normans in the late twelfth century, and he persuaded subsequent generations of scholars that its primary role was to aid the taking and securing of land.[85] Orpen based his argument on the historical record, but he also noted that the distribution pattern of mottes matched the pattern of early colonial landholding in Ireland. The number of mottes known on the island has increased in the intervening years, thanks to systematic survey work, but the distribution pattern has not been changed sufficiently by that work to query Orpen's attribution. Our understanding of the functions of mottes within the infant lordship is now a little more nuanced.[86] Unfortunately, there has been very little archaeological excavation of such sites in Ireland, so surprises may await under the sod. The rather simple timber buildings found on the summit of the small motte at Lismahon (Down) are consistent with the common view that such mounds were erected to meet the immediate needs of conquest and colonization.[87] But some mottes such as that at Granard (Longford), for example, which was inserted into a substantial earthwork enclosure of earlier date, obviously represent very different intentions and ambitions.

Motte numbers are greatest in the areas of the former lordship of Meath and earldom of Ulster. There, motte-building trickled down the Anglo-Norman social hierarchy from the greatest regional potentates to lesser lords, and even to some whose social rank barely qualified them for seigneurial description in the first place. In Anglo-Norman Leinster, motte-ownership was generally confined to lords of relatively high rank, so the number of examples is smaller than in Meath or Ulster.[88] The settlement of the area of modern Munster, beginning in the late twelfth century after the first

81 Desisle 1864, 19 (s.a. 1210), 87 (s.a. 1223), 155 (s.a. 1240).   **82** McNeill 1997, 59–60, 66–70. **83** See, for example, Biermann 2015.   **84** Van Strydonck and Vanthournout 1996, 451. Aarts 2015.   **85** Orpen 1906; 1907a.   **86** McNeill 2014.   **87** Waterman 1959. This is an example of what has been described as a *tour beffrio* (Mesqui 1991). This translates as 'belfry tower', a belfry (*berfrei* in Old French and *berfrey* in Middle English, from the Latin *berefredus*) being, among other things, a military watchtower.   **88** See McNeill 2014 for the most recent work on the status of motte-owners in eastern Ireland.

land grants and then continuing into King John's reign, was not facilitated by motte-building on a scale at all comparable with the 1170s and 1180s in eastern Ireland, so mottes are not common in east Munster and are very rare in Cork and Limerick. The motte was probably not used at all in the settlement of Connacht from the mid-1230s; any Anglo-Norman mottes which can be identified on the west side of the Shannon are likely to mark the invaders' unsuccessful early thirteenth-century attempts at settlement there. It was not that the motte went out of fashion as conquest and colonization progressed westwards (although that might be part of the explanation for the pattern in Connacht) but, rather, that each territorial unit within the greater lordship simply had its own settlement dynamic, shaped by the preferences of its barons and, more indirectly, by the lack of coherent royal oversight of the subinfeudation process.

In recent years, some mottes have been identified as native Irish works, but as post-1169 copies of Anglo-Norman examples.[89] Forty years ago, Chris Lynn invited speculation on the motte-like character of pre-Norman 'raised raths' (ringforts with elevated interiors) in the north of Ireland, suggesting that they are relatively late – the ninth century at the earliest, and the eleventh at the latest – in the history of the ringfort. But scholars have stopped short of describing as mottes, or even as motte-like, any ringforts with elevated interiors. In the minds of most Irish researchers, then, the motte remains a post-1169 phenomenon in Ireland.

The evidence from Ballinasloe and Athlone from 1124 and 1129 respectively should lead to a rethinking of the type's chronology and cultural contexts. If sceptics of extensive pre-invasion encastellation allow that there were two mottes in Ireland in the 1120s, how can they reject the *prima facie* case for others, even if the annalists did not record them? After all, if there were two in the 1120s, does that not leave forty years for others to have been raised before the invasion of 1169? And might there have been some before the 1120s?

Given the paucity of the evidence, one must be careful to police the boundary between reasonable deduction and wild speculation, but no progress will be made without some speculation. Let us accept as probable, based on the evidence of Ballinasloe and Athlone, that the known corpus of mottes in Ireland includes some native examples erected in the decades *before* the invasion. So, where are they? Why have they not been identified? Some may be invisible because they were appropriated and modified by the Anglo-Normans, causing them to be classified incorrectly today as colonial monuments in their entireties. Others might simply have been mis-classified as Anglo-Norman: the small undocumented mottes at Ardskeagh (Cork) and Killeshin (Laois), for example, are located suggestively close to pre-Norman churches – early and mid-twelfth century in date respectively – to which no alterations were made in the late twelfth or early thirteenth centuries.[90] It must be conceded, however, that the

---

89 McNeill 1997, 73–4; 2014, 246–8. The phenomeon is attested to in Scotland: see Oram 2008, 178–9. **90** Killeshin was once identified as the original castle of Carlow, but Kieran O'Conor has shown that not to be the case (O'Conor 1997). The nearby church was built under the patronage of Diarmait MacMurchada. European in outlook, he was an active patron of the

number of native, pre-invasion, mottes within the corpus must be relatively small, because if mottes were common in pre-Norman Ireland one would find them in western parts of the country where there was little or no colonial settlement. There, of course, some might be hiding in plain sight as 'raised raths': excavations in, say, counties Cork or Limerick, or Galway or Roscommon, might someday reveal ringfort interiors of above-average elevation to have been occupied, even constructed, in the eleventh and twelfth centuries, prompting a re-evaluation. But the point is important: one can argue that there was motte-building in pre-Norman Ireland, but, because of the paucity of sites in the western half of Ireland, one could not argue that the number of sites was big.

When and from where might the idea of the motte have entered pre-Norman Ireland? The term *caistél*, used by the annalists for Ballinasloe and Athlone, is of Anglo-Norman origin, so it could not have been used in Ireland before 1066. The word did not necessarily connote a motte, as was shown above, but it is entirely conceivable that the term and the monument type entered eastern Ireland around the same time, possibly even together, from Norman England. This might have happened in the late eleventh century. Both might have entered Connacht shortly afterwards. This would not be an unreasonable thesis, nor could it be particularly controversial.

Future research, especially archaeological, is likely to change how we understand the monuments discussed above. In anticipation of such work, I want to offer two adventurous speculations for future reflection.

First, if we assume the motte as a type to have been an importation into pre-Norman Ireland, can we rule out the possibility that it arrived directly from France (regardless of the linguistic evidence)? The case for direct importation from the Continent into the Ua Conchobair kingdom of Connacht, even in the eleventh century, deserves some consideration. The river Shannon connected the midlands and eastern Connacht to the Atlantic, from which seaboard France was more accessible than England. It might not be irrelevant that French influence is apparent in the sculptural decoration of some Irish churches erected in the Shannon region in the twelfth century.[91] The key to entertaining the possibility of a French origin, regardless of whether it was directly to Connacht or not, is to recognize that pre-invasion mottes in Ireland might *not* have been built to emulate the fortress-mounds associated with Norman or Anglo-Norman invasion and military colonization. Mound-castles in many parts of Europe were not actually associated with processes of conquest. There is also relatively little evidence, documentary or archaeological, that they were ever attacked, suggesting that they were generally not built with the primary intention of defending their owners from attack. Four mottes are depicted under attack on the Bayeux Tapestry, but the elaboration of the structures depicted on their summits (Fig. 8) suggest that they were not imagined by those who did the embroidery as military

reforming native church – his support for the Cistercians earned him a Certificate of Confraternity from St Bernard of Clairvaux – and he possessed at Ferns, his capital, the only documented pre-invasion castle in Ireland outside of Connacht (O'Keeffe 1997).   **91** Ibid. 2003, *passim.*

8 Mottes depicted on the late eleventh-century Bayeux Tapestry. For clarity, figures (men, horses) have been removed. That at Hastings is shown under construction, with the timber summit structure itself being assembled – it is known that prefabricated timberwork was brought to England with the invading fleet – as the mound is being raised.

buildings. The circular *domus* on top of a motte at Guines was sumptuously residential according to its contemporary description; it was not designed to withstand an attack.[92] It would seem, then, that the elevation of structures on mound summits was intended sometimes, if not mainly, to give them greater visibility, and by extension to give greater visibility to the associated rituals of lordship.

92 Coulson 2003, 73; Shopkow 2010, 111.

9 The mound at Kilfinnane, over 30m in basal diameter and under 10m high above the fosse. The ramparts have been levelled on this side – the north – of the monument.

Second, the 'language' of the motte as an object of visual culture that was associated with the display and performance of power might well have been understood before any formal introduction of the type from overseas in the late eleventh or early twelfth century. Power-display (including inauguration) mounds of non-sepulchral, but also non-military, character were known in Ireland well before 1100.[93] Assuming it not to have been a burial mound originally, *The Forradh* at Tara (Meath) – the mound on the summit of the Hill of Tara – belongs arguably in the conceptual ancestry of the motte.[94] The same might be said of the low, heavily-eroded, non-sepulchral mound inserted into the restricted space in the middle of a multivallate enclosure at the ancient royal site of Tlachtga (The Hill of Ward), near Athboy (Meath). The radiocarbon-derived date-range for the insertion is suggestive: AD 884–1029.[95] Another relevant mound is at Kilfinnane (Limerick) (Fig. 9). This large earthwork is in the middle of a (now partly-destroyed) multivallate enclosure, the inner rampart of which encircled it quite tightly. It is classified as an Anglo-Norman monument, but there is no record of the building of a castle at Kilfinnane, it is located in a region where mottes are very rare, and Anglo-Norman mottes do not have such contemporary multivallation. One hesitates to describe the mounds at Tara and Tlachtga as mottes, but the pre-Norman

93 See Herity 1993.   **94** O'Keeffe 2013a.   **95** My thanks to my colleague, Dr Steve Davis (UCD School of Archaeology), the site's excavator, for this information.

mound at Kilfinnane might merit it. There is an almost identical site at Rathmore (Kildare). It could not possibly be Anglo-Norman in its entirety, but its mound acted as a motte in the late twelfth-century colonization of the district, and it might have been altered for that purpose. As at Kilfinnane, it is conceivable that the Rathmore mound, in its original form, was a pre-Norman motte, closer in spirit and chronology to the mounds at Ballinasloe than to, say, *The Forradh* at Tara.

Looking at all of the sites just discussed, one is tempted to suggest that an indigenous mound-building tradition was locked into the DNA of the pre-Norman castle-mounds in Ballinasloe and Athlone, if not informing their physical morphology then at least allowing them to be understood in native Irish society as expressions of hegemonic power. The idea might seem far-fetched, but it is worth noting that no single place of origin for the high, flat-topped, castle-mound can actually be identified anywhere in Europe, even if the current chronology suggests that the type appeared first in France.[96] One can see at Der Husterknupp, for example, how a motte emerged from a gradual accumulation of soil on a settlement site during the tenth and eleventh centuries.[97] The simultaneous appearance of types of castle-mound in different parts of western Europe (alongside *petites enceintes circulaires*, types of *rocca* fortresses, stone-walled fortresses, and so on) allows the possibility of a largely independent genesis in different places of the basic morphological concept of the motte, albeit in the common context of post-Viking social change. Further research might someday place sites like Kilfinnane and Rathmore at the very centre of the European conversation on the origins of the motte.

Could Ballinasloe and Athlone have had baileys in 1124?

The enclosure attached to (or, less frequently, enclosing) a motte is known in English as a bailey. The resultant type, the motte-and-bailey, is fairly universal in western Europe, although the term motte-and-bailey itself, in which the mound and enclosure are 'coupled', is actually unique to English-language scholarship. The Latin *ballium* was used to describe this feature in England from the twelfth century.[98] We do not know what word was used before then, if indeed any was, but the feature already existed in essence as an appendage to a principal settlement focus: in Phase II at Der Husterknupp, for example, dated to between 950 and 1000, a fosse surrounded a bailey-like enclosure beside a very low settlement mound (see Fig. 4). So, could Ballinasloe and Athlone have had baileys in 1124? The short answer is yes.

The modern word, bailey, is understood to be derived from *baile*, the Middle English derivative of *ballium*.[99] This may have entered usage around 1200.[100] I am not aware of its Old French equivalent, *bai(l)le, balie*, being used in contemporary French contexts. Some modern French scholars use *baile* rather than the more common *basse*

---

96 Attempts to identify morphological and geographical origins have not been successful. For example, Jean-François Maréchal made the unimplausible suggestion that invading Vikings saw Freisen *terpen* (dry, tell-like, settlement mounds on low ground) and, settling in France as Normans, transformed the concept to invent mottes (Maréchal 1979; 1984).   **97** Herrnbrodt 1958.   **98** Latham 1965, 42. DMLBS s.v.   **99** Higham and Barker 1992, 361.   **100** https://quod.lib.umich.edu/m/med/.

cour (a low court),[101] but I have not found an example of its use in published primary French sources. In modern German literature the feature is described as *Vorburg* (the space, literally, 'in front of the castle'). This is a medieval word.[102] However, its use was not confined to castles (it was also used in respect of spaces outside towns), and that in turn would suggest that, unlike *ballium* or *baile*, it was not a specialized word in the context of castles.

Some twenty years ago the late Professor Francis John Byrne expressed to me his view that the modern word 'bailey' might actually have originated in the Irish *baile*, a word that connoted in Ireland either a settlement or a taxable land-unit.[103] He was tempted by its chronology: *baile* is first attested to in the native language around the turn of the millennium, which is considerably earlier than the words which, presumably, he regarded as cognates. Given that 'bailey' is not used in England until well into the Angevin period, and that *baile* has the same spelling in both Anglo-Norman French and Middle English as it has in earlier medieval Ireland, Byrne's suggestion of a borrowing from Irish seems unlikely. But he was correct in identifying the Irish word's potential importance within the wider cultural context. Rather than being its place of origin, it is far more likely that Ireland preserves evidence that *baile* emerged in medieval western European culture as a derivative of the Latin *ballium* at an earlier date than is indicated by English and French sources.

The burning of a *dún* and the 'breaking' of a *baile* in 1011 at *Dún Echdach*, now Duneight,[104] assumes special significance when one notes the evidence that a motte-and-bailey of Duneight had a pre-Norman horizon of occupation.[105] Charles Doherty, writing about *Dún Echdach*/Duneight, asked 'is there any reason why *dún* and *baile* should not be translated as "motte" and "bailey"?'.[106] There is no reason why it should not be, although it should be noted that the 'shape' of the settlement in the pre-Norman phase discovered in the very limited excavation at the site is not easily interpreted. *Dún Echdach* might have comprised a fort, a *dún*, to which was attached an enclosed settlement somewhat larger than a conventional bailey (and therefore larger than the present Duneight bailey), as indeed might have been the case in 1132 with the *caislen* and *baile* at Galway.[107] As a possible parallel, one might look to the castle at Betz-le-Château (Touraine), in use the same time as *Dún Echdach* was attacked. Its bailey, attached contemporaneously to the motte at the end of the tenth century, was extensive enough to enclose and give seigneurial protection to a village (including its church and cemetery), while there was an inner bailey beside the motte in which there were multiple pits, or silos, for the storage of food, possibly delivered to the castle as the product of 'feudal' service by the villagers (Fig. 10).[108] It is tempting to think that places like *Dún Echdach* and Galway in the early eleventh and early twelfth centuries respectively were similar.

How the word, *ballium* or *baile*, came to be attached to an enclosure beside a castle-mound is worthy of some reflection. Revealingly, its many medieval cognate nouns

---

101 See, for example, Deyres 1974.   **102** http://www.woerterbuchnetz.de/DWB?lemma= vorburg.   **103** O'Keeffe 2014a.   **104** AU 1011.6.   **105** Waterman 1963.   **106** Doherty 1998, 327.   **107** MIA 1132.21.   **108** Riou and Marteaux 2012.

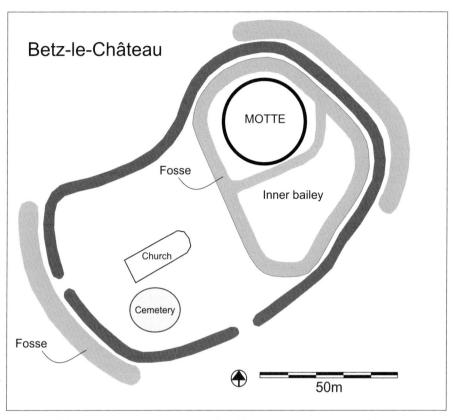

10 Plan of the castle and settlement at Betz-le-Château.

and verbs (in Latin, Old French, Anglo-Norman and Middle English) relate in some way to the possession and exercise of power over individuals or jurisdictions: they include relationships of bondage, captivity, custody and guardianship, the delivery of an individual into the custody of a mainpernor (bail, as we would understand it today), the authority of a seigneur to appoint to the office of *bailiff* someone who will have authority over a *bailiwick* (both cognate words themselves), and so on.[109] So, it must be wrong to regard a bailey, at least in its early history, as merely an enclosure intended to accommodate structures and functions for which there was no physical room on a motte's summit. Yes, it provided such accommodation, but it was surely also a jurisdictional entity originally, its rampart defining the space within which certain types of authority could be exercised and recognized, from imprisonment to the appointment of officials. In a sense, then, the (low) bailey functioned relative to the (tall) motte as the (low) hall functioned relative to the (tall) tower in stone castles (see Chapter 3). From the late eleventh century there is a reference from Segré (Maine-et-Loire) to a hall (*aula*) located *ad pedem motae*.[110] Noting the suggestion above that *The*

109 http://www.anglo-norman.net/, https://quod.lib.umich.edu/m/med/.

Forradh at Tara is conceptually in the tradition of the *mota*, one might be tempted to regard the enclosure at its foot (*ad pedam motae*), known by the name of the building once inside it as *Teach Cormac*, Cormac's house (or hall), as conceptually in the tradition of the *baile*.

BRINGING THE CHRONOLOGY BACK FURTHER? SOME OTHER 'CASTLE' WORDS

Various other words, some only distantly related etymologically to Latin words, were used in Ireland prior to the first documented appearance of *caistél* to describe places or sites that were protected or defended. Some of those remained in use contemporaneously with it. The contexts in which those words – *dún, dúnad, longport, rath* and *lis* – were used give no strong hint that they deserve to be compared with the royal or seigneurial *castra* or *castella* attested to contemporaneously in France, but that might be entirely a factor of the nature of the written evidence. Still, some speculation is called for.

Dún is an especially interesting word. Derived from the ancient 'Celtic' *dūnom* and with multiple cognates in several languages,[111] its use was probably fairly flexible for much of its early history at least. But from around the turn of the millennium, it *might* have acquired a new contextual purpose, being associated with fortifications of that militarized lordship which was first described by Donnchadh Ó Corráin almost fifty years ago.[112] There is reason to wonder whether it connoted a mound-form fortification or a fortification which featured a tower or some point of artificial elevation. First, the original term *dūnom* seems to be a more likely etymological origin for the word 'donjon', a tower, than the more commonly cited Latin *dominionem* ('dominion', signifying lordship).[113] Second, *dunio* or *dunjo* could refer to a mound as well as a tower: the circular *domus* of the castle at Guines built on top of a *dunjo*,[114] clearly a mound. The use of *dún* in the context of Galway and Ballinasloe in 1124 suggests the word was an acceptable alternative to *caistél*, and that raises the possibility that *dún* sites or places first mentioned around that time might have been understood contemporaneously as castles.[115] Ballinasloe had a mound for certain, as did some other *dún* sites documented in the period, such as Dunmore (Galway) where the mound is low and defaced,[116] but the mere presence of any dominant feature in a fortification – a tower, for example – might have sufficed to merit the use of the term for that fortification in its entirety.[117]

110 See Meuret 1998, 153.   111 Matasovic 2009, 108.   112 Ó Corráin 1972; O'Keeffe 2019a. 113 The point was made by Maréchal 1991, 269; for *dominionem* see Brachet 1873, 119. 114 *MGH* XXIV, 613, 624: 'a very high motte or lofty donjon' (*motam altissimam sive dunjonem eminentem*); Higham and Barker 1992, 115–16; Dixon 2008, 194.   115 O'Keeffe 2019a, 127. 116 Ibid., 122–3, 127. The motte-like monument known as *Dún Dealgan*, in Castletown, just outside Dundalk (Louth), occupies an ancient site which is well documented in the twelfth century (O'Sullivan 2006, 1). It is not documented as a fortress before the invasion but the mound is so unlike Anglo-Norman mottes that it might be a fortress of the same period. 117 Might the low motte-like mound on the rampart of a 'ringwork' have given the site known as 'the Duno' (Oosterbeek, NL) its name? For a summary of that site see Aarts 2012, 4–5.

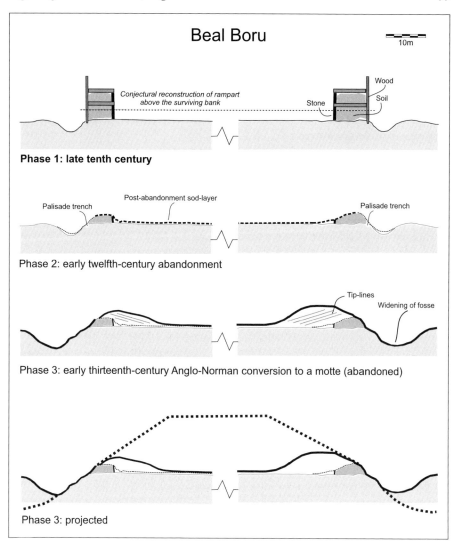

11 Cross-sections, based on the excavated evidence, showing the development of Beal Boru.

The word *cathair*, the uses of which in native sources indicate that it could be a type of fortification, or an ecclesiastical settlement, or a (fortified?) urban place,[118] brings us closer to the optional meanings of *castrum* and *castellum* in turn-of-millennium France. Kincora, at Killaloe (Clare), was named as a *cathair* right through the eleventh century, starting in 1012.[119] The evidence that Caherconnell (Clare) – note the name – was probably constructed sometime between the early tenth century and the mid-twelfth century is of considerable interest.[120] *Inis*, literally meaning 'island', could refer to a

118 eDIL s.v.   **119** For example, AIn. 1012.5; AU 1013.11, 1061.5; AIn. 1088.4.   **120** Comber

settlement on an island or to an artificial island (a crannog), and the contexts of the word's use in native sources suggest that they were perceived as places or monuments that were protected or fortified;[121] two of the castles named in the period after 1124 were apparently crannogs (see p. 39 above). The word *daingen* also connoted some sort of fortification. One possible indication of the purpose of the *daingen* (beyond merely providing protection for whoever or whatever was inside it) was the fact that the word could also apply to 'a bond, compact, covenant, espousal, security'.[122] Is this an indication that *daingen* referred to a place of homage, a place where fealty was sworn? It is interesting that in 1012/13 the *cathair* of Kincora is also identified as a *daingen*.[123] *Dindgna*, etymologically related, could mean an elevated spot.[124] It was sometimes used in conjunction with *dún* or *daingen*, suggesting that it might refer to an earthen mound associated with some form of coercive authority.[125]

Perhaps the most interesting terminology is used in a reference to military works created by Brian Bórama in 995: *Cumtach Cassil & Inse Locha Gair & Inse Locha Sainglend & dentai imdai archena la Brian*.[126] Doherty understood *cumtach* to allude to 'the enhancing or fortifying of pre-existing structures'.[127] *Dénta* is suggestive of a sophisticated architectural work, even in timber, made by an artificer.[128] This yields, then, the translation 'the re-fortifying of Cashel, Lough Gur, and Singland, and the fashioning of many structures besides, by Brian'. This might simply be hyperbole, but one could not discount the possibility that Brian commissioned elaborate timber architecture for his fortifications. Michael O'Kelly's excavation of the king's fortress of *Boraimhe*, now Beal Boru (Clare), produced a tantalizing clue (Fig. 11). The late tenth-century fort was unusual by Irish standards (as O'Kelly himself remarked). It was by no means a conventional 'ringfort'. A circular enclosure with an apparently shallow fosse, its bank of varying width was bounded on the outside by a palisade and on the inside by a stone wall.[129] The shallow settings of the palisade posts suggests that the bank could not have been retained without a substantial timber framework around it, even through it, similar perhaps to that reconstructed at Boves, *c*.900.[130] Although very different in design from the imposing *Dún Eochair Maige*, one could argue that Beal Boru is as deserving of the label 'castle'.

CONCLUSION

When did castle-building begin in Ireland? There are three approaches one can take in attempting to answer this question.

and Hull 2010, 157–8.   **121** For example, AT 985.1, 1132.8.   **122** eDIL s.v.   **123** AIn. 1012.5.
124 eDIL s.v. For a pillar-stone see AU 999.4.   **125** AFM 1084.8. See also Todd 1867, 114.
126 AIn. 995.6.   **127** Doherty 1998, 327. eDIL s.v.   **128** eDIL s.v.   **129** *Boraimhe* 'denoted a place where ... cattle-tribute was collected and counted' (Meyer 1910, 72); O'Kelly 1962.
130 For Boves see Racinet 2008, Fig. 63. Timber-lacing was also a feature of the Viking-age *trelleborgs*, royal fortresses of *c*.1000, around the Skagerrak and the Kattegat straits of southern Scandinavia (Dobat 2009, 80–3). Might the construction of *Boraimhe*'s rampart reflect influence from Scandinavian Limerick to the south? *Boraimhe* was destroyed in the early twelfth century; contrary to the view of various writers that it was re-edified as a ringwork castle in the early

The first is to follow, *to the letter*, the historical record. Interpreted literally, that record brings us back to 1124, the date of the first appearance of a word – *caistél* – which can be translated as 'castle' without dispute. That is a very late date indeed within the western European context. One might take the view that *caistél* was probably used in Ireland before it was committed to parchment, in which case its origin in the language of Norman England gives us a mid-eleventh-century *terminus post quem*. But there is no proof it was used before 1124.

The second approach is to look at castle-building outside Ireland for guidance, scrutinizing the histories of words, and identifying the individuals responsible for castles and the contexts in which they and their castles operated. An interrogation of the Irish record in such a light opens the door to the possibility that castle-building was a feature of Ireland in the age of dynastic warfare, at least in the eleventh century, and that native words used to refer to fortifications in that period effectively connoted 'castle', even though they were not derivatives of *castellum*. The scholar who follows this route will be buffeted by strong winds of scepticism ('where is the evidence?') and possibly even by assumptions of Irish exceptionalism. Fortunately, to counter claims of exceptionalism, we have for Brian Bóraime a record of a militant king whose exercise of hegemonic power in turn-of-millennium Ireland was not very different from that of castle-building potentates in Capetian France. The key here might indeed be France: too often, perhaps, Irish scholars think that the island of Britain is the more relevant place, but tenth- and eleventh-century Ireland had more in common with Capetian France than with Anglo-Saxon or Anglo-Scandinavian England in the late first millennium.[131] This is not to say that pre-Norman castle-building in Ireland reflects influence from France. Rather, it is to argue that tenth-century France provides a model for how we might interpret contemporary Ireland, even if the drivers of militarism and coercive lordship in each place – the collapse of Carolingian hegemony in one, the post-Viking rise of dynasties in the other – were different.

The third approach, which adheres to the second for most of its pursuit, is to look at the archaeological evidence in Ireland. That evidence is far from copius, but that might reflect a collective failure by archaeologists to ask the right questions, especially of non-sepulchral mounds. *Dún Eochair Maige*, which survives (just about), *Dún Echtach*, which might survive inside or beneath a motte-and-bailey, and Beal Boru, partly concealed below an aborted Anglo-Norman castle, are key sites in making a case for castle-building around the year 1000. Certainly, as was pointed out earlier (pp 19–20), no French scholar would have a difficulty identifying *Dún Eochair Maige* as a castle were it found in France and associated with lordship akin to that exercised by Brian Bóraime. It is a cliché, but more excavation is needed in Ireland to identify tenth- and eleventh-century sites which could be considered 'castles'.[132]

thirteenth century (see, for example, Barry 1987, 48–9), tip-lines, the irregularity of the bank, and the absence of a palisade trench indicate that O'Kelly was entirely correct in identifying the Anglo-Norman phase at the site as an unfinished motte. **131** O'Keeffe 2019a. **132** The problem is not unique to Ireland: Oram has noted 'how little work at any level, archaeological or historical, has been undertaken on Scottish tenth- and eleventh-century high-status secular sites' (2008, 168).

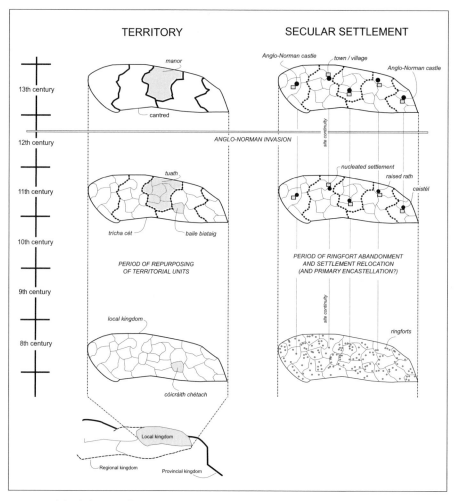

12 A model of the transformation of medieval territory and secular settlement in Ireland, 800–1200.

Finally, to the sceptic, reluctant to allow Ireland join the company of European places where castle-building is now known to have started in the tenth century or (at the earliest) the early eleventh century, I would make the observation that there is evidence in pre-millennium Ireland of the type of change that castle-building aristocracies effected on landscapes elsewhere. I submit that it deserves to be taken into consideration. That evidence is modelled in Figure 12.

The small Irish kingdom of the early Middle Ages was reimagined in the eleventh century, if not before, as the *trícha cét*, a spatial unit of royal tenure, taxation, local government, and military levy. At the same time perhaps, the *cóicráith chétach*, a five-farm unit, was transformed into the *baile biataig* (a taxable unit of land, held by families or family groups, and equivalent to the modern townland), a number of which constituted the intermediate-sized *tuath*. After the invasion of 1169, the *trícha cét* became the Anglo-Norman cantred, the *tuath* survived as the manor (and parish), and the *baile biataig* survived as its constituent lands.[133] Significantly, there was evidently a parallel process of secular settlement change.[134] Radiocarbon evidence makes clear that ringfort-construction ended, and existing forts were abandoned in their thousands, late in the first millennium. These processes, to which Irish archaeologists have been strangely reluctant to attach an explanation,[135] are most likely to reflect those very changes in social-political organization that led to the creation of the *trícha cét*, *tuath* and *baile biataig*. I suggest that in Ireland, as a process comparable to the *incastellamento* which transformed the central Italian landscape before the turn of the millennium, some older forts remained as centres of power within the new (taxation-oriented) territorial structure while some new centres of power were created at the same time, and that the population formerly in ringforts was relocated at that time to new nucleated settlements.[136] As was certainly the case with the territorial units, the Anglo-Normans might have reused the seigneurial monuments of the eleventh century, leaving them invisible; it is worth noting that the early fort at Beal Boru might not have been excavated had the Anglo-Normans completed the motte which they started to raise over it. Similarly, later settlements might overlay the settlements created in the eleventh-century reorganization of the landscape, which would explain why that former 'ringfort population' is not visible in the archaeological record.

133 This summary draws on the ground-breaking work of Paul MacCotter (2008).   **134** See O'Keeffe 1996.   **135** O'Sullivan et al. 2014.   **136** O'Keeffe 2019b.

CHAPTER 3

Signifying lordship in an age of medieval historicism: the rectangular donjon

Michel de Boüard discovered a remarkable sequence when, between 1968 and 1972, he excavated the motte known as La Chapelle in Doué-la-Fontaine (Maine-et-Loire). Inside the mound he found a long stone building for which he argued two phases: a first, later ninth-century, phase in which he believed the building to be a single-storeyed hall (*aula*), and a second, tenth-century, phase in which he believed it was extended upwards by a storey to become a form of tower, a *turris*. The structural evidence that one sees at the site today would suggest, *contra* his interpretation, that the building was actually of two storeys from the outset (Fig. 13). Be that as it may, the lower storey of the building was, in a subsequent phase, sealed within the motte, reconstituting the tenth-century upper storey as the ground-storey on the summit of the mound. That mound, dated by de Boüard to the start of the eleventh century, had been created by piling soil against its exterior. The lower storey was not filled in at that time in order to counter the (endangering?) weight of soil banked against the outside. Rather, it was retained as a dark basement.

Before discussing the structure discovered by de Boüard, it is useful to comment on its fate – its enmottement – in the earlier eleventh century. Sometimes regarded as a purely practical strategy to aid mound-building,[1] enmottement describes more properly the piling of a motte over or around an existing monument as a deliberate, symbolic, act of transformation. The extent to which it was done in the Middle Ages is uncertain: documents rarely give hints, while excavations into the cores of mottes, where enmotted structures will survive fossilized, have been too infrequent. But it might have been quite common. There is at least one documented example in Ireland. At Meelick, William de Burgh raised a motte over a church, but converted its upper part into an actual building, giving the church a powerful symbolic afterlife as an appropriated structure converted into a castle. The symbolism did not go unnoticed: the native annalists bemoaned William's consumption of meat during Lent within the new castle.[2] There is possibly a second documented example: the Annals of Ulster tell us that Hugh de Lacy was killed by an Irish man while 'building a castle in' Columcille's church [*cumdach caisteoil ina chill*] in Durrow;[3] *cill* might simply have connoted the monastery, but, if the translation should be literal, it is a parallel for Meelick. The enmottement of older ecclesiastical structures was actually not unique: at Villars-les-Dombes (Ain) part of a castle was converted into a church on a mound,

---

1 De Boüard 1981, 14–15; Flambard Héricher 2002, 124. **2** O'Keeffe 2019d. **3** AU 1186.4.

13 The *aula/turris* of Doué-la-Fontaine. The interior was divided into two spaces of unequal size by a latitudinal wall with a connecting doorway. The doorway on the left leads into the larger space, originally heated by a central hearth; the small doorway on the right leads into the narrower space, heated by a wall fireplace.

and part of that church was later converted into part of a new castle on a heightened mound.[4] In some acts of enmottement the transformation of an older structure was effected through its obliteration: at Mirville (Seine-Maritime), for example, sometime between 1087 and 1106 a motte was piled over a large wooden building (its bow-shaped ends reflecting a Scandinavian ancestry) which was no more than a few generations old at the time.[5]

Once a paradigmatic site, Doué-la-Fontaine is now more accurately described as an iconic site, a characterization that acknowledges its intrinsic interest but no longer imparts to it the singular significance which it once had in the historiography of European castellology.[6] It was paradigmatic because for a period after its excavation it was the site which provided, albeit by a certain amount of circular thinking, an archaeological illumination of the thesis that the decline of Carolingian public justice (taken to be represented by its original unfortified stone *domus*) saw the rise of an increasingly militaristic social order (taken to be represented arguably by the adding of an additional storey to the Carolingian *aula*, but certainly represented by the piling of the motte material against the wall of that *aula*). The *act* of enmottement was by its nature profoundly symbolic in any context, but its symbolic power depended on contemporary witnesses to the act, and on the durability of collected memory: the clock started to run down on the symbolism of the act from the moment that an

4 Poisson 1994.   **5** Le Maho 1984. Mesqui describes Mirville as an example of 'surmottement' (1991, 17).   **6** R. Allen Brown, discussing the genesis of the stone castle, suggested that at Doué-la-Fontaine we are in 'the very presence of the events we seek' (1976, 24).

original monument was concealed in whole or in part, and disappeared from both sight and memory. Still, one can easily understand how, as the implications of Georges Duby's work on feudalism were being still realized, the enmottement of a Carolingian structure at Doué-la-Fontaine, once discovered, was perceived in terms of epochal change.

Doué-la-Fontaine remains central to the castellological conversation,[7] but new discoveries and advances in dating-techniques are rendering it less revelatory. In terms of its history as a site of enmottement, the end product at Doué-la-Fontaine at the start of the eleventh century was actually not as unique as originally seemed to be the case. It was probably not unlike the finished monuments at, for example, La Marche (Nièvre), Semur-en-Brionnais (Saône-et-Loire), or Castelnau-Montratier (Lot). Mottes, removed within living memory without recording, were piled against the lower parts of tall stone towers at the first two sites named, and those towers have now been dated by radiocarbon to the tenth century.[8] These monuments, in their final enmotted phases, would seem to have been fairly exact parallels for Doué-la-Fontaine as it appeared after the turn of the millennium. In each case, the intention seems to have been to create a particular type: a stone building on a mound. That this was an actual type with both elements being of equal importance (as distinct from a mound that had a stone building on it, or indeed a stone building that had a mound underneath it) is suggested by the evidence at Castelnau-Montratier where a motte raised in the later tenth century and abandoned by *c.*1030 had at its core the lower 8m or more of a *contemporary* stone tower, indicating that the monument was conceived *ab initio* as a mound with a tower on it.[9]

The more important historiographical point to be made about the Doué-la-Fontaine discovery pertains not to the motte but to the structure which it part-concealed. This seemed at the time to be a unique survival, but it can now be described more accurately as a rare survival. Whether it was turriform through a process of conversion in the 930s (as its excavator suggested) or was entirely turriform from *c.*900 (as Edward Impey has suggested),[10] it is certainly one of the few surviving examples of a (once) tall, pre-millennial structure of domestic character. When it seemed to be unique, it was regarded as the earliest recognizable milestone on an evolutionary road which led from the late Carolingian unfortified *domus* to the post-Carolingian donjon.

But things are changing in the understanding of how Doué-la-Fontaine relates to the later donjons. Mapping the latter's prehistory and early history has been joyfully complicated by, for example, the identification of a three-storeyed residential block with an attached tower, both of *c.*900, at Mayenne,[11] and by the revised dating backwards of some donjons of demonstrable architectural-historical importance. The transformative effect on castellology of the redating of the donjon of Loches (Indre-et-Loire) by almost a century through dendrochronology has been reduced somewhat

---

7 Impey 2008a.   **8** Bonhomme et al. 2010, 14–18.   **9** Hautefeuille 2006. A similar sequence was found in the later motte at Farnham (Surrey) (Thompson 1960, 81–94). Low mottes were added as apparent after-thoughts to other sites (Jope and Threlfall 1959; Brewster and Brewster 1969; Saunders 1980). The phenomenon has yet to be noted in Ireland.   **10** Impey 2002, 197.   **11** Early 1998.

14 The west end of the donjon at Loches, outside (*left*) and inside (*right*).

by the discovery that other donjons, such as Ivry-la-Bataille (Eure) and Beaugency (Loiret), are now known to be older than originally believed, but it still startles to realize that this extraordinary structure, once dated to the 1120s, was built in the first half of the eleventh century (Fig. 14).[12] Mapping the development of the donjon has also been complicated in recent years by the recognition, painfully slow in coming, that the donjon's development as a type was not driven by military need.[13] Militarism was, after all, how Doué-la-Fontaine's suggested development from a hall to a tower was originally understood.

UNDERSTANDING THE DONJON

There is now, by contrast with the early 1970s, a substantial body of evidence that the evolutionary road leading from the age of Doué-la-Fontaine towards the classic post-millennium donjon, best represented in Ireland by Trim (Fig. 15), was not a single carriageway but had several lanes, that it twisted rather than ran straight, and that it was not paved with military considerations alone or even primarily. Still, one can

12 Durand 1996; Mesqui 1998 (Loches); Impey 2002 (Ivry-la-Bataille); Corvisier 2007 (Beaugency).
13 Dixon 2002, 9–10.

15 The donjon of Trim. The contemporary gate-tower (heightened *c.*1200) is visible in the background.

follow a general route from the donjons of Capetian France and Normandy of *c.*1000 as far as the donjons of later twelfth-century Ireland, which were certainly among the last to be built firmly in a tradition now known to have crystallized in the early decades of the eleventh century. I map that route below by selecting and commenting on key monuments along the way, but my account, while useful to contextualize the Irish donjons (which has never been done in the Irish literature), comes with a proviso that needs to be spelled out in some detail before proceeding.

The typology offered below is a typology of architectural space (or shape, more accurately) organized on a temporal axis. As such, it is predicated inevitably on the assumption that a donjon was conceptually a fairly singular thing, variously executed but always in the service to some degree of a core idea which was capable of realization through the spatial organization of rooms. It was indeed a single thing, but that thing was simply 'the embodiment of power',[14] something to which the spatial organization of rooms did not necessarily speak. In any case, such a typology cannot capture the functions for which those spaces were designed or the uses to which they were put (and these were not necessarily the same thing), even if it has the potential to be a tool by which function and use *might* be determined. Nor does it allow the possibility that the *image* of a donjon – what its visibility, either up-close within the courtyard or distantly in the landscape, was intended to connote to spectators – might sometimes have trumped whatever conventionally-practical functions it was intended to fulfil. Put simply, donjons were lots of things, did lots of things, and had lots of looks.

Pamela Marshall captured this complex reality very well by devising some descriptive labels for types or variations of donjons: '"palace" donjons'; 'predominantly ceremonial donjons'; 'hall-and-chamber format' donjons; 'solar/reception towers'; 'marker towers'; 'aspiration or emulation towers'; 'non-residential towers'.[15] These were not mutually exclusive types, as her commentary makes clear. Determining the principal or overarching function of any one donjon can sometimes be a challenge. Contemporary documentation rarely provides any guidance. Three particular functions account for the majority of donjons: 'fortification', 'residence', and 'display and status'.

The donjon as fortification

Castellologists have really dispensed with the theory that the donjon was conceived of as a last refuge, a myth to which the documented siege of Rochester (Kent) in 1215 has given the principal nourishment.[16] To be fair, donjons were probably recognized as last refuges in many castles, and their presence was therefore very reassuring to castle-communities, but the key point is that there is no evidence to suggest they were designed with last-ditch protection in mind.[17] The fortification which they offered was perhaps more frequently virtual, or symbolic, than actual. It might not be too ludicrous a metaphor to say that the donjon functioned in part as an elaborate 'beware of the dog' sign: the deterrent is not the sign itself but what the sign says.

14 Marshall 2015, 199. **15** Ibid. 2002. **16** Morris 2016. **17** For a contrary view, increasingly rare in the modern castellological literature, see Hulme 2007–8.

The donjon as residence

It is useful to begin by considering the meaning of the two words most associated with domestic activities in the Middle Ages, whether inside castles or not: *camera* and *aula*. These terms appear in many documentary records of activities and transactions, so they are as familiar to historians as they are to archaeologists. We will review them here as descriptive terms for structures and spaces. It should be noted, though, they were actually much more than that in the Middle Ages: medieval poets and *chansonniers de geste* knew their social and symbolic connotations and so used them imaginatively and metaphorically.[18]

The English translation of *camera* is 'chamber'. This suggests a single room. It might sometimes have been just that in the Middle Ages: the 'seigneurial minimum' was, in essence, a single-room *camera* above a service basement.[19] But *camera* was often accompanied by adjectives which signified differences in status between types of chamber; one encounters such self-explanatory pairings as *magna camera*, *camera principalis*, *camera ducis*, and so on. In some instances the term, though a singular noun, seems to have referred to a suite of rooms for private living.[20] The best evidence in Ireland for such variability in how *camera* was understood in the Middle Ages comes from the early fourteenth-century *Registrum* of Kilmainham, the chief house of the Knights Hospitaller in Ireland. This was a fortified priory rather than a castle in the Middle Ages, not that it matters, although the *Registrum* does record that it had at its core a *castrum*. Distributed around the priory complex were *camerae*, owned by corrodians and retired members of the Hospitaller community for whom the priory was essentially a retirement home. Some of the *camerae* were single upstairs rooms but some of them small two-storeyed houses (Fig. 16).[21]

The English translation of *aula* is 'hall'.[22] This is understood to connote a space of gathering, where almost all activities were in full view of everybody gathered there. The 'everybody' in question varied according to context, but that is a reflection of the multi-functionality of the hall's conception. In a medieval residence, as a general rule, any activity which was communal in nature, which involved the inner household at very least, and which required or was permitted communal witness, took place in a hall. Eating meals was one such function, and some halls were probably used mainly for such prandial activities. The administration of justice was another. Halls intended for that function were less likely to have doubled-up as eating places. The performance of power was important, so halls of justice were especially elaborate (Fig. 17).[23] Even residences 'below' the level of the castle are known from the sources to have had halls.[24] The case in Ireland of the dying Thomas Leon bequeathing his property to his son

18 Garner 2010.   19 Meirion-Jones et al. 1993, 176.   20 Salamagne 2012.   21 O'Keeffe and Virtuani 2020.   22 For the etymology of the term and its (suggested) cognates, see Thompson 1995. See also Ronnes 2012. Where original documents are gone, leaving only calendared references in English translation (as is the case with many references in CDI I–V), one is left to assume that 'hall' is a straightforward translation of *aula*.   23 For the importance of the visibility of the noble in entering a hall see Labbé 1987, 264–6. For records of halls being entered by elites on horseback see, for example, Bouillot 2000, 28; Garner 2010, 250.   24 The concept of 'below' the level of the castle comes from McNeill 2002.

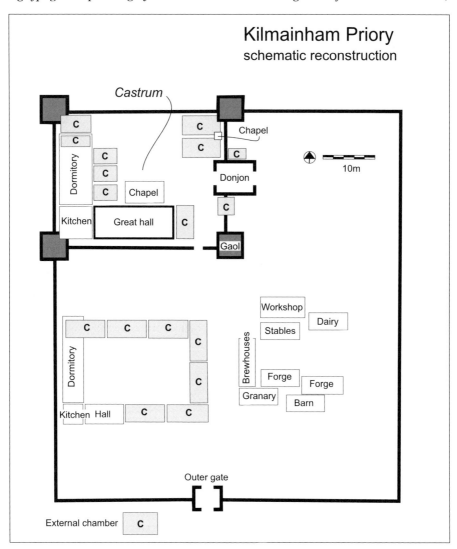

16 Schematic reconstruction of the layout of the chief priory of the Knights Hospitaller in Ireland at Kilmainham in the mid-fourteenth century, based on the description in the contemporary *Registrum*. Chambers were located inside and outside the (late twelfth-century) *castrum*. The evidence in the *Registrum* suggests that the chambers were mainly built in the early fourteenth century. The donjon, which seems to have contained the prior's chamber, had an entrance passage at ground-floor level.

merely by grabbing the handle of the door into his hall – a hall in an estate residence 'below' the level of a castle – illustrates how the power attached to a hall was legalistic: the hall was legal proxy for the entire estate.[25]

25 O'Keeffe 2015, 216.

17 The interior of the great hall (*c*.1200 and later) in the palace of Poitiers (Vienne), looking towards the dais. The roof dates from the nineteenth century.

It is now recognized that the concepts of 'public' space and 'private' space as captured in the terms *aula* and *camera* respectively are best understood as characterizations of degrees of inclusivity and exclusivity, of 'open' and 'closed', on a sliding scale. An *aula* was never completely open-access, nor was a *camera* always intimately private. On the contrary, the function of one often bled into the other; a *magna camera*, or 'great chamber', for example, could sometimes be an audience chamber, and increasingly served as one as the Middle Ages progressed.[26] Still, one might reasonably ask of any residential donjon the point on that sliding scale for which its focal spaces were better equipped. From there, one might begin to deduce what variety of residential donjon it was. But the task is not always easy. Determinations of room function based on window size, or the presence or absence of a fireplace, or the provision or otherwise of toilets, presuppose a fixed architectural language, but there is no reason to think that there was one. Accessibility – whether it be the ease-of-accessibility or the theatrical framing of a point of access – is probably the best criterion in making a determination of function. Basically, spaces at the 'public' end of the spectrum needed greater accessibility, so if one seeks to identify a hall within a donjon one should look at the entry-level floor. Upper-floor rooms were generally less accessible than ground-floor rooms, and were usually accessible by spiral stairs (discrete by their nature) suggesting that they were *camerae*. Where floor levels inside buildings were permanently partitioned to form two units of unequal floor area, the observation that the larger space was nearer the entrance would suggest that it was at

26 For an important analysis of the public/private dichotomy see Austin 1998. See also Hicks 2009, 61–3. For Ireland, see O'Keeffe 2014c; 2017b.

the 'public' end of the spectrum, and was probably the *aula*. In such configurations, the smaller space, further from the main door, was probably the *camera*. We will see this presently at Trim Castle.

The donjon as an object of display

The relative ease with which one might optimistically anticipate making a binary distinction between 'public' and 'private' when looking at any castle is ruptured, however, by a third function of the donjon: display. This refers to the display of the tower itself, its height and bulk, its architectural detailing, and so on. Tall donjons allowed the seigneurial presence be observed from the landscape, but also allowed that landscape to be observed.[27] Tall donjons must also have impressed observers by revealing the technical mastery of the masons whom wealthy lords could hire: to live in such a tower was to live dangerously and so to command not just attention but awe.[28] The concept and associated power of lordship itself was further displayed through performativity within the donjon. One might decide that certain open spaces within donjons were not halls, but one cannot assume them instead to have been chambers in the conventional sense of 'private' habitational rooms: some spaces were neither 'public' nor 'private' in the limited sense implied by the terms 'hall' and 'chamber'. A reception room, intended for an audience with a lord, might be regarded as semi-public and semi-private. Hedingham (Essex) is a classic example of a display donjon in both respects: it intentionally misled the outside spectator by rising much higher on the outside than it needed to for practical purposes, while its interior was an audience or reception chamber for its owner.[29]

EARLY ADVENTURES IN DONJON-BUILDING: THE ROAD TO IRELAND

Doué-la-Fontaine is still a useful starting point for a typology of donjons, the aim of which is not to reconstruct an actual developmental line, but, rather, to explain how the Irish donjons, once they started to appear in the 1170s, fit within the corpus of such towers in north-western Europe (Fig. 18). The account which follows here covers the ground covered by Edward Impey and Philip Dixon a decade ago in a major study of London's White Tower,[30] but with a slightly different perspective and with the incorporation of some information which has been published in the past decade.

The single-pile donjon: the road to Carrickfergus

Whether one- or two-storeyed originally, Doué-la-Fontaine was certainly large enough to provide comfortable accommodation at upper storey level, a claim that one cannot make so confidently for the enmotted towers at La Marche and Semur-en-Brionnais, now known to be of generally similar vintage. Doué-la-Fontaine seems to belong in the same general tradition as the tower in Langeais (Indre-et-Loire), dating

27 Creighton 2010; McManama-Kearin 2012. **28** The point is made by Renoux 1991, 297–8. **29** Dixon and Marshall 1993. **30** Impey 2008; Dixon 2008.

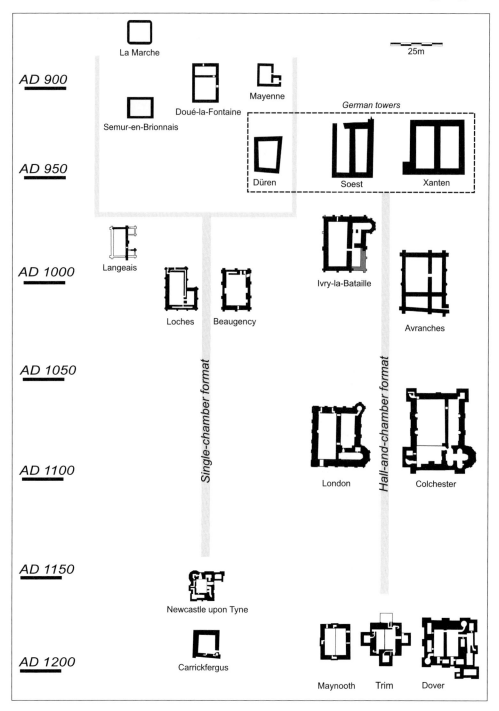

18 An outline of the morphological development of the donjon from the tenth to the late twelfth centuries using selected examples.

from *c.*1000.[31] Probably built by Fulk Nerra, Langeais also had a dark basement below its main residential space. It is the earliest reasonably intact example of a design-formula repeated with different levels of sophistication in later donjons. That Langeais, whatever about Doué-la-Fontaine, belongs in the genealogy of the classic donjons of the eleventh and twelfth centuries is attested to by its corner and mid-wall pilasters (articulating devices which often supported vaulted bay divisions in churches but which were of minimal structural value in vertical towers). However, its overall design – a pair of projecting towers on one side, linked by a wooden gallery at a high level – gave Langeais a somewhat idiosyncratic, and rather Antique, character. The turrets and connecting wooden bridge at Langeais suggest that its builders were alert to the need not merely to accommodate but to choreograph movement into and around the building. The builders of the later donjons had the same concern. But the two-turret solution at Langeais appears not to have been imitated.

Whatever uncertainty characterized Langeais, no uncertainty is evident in Fulk Nerra's donjon at Loches, started around 1013 and completed around 1035.[32] Here, a clear distinction was made between the hall, at first-floor level in the main block (the part known as 'le grand donjon'), and the private rooms, placed above the hall level in both the main block and the upper parts of the attached block (the part known as 'le petit donjon'). The communication routes into and around the building were carefully considered in advance. And whereas Langeais looked vaguely Roman (and has been described as *pré-roman*, pre-Romanesque),[33] Loches was as aesthetically advanced a castle building as was ever constructed in the so-called Romanesque tradition, with its soaring height, ashlar masonry, and elegant semi-cylindrical pilasters. The donjon of Beaugency, marginally less jaw-dropping visually and with simpler floor plans, is now known to have been built at the same time (1015–30).[34] Nogent-le-Rotrou (Eure-et-Loire) and Montbazon (Indre-et-Loire) are probably early eleventh-century too.[35] Scientific dating is beginning to indicate earlier-than-expected dates for other donjons.[36] Conceptually fully-formed when they were built, Loches and Beaugency stand, alone for now, at the head of a series of comparably tall and aesthetically accomplished *single-pile* donjons in the Capetian, Norman and earlier Angevin territories. They are probably evolved versions of the *turres* which are documented in the tenth century but no longer survive.[37]

The fact that these buildings are *single pile* is important. A single-pile building is one in which the outer walls are the sole load-bearing walls. That does not mean that internal spaces are not partitioned – Beaugency's interior certainly was – but that the

---

31 Impey and Lorans 1998, 37–8. **32** Mesqui 1998. **33** Impey and Lorans 1998, 321. **34** Corvisier 2007, 21. **35** Impey 2008, 231–2. **36** Radiocarbon dating suggests an early eleventh-century date for the earliest part of the donjon at Pouzauges (Vendée), bringing the early donjons deeper into France (see Béthus, 2019). There are mid-tenth century dates for a structure, possibly a donjon, predating the present donjon at Pons (Charente-Maritime) and later tenth-century dates from the donjon at Saissac (Aude) (Champagne and Mandon 2014; Cazes 2014). Radiocarbon dates in the tenth century from the donjon at Sainte-Suzanne (Mayenne) are assumed to have come from old wood (Bocquet 2004, 215). **37** Impey 2008, 228–9. For the role of the *turris* in the conversion of the Carolingian *palatium* into a *castrum* see

19 The heavily-ruined donjon at Corfe, with its tall (Loches-inspired?) fore-building projecting onto the down-slope.

partitions were not structural. In a single-pile donjon each floor level is likely to have been conceptualized as a single space (even if coded hierarchically in some way), so that movement from one grade of internal space to another within the tower – from a reception room to a chamber, for example – was vertical, not horizontal. Invariably, this meant that the donjons rose to at least three storeys: entry level was conventionally at first-floor level, above a service basement, so one more storey at least was needed. Fairly typical would be Moncontour (Vienne), for example, which was a three-storeyed donjon with two fairly simple rooms above a basement, all of them connected by a corner stairs.[38] Display or ceremonial donjons did not necessarily need vertically-disposed stacks of rooms, but ceremony and display often required such donjons to be tall anyway, even if that necessitated a degree of external subterfuge, like the 'pretend' upper storey at Hedingham.[39]

Single-pile rectangular donjons of three and more storeys in height were common in Norman and Angevin England, and some, like Newcastle upon Tyne, a royal tower, had floor plans of considerable sophistication. Corfe (Dorset), possibly of the 1080s,[40] was the earliest in England. It was the most Loches-like of all the English donjons, but the feature which made it especially so, the tall fore-building (Fig. 19), disappeared from the repertoire of the English builders immediately afterwards. It is probable that

Renoux 2002. **38** Châtelain 1973, 160–1, Pls. X, XXXIII. **39** Dixon and Marshall 1992.
40 Goodall 2011, 112.

20 The donjon at Carrickfergus.

there was not a single baron in late twelfth-century Ireland who had not set foot in one of these turriform donjons before crossing to Ireland. Yet, the late twelfth-century castle of Carrickfergus (Antrim) had the only properly multi-storeyed single-pile donjon in Ireland (Fig. 20).

One functional space which was apparently present in Loches was generally *not* carried forward as the tradition of the multi-storeyed, single-pile, donjon evolved through the eleventh and twelfth centuries: the hall. The removal of a main hall from the interior of a donjon reduced the number of people who might have an expectation of entering that donjon. This change in planning allowed the master masons who designed these great buildings to concentrate on creating spaces suited to more private, or exclusive, seigneurial performances. Stripped of the hall, the single-pile *residential* donjon was really a turriform *camera*. The importance of this observation for the interpretation of Irish towers will be apparent later (pp 92–5). The approximate date at which the hall 'moved out' of the single-pile donjon is not easily established, because it is conceivable that in some such donjons, at least before the second quarter of the twelfth century, the entry-level floor was simply allowed to function as the hall. But from an Irish perspective, the chronology of the change is not too important, because it had certainly been made in England by the time of the Anglo-Norman invasion of Ireland. The castle-building barons of later twelfth-century Ireland were familiar with halls standing alongside but physically detached from chamber towers.

The double-pile donjon: the road to Trim and Maynooth

The original tower of Ivry-la-Bataille, now dated to the period 990–1010, was a single-pile structure from which projected a conjoined chamber and apsidal chapel. The chamber was very soon extended – within a couple of decades of the tower's construction, perhaps – in a manner that resulted in one of the original external walls becoming a cross-wall inside the building.[41] Thus was contained within the one compact structure, at the same floor level, the three elements – the hall, the chamber and the chapel – which constituted what Jean Mesqui has described as the *programme palatial*.[42] In Ivry's case, the three elements were within the core of the building, with the apsidal chapel breaking the orthogonal shape, but in some other donjons of this 'palatial' type, a fore-building giving access to the main entrance contained the chapel. But the principle was the same: public, private and praying spaces were interconnected at the same (first-) floor level. Although donjons with that particular horizontal arrangement of spaces could be just two storeys high, because their footprints allowed them to contain all the spaces they needed, some rose an additional storey, most notably Colchester (Essex), which was later lowered, and the White Tower in London.

Ivry-la-Bataille had, then, in its altered state, a *double-pile* plan. In other words, a partition wall across the middle of the interior meant that each floor level had two principal side-by-side spaces (one of which was, in its case, further partitioned to define the chapel's space). It is the earliest donjon in the lands of Capetian, Norman and Angevin power with such an internal cross-wall. It might not have been fully load-bearing but it was solid in the manner of a proper double-pile dividing wall.

Assessing Ivry-la-Bataille's importance in the history of the donjon is complicated by the inadequacy of the information available for the tenth-century towers east of the Rhine, at least two of which were double-pile.[43] The Ivry-la-Bataille cross-wall is especially important because it was not a medial wall but was a little off the central axis of the building, thus giving the donjon two internal side-by-side spaces of unequal width, the wider one being identifiable as the hall. Ivry-la-Bataille might be the first actual building in the Norman and Capetian worlds in which the cross-wall was given a role in shaping the social topography of a donjon, and other buildings with the feature might be indebted to it.[44] The largely destroyed Norman donjon in Avranches (Manche), identified as *pré-roman* and probably of the first decade or two of the eleventh century,[45] is an early (and itself experimental?) descendent. Like Loches, which it probably pre-dates by a few years, Avranches has an early version of a feature which was not in Ivry-la-Bataille but appears commonly in later donjons and eventually became a signifying feature of English 'Romanesque' and 'Gothic' architecture, including in Ireland: the so-called 'thick wall passage' (Fig. 21).[46] So, between them, Ivry-la-Bataille and Avranches, alongside contemporary churches, point to the importance of Normandy as a place of architectural innovation around 1000.

41 Impey 2002.   **42** Mesqui 1993, 11.   **43** Fehring 1987, Fig. 36.   **44** Impey 2008, 239.
45 Impey 2002; Mesqui 2010.   **46** The term 'thick wall' (*mur épais*) was coined by Jean Bony (1939). Such wall passages are understood to have first appeared in the Middle Ages in churches of the early eleventh century (Fernie 2000, 270), but the chronology may need revision in light of the early dates for Loches and especially Avranches.

21 The 'thick wall passage' in the upper part of Trim donjon.

Although described as a *turris famosa* by Orderic Vitalis in the early twelfth century, Ivry-la-Bataille exerted influence principally through the most famous buildings descended from it, William I's donjons in London and Colchester. The use of the cross-wall to define parallel spaces within buildings survived well into the twelfth century in Norman and earlier Angevin donjons in England, with Middleham (Yorkshire) probably dating from as late as the last quarter of the century.[47] It was then brought into Ireland by the masons who started work in the mid-1170s on the donjons of Trim and Maynooth (Kildare), built as the double-pile tradition was finally dying. In these two cases, the structural form was essentially single pile, in that the partitions were not solid walls originally, but the internal spaces were organized around the concept of parallel rooms in the manner of double-pile architecture. Trim and Maynooth were not the last of the breed which descended from Ivry-la-Bataille. Among the truly great donjons of the era, that distinction probably goes to the great royal donjon at Dover (Kent), started as the first phase of work on Trim's donjon came to a close.

This review of donjon architecture in France and England prior to 1169 was written to provide a lead-in to a discussion of rectangular donjons in Ireland. Three Irish buildings were alluded to: Carrickfergus, and Trim and Maynooth. These are three of only five donjons in Ireland for which construction dates in the 1170s or early 1180s are either documented or can be argued from the architectural evidence. The other two are Dunamase and Castleknock (Dublin), the latter being of polygonal plan (and discussed in the next chapter). One can see from the discussion that the donjons at Carrickfergus, and Trim and Maynooth, represented two different lines of descent from the first donjons of late tenth- and early eleventh-century French and Norman origin. Their appreciation as works of architecture, and as historical sources in stone which graphically contextualize Anglo-Norman Ireland within the Capetian/Norman/Angevin cultural matrix, is enhanced by knowledge of the deep wells of tradition from which they sprung.

FIRST GENERATION RECTANGULAR DONJONS IN IRELAND

Donjons built by the Anglo-Normans in Ireland between the 1170s and as late as the 1250s can be used to restate a point made earlier (p. 65): donjon architecture is characterized by heterogeneity. That heterogeneity is especially striking among the earliest examples in Ireland. I discuss here in detail four incontestably early rectangular donjons: Trim and Maynooth, which were started in the mid-1170s, Dunamase, probably started in the later 1170s or, if not, the 1180s, and Carrickfergus, started in the early 1180s. It should be stressed that these are not the only late twelfth-century donjons in Ireland: as is shown later, the rectangular donjons of Glanworth and Ballyderown (both Cork) are probably pre-1200 in date, while the polygonal donjon at Castleknock was probably started in the mid- or late 1170s. In picking out these four buildings for an extended discussion, I am not suggesting that they were influential.

47 Kenyon 2015.

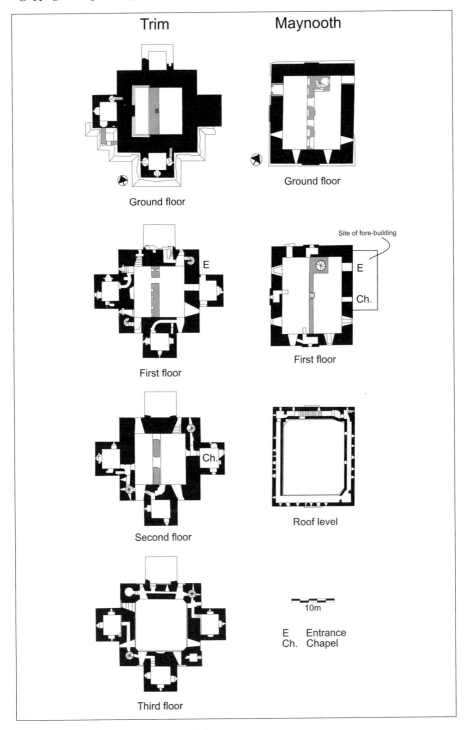

22 Floor plans of Trim and Maynooth donjons.

On the contrary, it seems that they were not influential at all, which adds to their interest.

The first two donjons of the four, Trim and Maynooth, are almost certainly the first two substantial Anglo-Norman stone buildings of any type in Ireland, and they are the two donjons in the group that converse most closely with each other (Fig. 22). They are clearly first cousins.

Trim

The stone donjon in the great castle of Trim was started after 1174. It was the third structure to have been built on the site since Hugh de Lacy, lord of Meath and the most powerful individual in the nascent colony, settled on Trim as his *caput*.[48] The donjon was two storeys high by the end of the 1170s, and, although later heightened again at some date after Hugh's death, it was entirely functional as a two-storeyed building.

It was quite a remarkable structure. It had a projecting turret which served as a fore-building but was accessed by wooden stairs, presumably open to the sky and therefore allowing, intentionally or not, de Lacy to be seen as he entered and exited. It was not a conventional fore-building by twelfth-century English standards because it was planned to be one of a group of symmetrically-disposed mid-wall towers. The first-floor space inside the body of the tower was divided by a cross-wall, originally in timber but replaced in stone at an early date. The two parts thus created were of almost-equal width, one connected to the entrance and the other further back and therefore more private, and both had their own roofs, the scars of which are still visible (Fig. 23). This was a classic hall-and-chamber scheme in the London tradition.

Movement through Trim was quite labyrinthine. At first-floor (entry) level, it was possible to access two of the projecting towers from the hall, and spiral stairs in one of the corners gave access, via a mural passage, to the chapel above the entrance. That chapel could be accessed from the hall (via the stairs) and directly from the second-floor level in the main block, but a door must have barred access to the main block because it would otherwise have been open to anybody who went from the hall to the chapel. The chamber beyond the hall at first-floor level had a wall fireplace, access to the fourth projecting tower, and a corner stairs leading upwards and giving access to the next floor level in both the main block and the projecting tower.

The raising of Trim from a low, two-storeyed block to a four-storeyed tower happened in two stages, apparently relatively early in its history. It has been asserted that the first new storey (the third, or the second floor) was added in the 1190s, and that the final storey was added around 1200.[49] Publication of the architectural survey of the donjon made at the time of its conservation is needed, and one must wait to see the evidence before addressing the matter of original intent: was it always intended to be a multi-storeyed donjon, or was there a change of plan? On the one hand, by the 1170s the fashion for halls inside donjons was in decline, so it would seem odd that Trim would have been given a rather anachronistic identity as a low-rise hall-and-chamber

---

48 S. Duffy 2011, 8–10; see also O'Keeffe 2013b; 2017a.   **49** Hayden 2011, 110–12.

23 The original first-floor chamber in Trim donjon, viewed from inside the original roof-space, with the cross-wall on the right-hand side. Note the outline of the original pitched roof on the opposite wall, cut through by a later window.

donjon were it intended to double its height within a generation. Its date is important here: the original donjon of the 1130s at Portchester (Hampshire) was also low-rise, and was extended upwards within twenty years (Fig. 24), but that change happened at

24 The donjon at Portchester, its earlier phase marked by the pilasters.

a time, the 1150s, when the type of design which was to be used at Trim twenty years later was going out of fashion. On the other hand, the second-floor chapel at Trim was probably intended from the outset, and the only way that it could have been accessed by de Lacy (without forcing him to take the scenic route via the hall, the spiral stairs and the mural passage) was to have a direct entry from a second-floor level.

Maynooth

The early history of Maynooth Castle is not documented. Long assigned a date of *c.*1200,[50] the date now sanctioned for its donjon (Fig. 25) by the National Monuments Service is the late 1180s.[51] There is no evidence to support either date. My own view is that this building was erected by Maurice fitz Gerald, one of the first Anglo-Normans in Ireland, and dates from the mid-1170s.[52] Discovery of occupation under the donjon[53] raises the possibility that the first castle was an earth-and-timber castle, but that does not preclude – as the evidence at Trim makes clear – a very early replacement with a stone donjon. As at Trim, the Maynooth donjon has evidence of alteration. Granite quoins can be observed at lower-storey level, but the heights off

---

50 See, for example, McNeill 1997, Fig. 21.   **51** Archaeological Survey of Ireland (https://webgis.archaeology.ie/historicenvironment/ q.v. Kildare: Maynooth).   **52** O'Keeffe 2013c.

25 The donjon at Maynooth. The original entrance at first-floor level is on the far right-hand side. The door in the middle of the wall at that level connected the hall to the chapel in the (now-lost) fore-building.

ground level to which such stone was used are too inconsistent to suggest that there was originally a single-storeyed building at Maynooth. There might have been a delay in building work, with a different stone – tufa – used upon recommencement. Whatever the case, the donjon, like that at Trim, was two-storeyed in height by 1180.

Maynooth was a simpler building than Trim but was no less unusual. It was arguably better built: blocks of squared-off, flat-surfaced, stone were set in beds of spalls, all tightly bonded with a mortar of unusual hardness, and almost perfectly flush. One can imagine local labour building most of the walls at Trim, because it was conventionally coursed, but the fabric at Maynooth is quite unlike anything that one sees in the native, pre-invasion, repertoire in Ireland. Oddly, there are few putlog holes, suggesting even a different scaffolding system from normal.

Viewed externally, Maynooth's pilasters place it a little more firmly in the 'Romanesque' donjon tradition than Trim, and their skilful integration into a multi-stepped plinth (Fig. 26) compares well with Norman and Angevin examples in England. However, the use of mid-wall pilasters *only* is unusual: the norm in Capetian, Norman and Angevin contexts was for such pilasters (if they were used at all) to be accompanied by corner pilasters. No donjon in England has the Maynooth scheme. Only one tower in Ireland has it, albeit a very different type of building: the tall west tower of the church in Baldongan (Dublin). Regarded as late medieval in date,[54] it is surely a candidate for an early thirteenth-century donjon, its upper room putting it in the tradition of donjons described by Marshall as 'marker towers'.[55] The builders at Maynooth availed of the pilasters to give the donjon tiny mural rooms at first-floor level, each lit by a single window. These rooms are so small that it is difficult to conceive of the pilasters having been built to thicken the walls to facilitate their installation in the plan. The intention at Maynooth might have been to give the donjon some visual similarity with contemporary Trim, where the mid-wall projections were actual towers.

The little mural rooms are not unique to Maynooth within the repertoire of eleventh- and twelfth-century donjon architecture. Similarly small rooms contained within the thickness of the long walls of donjons (as distinct from within their corners) are found in a number of English contexts, Norman and Angevin. Maynooth is unusual, though, in having those rooms partly occupy space within mid-wall pilasters. The functions of such small mural rooms are generally unknown. At Carlisle (Cumberland) one such room was associated with the castle's well, another was apparently a prison, and another probably a tiny kitchen. At Hedingham, similar small rooms might have been for the containment of paraphernalia related to ceremony.[56] In many other cases, though, such rooms might not have had specific functions at all.

---

53 Hayden n.d. 54 Archaeological Survey of Ireland (https://webgis.archaeology.ie/ historicenvironment/ q.v. Dublin: Baldongan). 55 For 'marker towers' see Marshall 2002, 33. There are some small donjons with only mid-wall pilasters in western France: Tour-aux-Cognons (Vienne) and Chalucet (Haute-Vienne), where in each case there are two, and Paunat (Dordogne) where, as at Baldongan, the tower, which has pairs of mid-wall pilasters, is part of a church (Châtelain 1973, Pls. XI, XV, XIX). 56 Dixon and Marshall 1992.

26 One of the mid-wall pilasters, the plinth, and the 'display doorway' (with its corbelled balcony) in the north wall of Maynooth donjon.

Entry into Maynooth's donjon was by a fore-building on the east side, with the original entry vestibule partnered by a chapel at first-floor level. The arrangement can be paralleled at Portchester in the 1130s, even down to the likelihood that the Maynooth fore-building also had a prison in its lower part. One difference, however, is that at Maynooth the chapel was accessible from inside the main block whereas at Portchester it was not (see Fig. 43). The large first-floor space at Maynooth was partitioned longitudinally from the outset, with its partition – originally of timber – positioned directly above an arcuated medial wall in the basement. The resulting spaces were of equal width (which is a contrast with Trim where there was a very slight difference in width) but differences in their plans suggest that, *contra* McNeill and Sweetman, they did not together constitute a large first-floor hall with a spine wall to carry its roofs.[57] Rather, the layout suggests two spaces of different but connected function, that nearer the doorway being the hall and that beyond the partition being a chamber (with the small pilaster rooms opening off it). The latter's identification as a chamber is also secured by the presence of a doorway leading originally onto a balcony (see Figs. 26, 27) from which the deerpark to the north of the castle could be viewed. Such doorways are known in donjons in England and France.[58] The best

57 McNeill 1997, 37; Sweetman 1999, 68.   58 For parallels, see Marshall 2012; O'Keeffe 2013c.

27 Interior view of the 'display doorway' at Maynooth. The challenge of understanding Maynooth's late twelfth-century roofing system is apparent in this photograph.

28 Plans of the donjons at Falaise, Rising and Maynooth, showing the positions of the display doorways relative to their main entrances, halls and chambers.

parallels for the Maynooth arrangement are Norman rather than Angevin, which reveals it to be quite an old-fashioned building for its date in the 1170s (Fig. 28).

The key to understanding Maynooth is the lack of provision for accommodation. One can imagine a central hearth, or maybe two (one per first-floor space), but the option of having a fireplace in the long wall of the chamber – a feature of Trim – was eschewed, even though the mid-wall pilaster thickened the wall sufficiently for one (such as one sees at Portchester). More critically, there were no toilets. The chamber was not, therefore, an inner, residential, room equipped for private living but was, rather, some form of great chamber, a space at the private end of the spectrum of spaces to which some access to non-household members was allowed. Unlike Hugh de Lacy at Trim, therefore, Maurice fitz Gerald could not emerge into the chamber from an even more secluded space after a night's sleep; his place of actual residence must have been elsewhere in the castle in the 1170s.

So, Maynooth's scale and simplicity both point to it falling within the spectrum of the ceremonial donjons described by Pamela Marshall; it was, in essence, a great audience building, intended to impress on the outside and designed on the inside for the presentation and performance of power, but capable of little else. Accordingly, it was modestly in the tradition represented widely and often more spectacularly in the neighbouring lands, as at Pons (Charente-Maritime) in the 1180s, and even further afield, as in the Norman-built Pisana Tower of *c*.1130 in the palace of Palermo in Sicily.[59]

Identifying the master mason at Trim and Maynooth

Within a decade of the invasion, then, there were two stone-built castles within 30km of each other, and they almost certainly had the only two completed donjons in Ireland at the time. Both of them were two storeys high, with upper-floor entrances. Both were built using units of 0.7m.[60] In plan, both had mid-wall projections containing rooms: Trim had its four strongly projecting mid-wall towers and Maynooth its shallow pilasters. And, although neither was strictly a double-pile building, both had cross-walls defining spaces of different function; both were, in other words, in the long line of descent from Ivry-la-Bataille. Given that de Lacy and fitz Gerald knew each other well, and had been in Dublin together at one stage,[61] there is a good argument that both men hired the same master mason to design their buildings. There is one very important difference between the two donjons, but it does no violence to the suggestion of a shared master mason: Trim was primarily residential and Maynooth was primarily ceremonial.

I want to argue that the master mason who designed these donjons came from a royal yard, where exposure to some great Henrician projects inspired him to create bespoke (and, in the case of Trim, vaguely royal) designs.

In analysing the plan of Trim's donjon, Roger Stalley drew attention to its unusual shape and speculated on its symbolism. He noted Sandy Heslop's then-recent analysis of the geometrical shape of the donjon at Orford (Suffolk), built 1165–73, and he described Trim's geometry as 'more straightforward'.[62] Since then, the geometry of Trim has been worked out by Willie Cumming and Kevin O'Brien, who found it to be closely aligned with that of Orford.[63] I think it is unlikely that, in contrast to what has been argued for Orford, Trim's geometry was intended to evoke anything symbolic. On the contrary, I think that the donjon was built to the design of a mason who had training in geometry, and knew that the principles of geometry helped the processes of designing and building. Still, the implications of the proportional similarities with Orford are very important. Other donjons were built using the same units of measurement and similar proportions, including Rochester and, interestingly, Portchester. But the Orford and Trim donjons are unique in having projecting towers

---

59 Châtelain 1973, 184–5; Chiesa 1998, 321.   **60** Hayden 2011, 106, 143–5.   **61** O'Keeffe 2013, 26–7.   **62** Stalley 1992, 18; Heslop 1991.   **63** Hayden 2011, 59, 105–6.

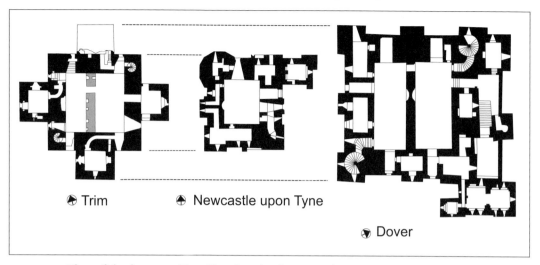

29 Plans of the donjons at Trim (first-floor level), Newcastle upon Tyne (second-floor level) and Dover (second-floor level), showing the similarities in their proportional systems.

from the middle of each face (Orford's geometry reveals its three towers to have been conceived from the outset as were those in Trim). And Maynooth, with its unusual mid-wall pilasters, can be added to make a triumvirate of unique donjons with mid-wall projections. It is surely relevant that Orford's now-lost curtain wall had towers resembling in plan those in Trim's first-phase curtain wall.[64]

Orford was a royal castle. Two other royal donjons in England encourage the identification of the Trim and Maynooth master mason as a sometime employee of a royal workshop. The donjons at Newcastle upon Tyne, built 1172–8, and Dover, built 1179–88, were designed by one Maurice, described variously as a *cementarius* and *ingeniator*.[65] Both towers were built to the same metrical template as Trim (Fig. 29). In plan the two are rather different from each other, but they share the phenomena of second-floor entrances via complex-plan fore-buildings, staircase chapels, and lead pipes distributing water to the floor levels. That latter feature is a link with Trim, where attention was also paid to water control within the donjon.[66] There are clear comparisons in layout between Dover and both Trim and Maynooth. Upon entering Dover's hall, spiral stairs ascend in the corner to the right, as at Trim. Access to the chapel above the entrance stairway at Dover is from the hall; at Trim the access is also from the hall, albeit via the spiral stairs, but at Maynooth it is via a doorway in the manner of Dover. Beyond the partition at Dover is a more private space, off which are small rooms. These are akin to what one finds in the projecting towers at Trim, but they parallel more exactly the small pilaster rooms at Maynooth: the rooms are only partly within the mid-wall pilasters at Dover, but, as at Maynooth, they are lit by windows in those pilasters. Finally, as at Trim, the spiral stairs in the private part of the Dover donjon is in the corner diagonally opposite that in the public part.

64 O'Keeffe 2007b, 127.   **65** Hislop 2016, 107–9; Dixon 2018, 382.   **66** Hayden 2011, 113.

These close comparisons between the two Irish donjons and Dover suggest that, at very least, the master mason in Ireland in the 1170s came from Maurice's circle. That mason had possibly worked on the early stages of Newcastle before coming to Ireland, and before returning to England to work on Dover. Given that the Trim design in particular anticipates by a few years some of the plan-features of Dover, is it possible that the Dover plan was developed from the plan which this master mason created for de Lacy's donjon?

Going further, and noting how differences between Newcastle and Dover reveal him to have been capable of producing works of different character, could we identify Maurice himself as the master mason who worked briefly in Ireland in the mid-1170s? Maurice was at Newcastle in the early 1170s but his presence might not have been needed there all of the time. Payments to him for work at Newcastle are recorded in the pipe roll for 1174–5,[67] which is exactly the time that work was starting at Trim and Maynooth. The timing of the payments might be significant: they might mark his departure from Newcastle in pursuit of work elsewhere. Hugh de Lacy's standing with Henry II in the early 1170s allows us to envisage Maurice, clearly a man who was highly regarded by the crown, enjoying a commission in Ireland. Not intending to fortify the new lordship himself, Henry might well have been directly responsible for forging a connection between his master mason and both de Lacy and fitz Gerald. The suggestion is not far-fetched. That Henry took some interest in the design of castles owned by his lords and barons in Ireland is suggested by the evidence at Castleknock. As will be seen in the next chapter, Hugh Tyrel's donjon there, under construction in the later 1170s, was built to a design briefly favoured by Henry II in England in the earlier 1170s. Henry had made Hugh a direct tenant of the crown earlier in that very decade.

Dunamase

The focal building at Dunamase is likely to be contemporary with Trim and Maynooth. It was not a typical donjon by any means. Rather, it was a hall with a chamber at one end. It is described here as a donjon because, thick-walled, rectangular, and free-standing on the highest ground within a castle enclosure, it occupies the space which was normally reserved for a donjon. It is not dated, but its architecture suggests that we look in the early history of the district under Anglo-Norman control for a context in which it might have been built. Goddard Orpen believed that Strongbow (Richard de Clare) built the first castle on the site between 1173 and 1175.[68] From *c.*1176 until his death, probably in 1181, Geoffrey de Costentin was in the district, courtesy of a grant from Strongbow. Being resident on the site, he is probably better identified as the donjon's builder.[69] The structure was not so elaborate that it was beyond Geoffrey's means to build it, and stone was freely availably on the site for quarrying. The alternative is to attribute it to Meiler fitz Henry, who was granted the district in 1181.[70] Whether built by de Costentin (my choice) or fitz Henry, Dunamase was the first major stone castle in Ireland to have been built by a lord who was not of the very

---

67 Hislop 2016, 107.   **68** Orpen 1911, 329, 375.   **69** Hodkinson 2003, 47–8.   **70** Scott and Martin 1978, 195.

30 The remains of the end-tower at the north end of Dunamase donjon, viewed from outside the line of the east wall of the hall.

highest rank; although very senior figures in the world of early Anglo-Norman Ireland, neither de Costentin nor fitz Henry had the top-tier status of Hugh de Lacy or Maurice fitz Gerald. That should disabuse us of any presumption that the power and financial capacity to build castles in stone so early in the history of the lordship was confined to those very few men whose territorial possessions were provincial in scale.

The building at Dunamase comprised a two-storeyed, rectangular tower (a room over a basement, basically), to which was attached contemporaneously a ground-floor hall, equal in width to the tower but with its long axis running at a right angle (Fig. 30). The two elements were thus contained within four outer walls, and therefore constituted a single structure.[71] The distinction between the two parts was probably visible from the outside in the fenestration, as well as at roof level (where, at very least, water outlets would have signalled roofs running in different directions). The hall was entered through opposed doorways at ground level at the end closest to the tower, and stairs linked the western entrance (the larger of the two entrances) to the wall-walk.

71 A parallel is Bowes (Durham), a building of much better quality (see Mercer 2019–20).

The nature of the entry from the hall to the end-tower is not known. One or two doorways in the wall separating it and the hall can be presumed – the present wall foundation between them is not original – and if there was a separate entrance to the tower's first-floor level it can only have been on the west side. Dunamase's limited provision for accommodation leads one to suspect that, as at Maynooth, the main residence was somewhere else on the site.

Carrickfergus

A different model again was deployed at Carrickfergus, the next donjon in chronological sequence. This was a near-square chamber donjon with no provision for an internal hall. Intended from 1177 or 1178 when part of curtain wall was built in order to enclose the promontory site, major construction work on this donjon probably started in 1181 or 1182. A slight change in plan was made almost as soon as building work began: after the south wall had been started, the line chosen for the donjon's east wall was abandoned in favour of a new line very slightly to the west, thus narrowing the donjon, and this was done perhaps in order to leave as much room as possible for the external hall.[72] Entry to the donjon was directly into a rather plain first-floor room via 'a showpiece stairway' which has been compared with that at Hedingham, built forty years earlier.[73] Spiral stairs gave access to the next floor up, which was more elaborate, and above that again to the principal chamber at third-floor level. There are many parallels in England for Carrickfergus's turriform character, but there are few Angevin parallels for its number of storeys. While no English building stands out as a specific model, it is appropriate given John de Courcy's life and career that Carrickfergus's closest cousin is probably the donjon of Appleby (Westmoreland), built a decade or so earlier.[74]

The 'Englishness' of these four donjons

One could fashion an argument that these donjons, alongside some other very early thirteenth-century structures still to be discussed here, represent a horizon of 'Englishness' which petered out in Ireland within a decade or two after the turn of the century. After all, while the political bond to the English monarch remained strong among the colonial families for decades, cultural links between the aristocracies of Anglo-Norman Ireland and contemporary England would surely have weakened once the scions of the original invaders, born in Ireland in the late twelfth century and never to set foot in England, outnumbered any new arrivals of castle-building aristocrats from England after 1200.

However, at the risk of being pedantic, there is a roadblock to describing these donjons as simply 'English'. 'Englishness' in late twelfth-century England, however coherent it might have been as an identity,[75] was not a stable and coherent bundle of behaviours. While it is not possible to measure the distance from 'Englishness' which

---

72 McNeill 1981; 2014–15, 20; Donnelly et al. 2005.   **73** Donnelly et al. 2005, 317.   **74** Both towers have spiral stairs immediately beside their points-of-entry, and further stairs at the far end of the same wall. For de Courcy's career, see Duffy 1995.   **75** Genet 2010.

was travelled by Anglo-Norman settlers in Ireland once they started families here, it is apparent that some distance was travelled. Bearing witness to that is the astute testimony of Giraldus Cambrensis in a speech he attributed to Maurice fitz Gerald (Maynooth's owner): '... just as we are English as far as the Irish are concerned, likewise to the English we are Irish, and the inhabitants of this island and the other assail us with an equal degree of hatred'.[76] The implication here is clear: the act of relocation was immediately transformative of the invaders' sense of identity, which renders moot the value of regarding them as more 'English' than their Irish-born scions a decade or two later.

So, to describe these four buildings as 'English' is not entirely correct. Of the group, Carrickfergus is actually the only one which could pass scrutiny as a straight transplant from contemporary England, albeit from an England in which donjons of its type were in the late autumn of their fashionability. The other three are idiosyncratic. All four are somewhat archaic. One might attach some importance to the symbolic meanings of their archaisms to their *colonial* audiences in Ireland.[77] Perhaps it was a strategy to express to fellow colonists the rootedness of their owners in a long tradition of power as manifest in castle-design. At Trim, Hugh de Lacy's master mason arguably referenced explicitly both Henrician royal castles of a generation earlier (particularly Orford) and Norman castle-palaces of the more distant past (such as London); he seems to have been involved in Henry II himself doing exactly the same again in Dover a few years later. At Maynooth, the same master mason created for Maurice fitz Gerald a building which might not have looked particularly out of place in England before, say, 1140. At Carrickfergus, John de Courcy's master mason effectively imported mid-twelfth-century Cumbria into later twelfth-century Ulster. And at Dunamase, finally, Geoffrey de Costentin's master mason simply produced the sort of donjon which early experimentalists in France or England might have produced but not regarded as viable.

THE DESCENT OF THE DONJON

These first generation donjons in Ireland, completed before 1200, were soon sealed off as a group – none of the designs appears again – by two changes in practice in the period between 1190 and 1210. Both changes were driven mainly by the arrival of new land grantees from across the Irish Sea, but King John's engagement with the lordship after he took the throne in 1199 was also critical. First, new donjons reflecting late twelfth-century 'modernist' developments in Capetian and Angevin architecture in France began to be built in Ireland after the turn of the century. These will be discussed in the next chapter. Second, free-standing, single-pile, two-storeyed (or, more rarely, three-storeyed) residential donjons of rectangular plan began to appear in the late twelfth century in Ireland.

In brief, in these latter buildings, which are discussed below, the first-floor rooms were the main residential spaces. A selection of examples is illustrated in Figure 31.[78]

---

76 Scott and Martin 1978, 81.   **77** O'Keeffe 2007b.   **78** The plans are mainly derived from Mike Salter's invaluable – and underappreciated – books (2004a; 2004b; 2004c).

Compared with those donjons of the 1170s and 1180s which were discussed above, these buildings are small – and sometimes extremely small – in both footprint and superstructure. The non-Irish reader might even wonder whether all of these buildings were even castle buildings. Aside from their sizes, almost all of them stand alone now, their enclosures long gone. Were some of them 'manorial'? That is a poor adjective, of course, because almost all castles were manorial to some degree, but it is often used to refer to residences that were owned by free tenants rather than by lords, and which were therefore 'sub-castle' in status. So, could some of the buildings illustrated in Figure 31 be 'sub-castle' houses? The question is difficult to answer because so few of the places where these structures are found are mentioned explicitly in contemporary medieval sources. But they were generally described as 'castles' in the seventeenth-century land surveys, and all were recorded as 'castles' by the Ordnance Survey field-workers who enquired of them while preparing maps in the mid-nineteenth century.

The myth of the 'hall-house'

Before looking at these buildings in detail, it is necessary to divert to the question of their classification. I am describing them in this book as donjons, but Irish castellologists since the early 1990s have been describing most of them as 'hall-houses'.[79] Characterized repeatedly in the literature as socially-lesser buildings than donjons, 'hall-houses' are understood to be

> essentially free-standing halls which have been elevated to first-floor level and thus provided with storage facilities below. Some hall-houses may also have contained a limited amount of high-status private accommodation, but at this time halls were multifunctional spaces and so served as communal dining chambers for the entire household, as manorial administrative centres where monetary and judicial matters were resolved and, probably, as sleeping quarters for servants and low-ranking visitors.[80]

Readers of Harold Leask's classic book on Irish castles will know that he did not use the phrase 'hall-house'. How and when, then, did it achieve such currency in Irish castellology?

In the late 1980s, Patrick Holland, in an important (and much undervalued) paper, described thirteen two-storeyed Anglo-Norman castle buildings in the west of Ireland as having 'first-floor stone halls'.[81] Many of these buildings were unknown to Irish castellologists before his work was published. The Archaeological Survey of Ireland was recording similar buildings elsewhere, but they were not widely known because the Survey's county inventories were slow in being published. As an aside, prior to these new discoveries some thirty-odd years ago, rectangular castle-towers of the

79 McNeill 1992; 1997, 49–55; Sweetman 1998; 1999, 89–104; 2003; Sherlock 2014a.   **80** Sherlock 2014a, 353.   **81** Holland 1987–8; 1997.

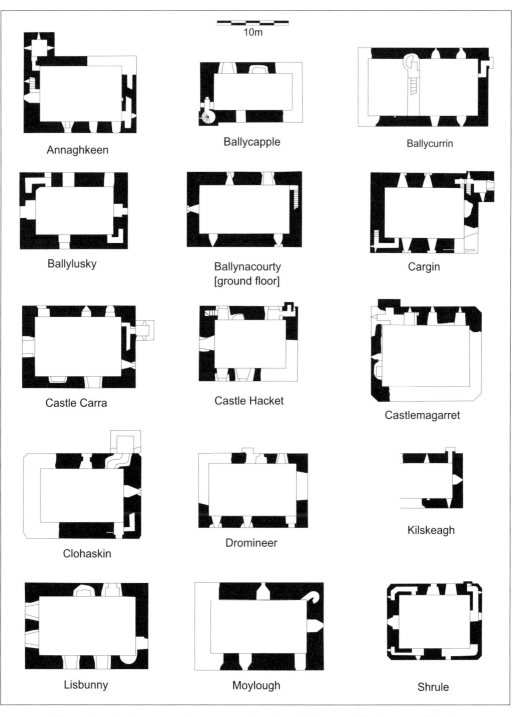

31 Plans of single-pile, two- or three-storeyed residential donjons. All plans are of first-floor levels except as indicated.

Anglo-Normans seemed to be quite rare. Leask listed the relatively few rectangular-plan Anglo-Norman 'keeps' which he knew about, and he gave the impression, probably inadvertently, that there were no others. That impression survived into the 1990s. So, when in the late 1960s Dudley Waterman identified Grenan (Kilkenny) and Glanworth (Cork) as additional examples, he published them in a national journal.[82] Similarly, when I identified Ballyderown as yet another example in the early 1980s, it was deemed worthy of publication in a national journal.[83]

In the early 1990s, as the corpus of Anglo-Norman 'keeps' was expanding through survey work, the label 'keep' was dropped in favour of 'hall-house' for the newly identified examples. This followed terminology used – problematically, it must be said[84] – in Scotland for buildings which were not dissimilar. When McNeill discussed the 'hall-house' as a type in 1997, he presented it as one which was largely concentrated in western Ireland,[85] reflecting the continued influence of Holland's important work. Two years later, David Sweetman devoted a chapter of his book to 'hall-houses'.[86] A respected and influential figure in Irish castellology, and director of the Archaeological Survey of Ireland, he single-handedly elevated the type from a small, geographically-restricted, sub-category of 'keep' to a major category of building in its own right. As the type became more firmly rooted in the thinking of Irish castellologists, many buildings which had earlier been described without contestation as 'keeps' or donjons were reclassified as 'hall-houses'.

Almost from the very start, however, the processes of classification and reclassification that have increased 'hall-house' numbers in Ireland – the Archaeological Survey of Ireland now lists fifty in the Republic – have actually been wildly inconsistent and betray an utter lack of logic. In some instances, the buildings do not merit having the term 'hall' attached to them in any way. For example, the upper room in the tiny 'hall-house' at Kilskeagh (Galway), internally only 4.5m wide and originally about 8m long, could not possibly have accommodated a hall and some cordoned-off private space. The 'hall-house' at Kinlough (Mayo) is a three-storeyed tower (later heightened) with an almost-square interior ratio of 1:1.25. In other instances, the classification is self-contradictory. For example, the near-identical and contemporary (1235–40) towers of Athenry and Moylough (both Galway) now have different classifications, with the former retaining its traditional label as a 'keep' and the latter now listed as a 'hall-house'; non-Irish readers will wonder how Moylough (see Fig. 34) could possibly be denied the label 'donjon'. The contemporary, sibling-built, towers at Coonagh and Castletown Conyers (both Limerick) are now categorized, respectively, as a 'keep' and a 'hall-house';[87] the latter is very ruined but was almost identical in scale and design to the former (see Figs. 41, 42 below) so one wonders here too why it is denied the same designation. There are other examples.

As a model which shifted the interpretation of Anglo-Norman donjons away from the military towards the domestic, the 'hall-house' had interim value in Ireland, given

---

82 Waterman 1968.   **83** O'Keeffe 1984.   **84** Stell 2014–15.   **85** McNeill 1997, 149–55.
86 Sweetman 1999, Ch. 3.   **87** Archaeological Survey of Ireland (https://webgis.archaeology.ie/historicenvironment/ q.v. Galway: Athenry, Moylough; Limerick: Coolbaun; Castletown Conyers).

that the military interpretation of castles still held sway up the 1990s. But John Blair was suggesting as early as 1993 that somewhat comparable – though admittedly 'non-castle' – structures in England, known as 'first-floor halls' since Margaret Wood's seminal paper in 1935, were actually chambers or chamber-blocks, and that their associated halls stood separately from them.[88] Subsequent research confirmed his hypothesis.[89] The historiography of the 'hall-house' in Ireland shows that Blair's paper went unnoticed among Irish castellologists (as indeed did the expressions of opposition to his view, especially by Michael Thompson and Anthony Quiney).[90]

To this day, the 'hall-house' remains in the vocabulary of Irish researchers. I have discussed elsewhere how its definition in Ireland is still informed by a misunderstanding of the character and function of the *aula* in Norman and Angevin culture on the one hand, and by a lack of awareness of that relevant English evidence on the other. And I have argued that the myth of the 'hall-house' has contributed in turn to a fundamental misunderstanding of the use of space in later tower-houses in Ireland.[91] The low towers so misidentified in Ireland were all small residential donjons. Halls were external to them, and were usually of perishable material. Such halls are documented.[92]

Noting the low height of the original donjon at Adare (Limerick), discussed below (pp 105–6), Tom McNeill described it as 'an unconvincing great tower'.[93] At least neither he nor the Archaeological Survey of Ireland succumbed to the temptation to relabel it a 'hall-house'. But his words capture the essence of many of the castle buildings identified as 'hall-houses': they are relatively small in footprint and in superstructure. They are indeed 'unconvincing' as 'great towers' according to modern understandings of the Latin root words, the noun *turris* and (especially) the adjective *magna*. But that is what they were in essence. They represent – as the heading of this section indicates – a line of *descent* of the great tower or donjon. In a sense, they represent in their simplicity a return to structural and functional first principles. Each was a later version of the timber-built *turris* in La Cour-Marigny (Loiret) of which it was written around 1080 that it had 'in its upper part a solar, where Seguinus and his family stayed, met, talked and ate together and slept at night', and that 'it had in its lower parts a cellar of various compartments to receive and store vital foodstuff'.[94] To deny them the label 'donjon' because they do not compare with the likes of Loches or Hedingham would be akin to denying a small single-cell church that label, 'church', because it does not compare with a great cathedral church or abbey church. I continue to advocate for the removal of the phrase 'hall-house' from the literature.[95]

From Glanworth to Tomdeeley

For evidence that two- and three-storeyed residential donjons first appeared in Ireland before the end of the twelfth century, we might turn to north Co. Cork. The manors

---

88 Blair 1993; Wood 1935. Boothby Pagnell (Lincolnshire) is the iconic site in the category. **89** Impey and Harris 2002; see also Hill and Gardiner 2018, 4. **90** Thompson 1995, 34–49, and Quiney 1999. **91** O'Keeffe 2013–14; 2014c. **92** O'Keeffe 2015, 210–17. **93** McNeill 1997, 38. **94** Mortet and Deschamps 1929, 10 (my translation). **95** For further critical appraisals

32 The donjon at Glanworth. The original entrance is at first-floor level on the right-hand side. The small slit window at the top of the wall was originally just under the roof.

of Glanworth and Ballyderown were both possessions of the de Caunteton (later Condon) family, enfeoffed in the Fermoy district by Raymond le Gros, probably in the 1180s.[96] The latter was a sub-manor of the former for the first century after the Anglo-Normans arrived in the district. Each manor had a castle with a donjon. The donjon at Glanworth is likely to be the older of the two, if the relative status of the manors is an indicator. If the architecture of Ballyderown suggests a late twelfth-century date, based on its moulded stonework, so too must Glanworth pre-date 1200, and possibly even date from as early as the 1180s.[97] Having said that, the two donjons, built by siblings, are very different in character from each other.

Glanworth was the simpler of the two, and it had a simplicity barely rivalled among Irish donjons (Fig. 32). Its basement could only be accessed from above by wooden stairs. Its first-floor room had the entrance doorway (with no fore-building) in one of

of 'hall-houses', supportive of my scepticism, see Stell 2014–15; Dempsey 2016a; 2017. **96** MacCotter 1997, 89–94; 2009, 1–3.   **97** For Ballyderown see O'Keeffe 1984. Con Manning has suggested the Glanworth tower could date from *c.*1190 (2009, 140). I concur. But I am not convinced by his suggestion that the 'partial ringwork' suggested by aerial photographs of the site existed before the stone buildings were erected (and might therefore be the work of

33 The donjon at Ballyderown. The two large windows are visible on the left-hand side. The walling on the far right-hand side belongs to a late medieval toilet turret, making the tower look slightly longer than it was originally.

the short walls, a small mural toilet in the short wall opposite, and plain side-wall windows. A small window below the parapet suggests a (cramped) attic,[98] but I am not sure that this plain donjon even had that feature: the absence of a fireplace in the main room below means that there must have been a central hearth, in which case a fully-floored attic above would not have been possible. The castle also had a detached hall to the north of the donjon. That appears to have had some residential element at its east end, which is the end towards which the doorway of the donjon faced. It would seem, then, that in the 1180s or 1190s Glanworth Castle had an exclusively private though relatively low-grade seigneurial residence in a small tower, a hall for 'public' activities, and a space of short-term habitation at the end of the hall from which the lord could enter from under the same roof.

Glanworth gives us our earliest glimpse of the model for a donjon which was favoured in the encastellated landscape of Ireland after 1200. No single point of origin for that model can be identified outside Ireland, nor should one search for one. In a sense, the Glanworth donjon represents the ultimate reduction of all residential donjon variants – Capetian, Norman, Angevin – to their common denominators: a dark basement, a habitable room above, a doorway into it, a toilet off it, and a hearth in the

Raymond le Gros); the line of the arc suggests that the hall was at least under construction when a ditch was being dug around the site.   **98** Manning 2009, 17–18.

middle of it. Glanworth is probably the only surviving example in Ireland of this simple scheme from before 1200, but it was almost certainly not the only one to have been built around that time. One should not regard it as having had any particular influence. The next *surviving* donjon of its type in chronological sequence is probably that at Adare (see below), built just after the turn of the century by a mason who probably never saw Glanworth. Whatever is the next one in chronological order, it is possible that its mason saw neither Glanworth nor Adare. And so it goes. There is no reason to think, in other words, that any one donjon is the *paterfamilias* in Ireland.

Ballyderown was a superior donjon, and by some distance (Fig. 33). It was higher, its footprint was larger (by about two-thirds), and it had moulded stone. Its chamfered quoins, executed in a soft stone which outwardly resembled oolithic limestone in colour, indicate that it was a building to be seen and admired. The basement was linked to the first floor by stairs in a vaulted mural passage. At first-floor level, one wall – the end wall opposite the mural stairs just mentioned – had two large windows, probably each a twin-light, set externally in roll-moulded 'Romanesque' frames and set internally in very wide embrasures which took up almost the entire internal width of the wall.[99] It would seem, then, that there was an upper/lower division of space in Ballyderown's first-floor room, something which was not possible in the more confined space in Glanworth. If the remains at Ballyderown suggest a room of hall-like character, its position at first-floor level makes that unlikely in an Angevin context. It was, though, more sumptuous than most other first-floor chambers in Ireland. There was an upper floor in the building as well, but it was more thinly walled, and evidence of how it was accessed from below no longer survives.

The variation between these two donjons, built almost simultaneously, is instructive. Just as the builders of the first donjons in Ireland in the 1170s and 1180s had options, as was noted, so too did the donjon-builders of *c.*1200 in Ireland. The de Caunteton brothers chose different designs, possibly even from the same master mason, just as Hugh de Lacy and Maurice fitz Gerald seem to have done at Trim and Maynooth respectively. The cylindrical option, discussed in the next chapter, was introduced to Ireland after 1200 so it was not available to the de Cauntetons.

The basic design-concept represented with different degrees of sophistication by Glanworth and Ballyderown must have entered Ireland a few times around the turn of the century, but the variation within the corpus is not so great that one needs to posit multiple independent points of entry. The likelihood is, I suggest, that a small number of masons arriving in Ireland around 1200, each tasked with building relatively simple chamber towers for Anglo-Norman lords of limited resources, planted stylistic roots. Those roots then tangled as new commissions emerged and as new Irish-born masons of English descent, trained on those initial projects, took on the responsibility for designing and managing projects. That process of entanglement then yielded a harvest

---

99 I know of only one parallel for such embrasures in Ireland: at Woodstock (Kildare), a single-pile donjon which was heavily modified in the late Middle Ages, two small first-floor windows in one of the end walls are set within large internal frames which take up most of the width of the wall.

of simple-plan rectangular donjons which, through three generations up to the 1250s (when donjon-building stopped), resembled each other in plan, even though some of the donjons were more robust that others in appearance. To illustrate this point, four donjons – two pairs of two – are selected here (Fig. 34).

The plain, two-storeyed, donjon at Mullinahone (Tipperary) dates from early in the thirteenth century. Nothing else survives of the castle, including its hall. This donjon was very close in spirit to that at Glanworth, although it was bigger and more thickly-walled. There is no reason to think it a derivative of Glanworth, but they had a kinship. They represent one design-type, possibly introduced just once or twice around 1200. Similarly muscular is the three-storeyed donjon at Moylough, dating from the mid-thirteenth century.[100] It is one of a group of moderately large residential donjons in Connacht, of which Athenry is the best preserved. The colonization of Connacht from the mid-1230s was an internal process; it involved individuals and families already in Ireland. Therefore, the roots of Moylough, Athenry and other buildings like them are on the east side of the Shannon. One can see that the Mullinahone-type (to coin a phrase) is somewhere within the DNA of Moylough, but it alone does not explain every aspect of Moylough.

At the other end of the spectrum from these strong donjons is the smaller and thinner-walled Cargin (Galway), also of the mid-thirteenth century. Its scale tempts one to suggest that its accompanying hall was timber-built.[101] Although less imposing than Moylough, and more discrete on the landscape, its interior 'worked' the same way: it had a residential first-floor room above a basement, all within a simple rectangular shell. There is little of Mullinahone in its DNA. One or two buildings erected east of the Shannon in the 1230s (when Connacht was annexed to the lordship) might have planted the seeds which explain why Cargin resembles Moylough in aspects of its plan and yet differs from it in outward appearance. Finally, of the four, the building at Tomdeeley (Limerick), undated but possibly of the second quarter of the thirteenth century, is similar but slightly larger than Cargin. In plan and elevation, it is closer in design to donjons in Connacht than elsewhere, and the wide chamfers on its external corners link it specifically to the mid-century donjons of Castle Magarret and Shrule (both Mayo). This feature was probably an invention of a single mason but we cannot say where it first appeared.

To conclude, it is probable that the origins of the corpus of single-pile rectangular donjons in Ireland illustrated in Figure 31 can be traced to a small number of buildings erected around 1200, probably by a small cohort of masons. Some innovatory donjon designs did enter Ireland after 1200, as is discussed in the following chapter, but most Anglo-Norman lords in the thirteenth century were satisfied with the traditional square or rectangular, single-pile, format, if indeed they were aware of the alternative designs.

---

100 Waterman 1956. **101** At the manor of Inch (Kerry), for example, there was in 1298–9 a hall 'of pales with an earthen wall and thatched' and a chamber 'with a cellar built of stone and thatched' (CDI 4, no. 551).

34 The donjons at (*above*) Mullinahone, (*below*) Moylough, (*opposite top*) Cargin and (*opposite bottom*) Tomdeeley.

35 The interior of Tomdeeley donjon. Note the small fragment of an engaged shaft to the left of the doorway. It is unlikely that there was an arch above this, so the spatial division might have been effected by articulation on each side wall, with a less permanent screen between.

Tomdeeley, Grenan and Greencastle: the problem of the 'chamber-block'

At first-floor level in Tomdeeley, on one side of the doorway, one can see remains of articulation intended to demarcate the boundary between two spaces of unequal size (Fig. 35): a larger and more open floor space into which that door gave access, and a narrower floor space occupying the western quarter of the building. Here is clear if fragmentary evidence, rarely seen in these simple buildings, that the upper-floor levels were (sometimes, at least) partitioned to create inner and outer rooms.

This observation at Tomdeeley raises a problem of terminology. I have described the building as a donjon. It is, arguably, a more elongated version of what one sees manifest at Glanworth, Ballyderown, Moylough, and elsewhere. Its elongation might have been for the explicit purpose of accommodating at upper-floor level the two spaces which that partition created. It was, in other words, a bicameral rather than a unicameral structure. Others were probably the same, but the evidence is lost. Were Tomdeeley found in England (or indeed in Normandy), it would almost certainly be

36 The donjon at Grenan. The toilet chute from the big first-floor room is visible in the short wall. The ground-floor entrance to the tower (with a small chapel above it at first-floor level) was at the opposite end, facing the probable site of the hall.

described as a chamber-block rather than a chamber tower or donjon.[102] That issue needs to be addressed.

'Chamber-block' is a modern term, so we should be careful not to try to shoehorn buildings in Ireland into the category which it purports to describe in England and Normandy. There are two Irish monuments of the thirteenth century for which that term works particularly well in a purely descriptive sense, but each was a complex of structures rather than a single free-standing structure. One is the heavily ruined 'manorial' complex at Rincrew (Waterford), probably of the early part of the century. There, a small and modest two-storeyed residential building with an annexe was placed at a right-angle to a small stone-built hall.[103] The other is Clonmore Castle (Carlow), where a complex of late thirteenth-century domestic structures with a curiously staggered plan lines the east side of a courtyard.[104]

Although he did not explicitly state it, most of the structures identified as chamber-blocks in England and Normandy by Edward Impey in a seminal survey of two decades ago[105] share two characteristics, regardless of whether or not they are compact and free-standing. First, evidence of internal partitions at their elongated first-floor levels indicate that there was social gradation among those with access to those levels.

102 For chamber-blocks see Impey 1999.   **103** Cotter, MacCotter and O'Keeffe 2015.
104 O'Keeffe 2001b, 187.   **105** Impey 1999.

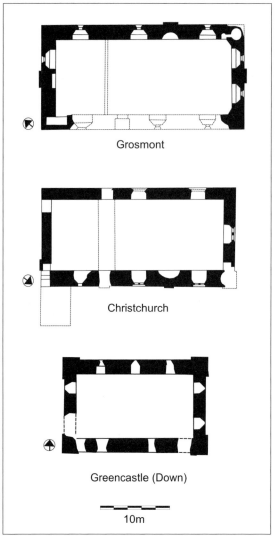

Grosmont

Christchurch

Greencastle (Down)

10m

37 Plans of the first-floor levels in the focal buildings at Grosmont, Christchurch, and Greencastle (Down).

Second, the structures in question were physically attached to halls or, if physically separate, were positioned relative to halls in a manner which underscores the functional and performative relationships between them. Based on these criteria, Ireland has at least three free-standing structures which would probably be described as chamber-blocks by English scholars. The first is Tomdeeley itself. An English scholar expecting a detached ground-floor hall would focus attention on the evidence that, in addition to its first-floor entrance, it had a ground-floor doorway facing where a hall might once have stood. The second is Grenan (Kilkenny), an exceptionally fine building dating from the 1220s (Fig. 36).[106] Its first-floor level offered very comfortable

106 Waterman 1968, 67–72.

accommodation, complete with a small oratory for private prayer. Unusually, there was no direct entry to this level from outside. Mural stairs gave access to it from a gable-end doorway at ground-floor level. That doorway faces a platformed area large enough to have accommodated a second building – a hall – at a 90 degree angle. The third is Greencastle (Down), dating from the second quarter of the thirteenth century. It is a difficult building to read,[107] but it seems to be in the tradition of, for example, Christchurch (Dorset), dated to *c*.1160, and Grosmont (Monmouthshire), dated to 1201–4, two of the many chamber-blocks identified by Edward Impey (Fig. 37).[108] Significantly, parallel to it and a matter of metres away was a small stone hall of single-storeyed height. Despite all this evidence, though, I would argue that labelling any of these buildings as chamber-blocks would be to introduce an unnecessary level of complication. They are better regarded as chamber donjons.

A family affair: de Marisco donjons

Adare lies at the chronological head of a very interesting group of donjons associated with a single Anglo-Norman family in Co. Limerick, the de Marisco family. There are (or, rather, were) four buildings in the group, one of them erected by Geoffrey, the justiciar, two erected by one of his sons, John, and one erected by another son, William.

Adare itself had a castle before the Anglo-Normans arrived in rural Limerick at the very end of the century. A reference in *An Leabhar Muimhneach* (*The Book of Munster*), an eighteenth-century genealogical manuscript based on early seventeenth-century materials, themselves derived from older sources now lost, informs us that Domnall Mór Ua Briain, king of Munster, 'built the Black Castle of Adare and the great hall to the south of the Castle'.[109] This would have been in the last decade of the twelfth century. The description tallies with the plan of the site (Fig. 38).[110] The 'Black Castle' corresponds to the small inner ward where the donjon is located. That donjon is Anglo-Norman, as will be shown. The curving wall to which it is attached is early but of uncertain date; the open-backed tower is mainly a late twelfth- and early thirteenth-century type (see below, p. 127), and could remain from Domnall Mór's castle. The 'great hall' can be identified as the first-floor hall overlooking the river from the outer ward. Being at first-floor level (above a full-height basement), it was unlike other early halls in Ireland, and that makes one wonder whether it reflects a native hall tradition for which no other physical evidence remains.

Geoffrey de Marisco acquired Adare at the very end of the twelfth century and the donjon can be assigned confidently to him. It was originally two-storeyed, apparently with a low attic above which was a roof which seems not to have been fully counter-sunk but was still largely concealed from external view. The tower was later heightened by two more storeys; McNeill suggests that this was done in the late Middle Ages,[111] but I think it is possibly a thirteenth-century alteration (to which

---

107 Tom McNeill described it as 'a first-floor great hall' (1997, 91), but I would argue that its upper room was not a hall.   **108** Impey 1999, Fig. 18.   **109** Devane 2013, 9.   **110** Lord Dunraven's plan of the castle from 1865 is reproduced most accessibly in Dunne and Kiely 2013, 37.   **111** Ibid.

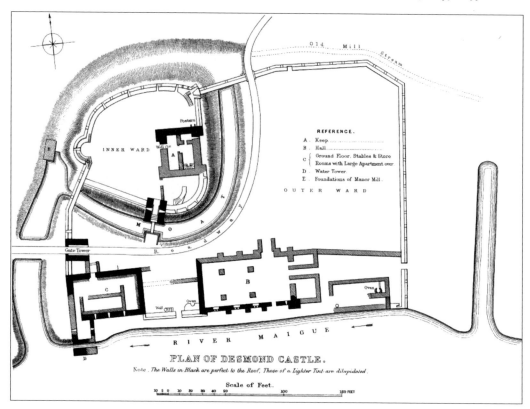

38 Lord Dunraven's very accurate plan of Adare Castle in 1865. The site of the pre-Norman 'Black Castle' is the inner ward, and the pre-Norman great hall is the smaller of the two halls in the outer ward; the larger hall is a rare Irish example of a three-aisled hall, and probably dates (on comparative grounds) from the middle decades of the thirteenth century.

changes were later made). The most curious feature of the donjon is how its pilasters project in single directions from the end walls past the side walls. They did not clasp the corners, in other words.

Adare's master mason does not advertise his presence to us in any building project before the donjon was built, but he, or at least his mason's yard, is represented in some of the other, slightly later, buildings associated with the family.

Geoffrey's son, John, acquired the manor of Bruree early in the thirteenth century and it is likely that he added a very small residential tower to the fortress of *Dún Eochair Maige* in Lotteragh Upper.[112] In laying claim to a native Irish fortress, albeit a more ancient one, he copied his father's action at Adare. His tower at Lotteragh Upper no longer survives, but descriptions and photographs (Fig. 39) suggest another two-storeyed tower, taller externally than it was internally (indicating a counter-sunk roof). It had no pilasters. Thomas Westropp's description[113] indicates an inserted double-vault

112 O'Keeffe and MacCotter 2020. **113** Westropp 1916/17, 489.

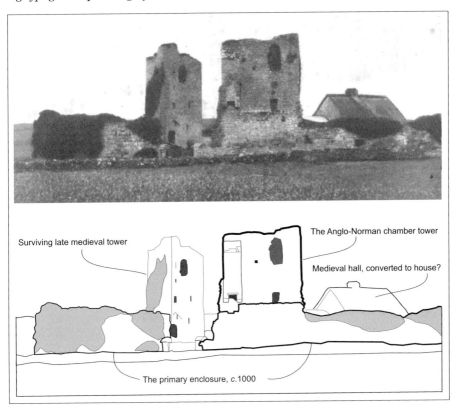

Surviving late medieval tower

The Anglo-Norman chamber tower

Medieval hall, converted to house?

The primary enclosure, *c*.1000

39 An interpretation of Thomas Westropp's published photograph of Lotteragh Upper Castle in the early twentieth century, identifying John de Marisco's chamber tower.

in the basement – the two compartments produced by this must have been quite tiny – and an upper storey which had mural openings clustered in its short northern wall. One opening was for stairs (its destination not recorded) and the other was for a toilet with an external machicolation.

The next work in chronological sequence with a link to Adare is the donjon of the royal castle at Clonmacnoise (Fig. 40). Its morphological connection with Adare is simply its corner pilasters. Such features are rare in Ireland and the Adare examples are odd to boot, but the Clonmacnoise examples compare well with those in two donjons built by Geoffrey's sons (see below). The date of Clonmacnoise is uncertain. An earth-and-timber castle was constructed there before 1215, in which year it was delivered into the custody of Geoffrey in his capacity as justiciar, who then surrendered it to the king in 1221.[114] There is no record of any building work by Geoffrey or any successor, but a date between 1215 and 1221 for the stone castle would not be unlikely.[115] A viable alternative to Geoffrey as the donjon's builder is Richard de Burgh, and the

---

114 CDI I, nos 600, 1015.   **115** O'Conor and Manning do not commit on its date but concede that it might date from the later 1210s or early 1220s (2000, 157).

40 The collapsed corner at one end of Clonmacnoise Castle, showing the pilasters at the narrow end of the donjon; the remainder of the donjon extended to the right.

identification of him as the builder does not weaken the link with the de Marisco family. Richard had possession of Clonmacnoise between 1228, when he was appointed justiciar, and 1233, when (some months after being stripped of the justiciarship) he was ordered to deliver the castle to his successor.[116] If he built the donjon, it was between 1228 and 1232. That date-range is important because Geoffrey's sons were already building rectangular donjons with pilasters at that very time. If Richard built Clonmacnoise, it was with cognisance of the work of, if not actual input from, masons working on de Marisco projects. But even if he was not involved in the work at Clonmacnoise, there is evidence that he was familiar with de Marisco buildings: Castlekirke (Galway), a native-built donjon of the early 1230s resembles to some degree the donjons built by Geoffrey's sons in the 1220s, and was built with his political support.[117]

By the 1220s John de Marisco had moved from Bruree to a new caput at a place which is now identified by the townland name Castletown Conyers but was known

116 CDI I, no. 2009.   117 O'Keeffe 2011a, 119–20. The date of the Castlekirke (*Caislen-na-Circe*) is disputed. Holland suggested a post-1237 date (1997, 164) and Mike Salter a date of *c*.1235 (2004, 28). McNeill was surely correct in identifying it as one of two Irish-built castles, both constructed with Anglo-Norman support, which were 'destroyed' by Fedhlim Ua Conchobhair in 1233 (1997, 161). Its construction should probably be attributed specifically to Áed Ua

41 The interior of Coonagh donjon. The two doorways at different floor levels in the end wall are original. As with Maynooth (see Fig. 27), the fabric does not allow an easy reconstruction of the original roofing.

in the thirteenth century as *Corcomohide*. He built a new castle there. His brother, William, hitherto unseen but later to achieve infamy as 'the pirate of Lundy', built a castle at Coonagh, located on church land which he and his wife, Matilda, obtained rather controversially as a marriage gift from her relative, the archbishop of Dublin.[118] The precise dates of the two castles are not known, but historical evidence suggests that Coonagh was probably built between 1225 and 1230. *Corcomohide*'s date cannot be much different; it certainly existed by 1234.[119] Much of the lower storey of John's donjon survives but vegetation hides its exterior. More than half of William's donjon survives almost to its full original height, but it is missing all of one of its end walls and parts of the adjoining walls (Fig. 41). The two donjons were almost identical in plan, and were quite unlike any other donjons of the period in Ireland, so we can regard them as a pair, and we can turn to Coonagh, the more complete of the two, to understand them. The morphological link with Geoffrey's donjon in Adare is manifest in the presence of pilasters in both donjons, with those in John's donjon closely resembling those at Adare in the curious nature of their projection.

Conchobhair to whom Richard de Burgh restored the kingship of Connacht in 1232 (AC 1232.10). **118** O'Keeffe 2011a. **119** Ibid., 121–2.

42 The donjon at Coonagh, showing the projecting turret. The arch on the right opens into the turret, and that on left is a recess. There are very slight traces of scarring from the original timber roof above the two features. There are signs on the mortar plaster that the fore-building wrapped around the turret on the left-hand side. An original window at ground-floor level in the turret suggests that the fore-building was partly open-framed.

43 The donjon at Portchester, showing the recess for a seat inside what was originally the fore-building chapel.

The arrangement of space within Coonagh's main block is puzzling because there are no traces of the original roof to indicate how many floors it had. There may have been only two, a lower one which was probably partitioned by an arcade to support the floor timbers, and a very well-appointed first-floor room with a canopied fireplace and seated windows. Wall-scars suggest a ceiling above the first-floor room, and there is a single surviving window to suggest that there was a floor above that again. Evidence of original crenellations on the exterior – the tower was heightened in the later Middle Ages – indicates that this was a tall building (only surpassed in height among Ireland's Anglo-Norman donjons by Trim, in its completed form, and Carrickfergus), so an upper floor is possible, but a low ceiling would have killed some of the visual impact of that first-floor room. Stone-by-stone survey from scaffolding might resolve the problem.

The most interesting feature of Coonagh is the evidence for how it was accessed by William and Matilda de Marisco. Entry was through a remarkable structure unparalleled in Ireland except at *Corcomohide*. It was a projecting stair turret, entered via a (stilted?) wooden fore-building at a height approximately equivalent to roof level inside the main block. Within the fore-building at the point of entry was a tiny oratory, its back wall having an arched recess cut into the masonry of the turret (Fig. 42). A parallel for an entrance and a chapel side-by-side, the latter also with an arched recess in its back wall, is Portchester (Fig. 43). From the turret, the de Mariscos

44 Chambois donjon in the late nineteenth century, prior to its restoration.

could move along a mural corridor linking two small rooms in the main block's corner pilasters – this is a feature exactly paralleled only, to my knowledge, at Clun Castle (Shropshire),[120] probably of the late thirteenth century – or they could descend into the tower's first-floor room. The descent ended at a doorway of high quality, suggesting that the first-floor room was a space of reception rather than of private retreat. The pattern at *Corcomohide* was probably the same.

Coonagh and *Corcomohide* were as rooted in earlier twelfth-century thinking as any donjons in Ireland, even Maynooth, perhaps the most archaic of all. But their joint pedigree, beyond Adare of course, is impossible to trace. Coonagh's better preservation permits some speculation. It has two parallels with Trim: entry via a projecting turret, and corners which rose higher than the walls between them. But one needs to go outside Ireland for a more exact parallel. Chambois (Orne) has an English donjon of the 1170s which is larger but of comparable proportions, and shares with Coonagh the use of clasping pilasters with small internal rooms, a projecting mid-wall turret (also slightly south of centre) with an entrance and a chapel, and a long-wall positioning of a hooded fireplace in its main room (Fig. 44).[121] One hesitates to describe Chambois as an inspiration, but identifying it as a parallel underscores both the ambition and archaism of Coonagh's basic conception.

The remarkable choreography of entry and movement at Coonagh, imposed by a wooden fore-building and a descending stairs, is unparalleled exactly anywhere outside

120 Guy 2016–17, 100.   **121** Decaëns 1997. The pre-restoration drawing is taken from Joanne 1892, 1461.

Ireland, to my knowledge. Entry at a high level, followed by descent, into the body of a donjon, is not unknown,[122] but it was uncommon. Coonagh's master mason might have recognized the symbolic power of a patron being seen to climb high within a fore-building, pass a chapel, and then descend into an audience room, and he might then have created the Coonagh scheme from his own imagination to allow that happen. There was possibly another reason. Being so tall, the top of the wooden fore-building was visible from the local parish church to the east. Given that the castle was built on church land, the alienation of which made it a subject of prolonged legal proceedings,[123] William and Matilda de Marisco might have desired to have an elevated chapel visible to the outside world in order to show that 'the church' was embedded in their seigneurial residence.

CONCLUSION

Ireland's rectangular donjons, built in almost every case under Anglo-Norman patronage (Castlekirke is an exception), follow in traditions which one can trace through Angevin and Norman England, and from there back into Normandy before 1066, and back again into tenth-century Capetian France. There is no obvious *direct* influence from France in the corpus of these donjons in Ireland,[124] but that does not negate the value for Irish scholars of knowing the French material, especially as French influence was to inform some of the castles built in the new 'modernist' age (see Chapter 4).

Knowledge of the ancestry of the Irish donjons is critical to their comprehension. The first donjons, built in the three decades or so after the invasion, follow some of the different lines of development of the donjon as a type, and they wear their ancestries on their sleeves. They possibly fall into two groups: the conservative (either in style, as at Carrickfergus, or in ambition, as at Glanworth and Adare), and the archaic (as at Trim, Maynooth and Dunamase). The distinction between conservatism and archaism is a subtle but important one: the former is a form of stasis, an architecture of the status quo, whereas the latter is an architecture that recognizes the momentum of stylistic change but chooses to think about it from a perspective that is historicist and maybe nostalgic, rather than forward-looking and innovative.

Large rectangular donjons were built in small numbers in Ireland into the 1220s, at Grenan and Coonagh. But by the middle of the thirteenth century, the conservatism represented by the 'seigneurial minimum' was itself an archaism, as simple chamber towers offering modest and traditional accommodation to their owners – Glanworth seems to be the earliest surviving example – came to dominate the encastellated

122 It is found at Dover and Newcastle upon Tyne, for example. A second-floor reception room is suggested at Sainte-Suzanne (Mayenne): Bocquet 2004, 214.   **123** O'Keeffe 2011a, 95–100.
124 The rounded corner-pilasters of the small, undocumented, thirteenth-century tower in Ballyboy (Tipperary) are very French in character (for parallels see Châtelain 1973, *passim*) but it is difficult to imagine how French influence could have permeated as far as this rural location in Ireland and not left traces along the way.

landscape. Such architecture was archaic because new 'modernist' ideas about castle-planning had begun to appear early in the new century, offering lords alternatives *if they chose*.

From a north-west European perspective, the rectangular Irish donjons lie at the end, chronologically, of the broadly defined architectural tradition described as Romanesque. If England and France are 'core' areas in the development of castles during that period of 'medieval historicism', as Marvin Trachtenberg has described it,[125] Ireland has intrinsic interest to all European castellologists as a locale on the 'periphery' where one can see the architectural tradition of the eleventh and twelfth centuries simply peter out in the thirteenth, its patrons no longer looking over their shoulders at architectural developments in their ancestral 'homelands'.[126]

125 Trachtenberg 2001.   **126** In this sense, Ireland is worth comparing with Sicily, where Norman great towers often deviated from the 'homeland' tradition in the Duchy in being multi-storeyed, and in having ground-floor entrances and cross-walls which rise from basement to roof level. For some descriptions, see F. Chiesa 1998.

CHAPTER 4

After *Romanitas*: castles of the new medieval modernism

In his magisterial survey of English castles, John Goodall devoted a chapter to the works of the reigns of John (1199–1216) and Henry III (1216–72) under the title 'The Gothic Castle'.[1] 'Almost overnight', he wrote, 'around 1200 the rectangular tower favoured in the Romanesque period passed out of fashion from new English castle building for a century. In its place circular or semicircular, and more occasionally polygonal, designs reigned supreme. So complete is this change that the circular and semicircular tower should properly be understood in the abstracted sphere of castle design as no less characteristic of English Gothic architecture than the pointed arch.'[2] Goodall should really have entitled the chapter 'The Earlier Gothic Castle', simply because conventional thinking brings Gothic into the fifteenth and earlier sixteenth centuries, but his point was well made.

The new architectural style known as Gothic, the 'modernist–medieval' style as Trachtenberg characterized it, was born as an ecclesiastical architecture in the Paris Basin, and it appeared first in England with the rebuilding of the choir of Canterbury Cathedral after a fire in 1174. It then snuffed out the stylistic preference – 'Romanesque' – of Norman and early Angevin England. By the time John took the crown, the die was cast: most patrons had abandoned what had been the architectural style in the kingdom of England from at least the mid-eleventh century. One might ask, as has Richard Hulme,[3] what relationship there could possibly be between the development of a new architecture for great churches and the development of a new military architecture, given that many of the features which characterize one are generally not found in the other. But such a question is predicated on a narrow understanding of the nature of style. To think of architectural style as a set of common, formal attributes is to misunderstand the creative processes which generate aesthetic and technical coherence, and to misunderstand how new thinking about architectural design in one context could liberate thinking about design in another. It is apparent that castle-builders from the later twelfth century did not seek to imitate the full range of what they observed in contemporary churches, even if they too used pointed arches. But they clearly saw what engineering was capable of producing for churches. They clearly identified in those same churches the capacity of architecture to convey new meanings through breaking the mould of *visual* culture. So, given that the new adventurism in the planning of military architecture probably owed very little

1 Goodall 2011, Ch. 6.   2 Ibid., p. 154.   3 Hulme 2013–14, 204.

to Frankish experiments or experiences while on crusade,[4] one must regard Goodall's 'Gothic castle' as a home-grown, north-west European, Capetian/Angevin phenomenon. It was made possible to a considerable degree by the genius master masons of 'Gothic' churches, from St Denis to Canterbury, from Laon to Wells.

The relationship between England and France, and England and Ireland, in the matter of this ecclesiastical architecture after the mid-1170s is worth exploring briefly as a prelude to considering the castles. French and English aesthetic tastes in the new 'Gothic' architecture diverged quickly in the late twelfth century, leaving the Canterbury choir as an isolated item of French character in England. The tastes remained divergent until the middle of the thirteenth century, when, with their respective 'Rayonnant' and 'Decorated' styles, they converged around a desire to embellish both wall surfaces and openings with flowing motifs. But they diverged again a century later, and dramatically so. The French 'Flamboyant' style remained in the tradition of the 'Rayonnant'. However, the English 'Perpendicular' style, developed in the second quarter of the fourteenth century, privileged the vertical and horizontal line over the flowing (or 'flaming', *flamboyante*) line.[5]

In Ireland, church-builders followed English fashion from the twelfth century on, albeit with a different rhythm. The first English 'Gothic' style – the so-called 'Early English' – was introduced into Ireland in the 1190s, probably via the royal abbey of St Thomas the Martyr in Dublin.[6] It remained in vogue through the thirteenth century, mainly in window designs and arch-types. The 'Decorated' style, developed in England in the mid-thirteenth century, was then adopted near the end of the thirteenth century in Ireland. It remained in vogue in Ireland until the end of the Middle Ages, albeit with some design features of English 'Perpendicular' origin. It is worth noting that there is nothing of *direct* French origin in Ireland's ecclesiastical architecture from the time of the Anglo-Norman invasion. That is a change from the previous century, when some forms and motifs of western French origin entered the Irish architectural and sculptural repertoires.[7] And it also stands in contrast to the castles in the thirteenth century, as will be seen in this chapter.

The Channel separating England and France served to demarcate boundaries in taste in castle architecture as well as in church architecture through the Middle Ages, but the trajectory of stylistic convergence and divergence for the two categories of building in the two territories was very different. Churches were tied to liturgies from which their ground plans could not venture too far, but national identity could find a powerful expression in how their superstructures were designed and executed. That probably explains why English church-builders 'personalized' the new French style so quickly from the late 1170s, accentuating horizontal articulation over vertical articulation, for example, and retaining the Norman 'thick-wall' passage. Some consciousness of how style expressed a national identity probably explains also why

---

4 Colin Platt argued that crusader experiences were critical to the 'growing sophistication' of castles at this time (1982, 46–9). However, cylindrical forms were rarely deployed in the crusader lands before the start of the thirteenth century (Kennedy 1994, 86–7, 115; Boas 2005, 111–16). **5** The literature is vast. See, for example, Wilson 1990; Draper 2006. **6** Carey Bates and O'Keeffe 2017. **7** O'Keeffe 2003, *passim*.

English masons developed and adhered to the 'Perpendicular style' in the fourteenth century.[8] Castles, by contrast, were monuments of ever-changing pragmatism, and therefore were not rule-bound in their designs. That is not to say that identity found no expression in castle architecture – it clearly did in Capetian France in the early thirteenth century, for example, as will be seen here – but, rather, to assert that designs which appeared successful for whatever reason in one polity were always likely to be copied in another. In castle architecture, pragmatic concerns were presumably the equal of, and maybe even trumped, the desire to make identity statements.

The spread of stylistic ideas required political boundaries to have some permeability, and that was most likely to be the case where the territories were contiguous and the political cultures comparable. Thus, the addition of large parts of modern France to the territorial holdings of the kingdom of England following the accession of Henry II in 1154 provided an opportunity for the transfer of ideas between Angevin and Capetian barons and knights. The adoption by the Angevin lords in these islands of architectural ideas developed in France, within *both* the Angevin and Capetian jurisdictions there, probably peaked during John's tumultuous reign (1199–1216).[9]

Before looking at the evidence, the matter of Richard I (1189–99) and his role in the story of the 'modernization' of castle architecture in these islands merits a brief comment.[10] Richard was hardly ever in England, instead spending part of his reign in prison, part of it on crusade earning his moniker 'the Lionheart', and most of it in France. And his signal architectural achievement as a castle-builder – Château Gaillard (Eure), built 1196–8 – was on modern-day French soil.[11] But he is a critically important figure. Men like William Marshal were soldiers in royal service with him in France, absorbing ideas of architectural design which they would then reuse in England and, as we will see, in Ireland. From the perspective of the architectural history of castles, that decade in which Richard was (often only nominally) in power in the Angevin 'empire' should really be viewed more as a prequel to the reign of John than a sequel to the reign of Henry II.[12] The two decades from 1190 to 1210 saw such an acceleration of experimentation and innovation in castle architecture that the pace of progression over the previous two centuries seems almost glacial by comparison.

FIRST WORKS IN IRELAND, 1190–1200

The creation of a new lordship in Ireland in the late twelfth century was an opportunity for Angevin lords to build stone castles *de novo*. The previous chapter

---

8 Although it was quintessentially an English medieval style, the best-known scholarly work, Harvey 1978, exaggerates considerably the degree to which its practitioners rejected and remained unaffected by contemporary French Gothic. **9** O'Keeffe and Liddiard 2016. **10** Colin Platt used the word 'modernization' in this context (1982, 50). **11** Château Gaillard was 'English' only in a political sense. As a work of architecture, it was rooted firmly in the tradition of the land in which it was built, its polylobate inner curtain and its beaked-plan donjon being among the many features which are not found in England. See Corvisier 2001. On the question of its relevance to England, I side with Goodall's scepticism (2011, 144, 153) over Richard Hulme's conviction (2013–14). **12** This is *contra* Goodall (2011) who excluded

documented how in the final thirty years of the twelfth century castle-builders adopted a conservative, even nostalgic, approach. But those lords who were thinking about building castles after the turn of the thirteenth century had two other choices. They could exploit the results of those design-experiments, or they could experiment for themselves. The evidence presented in this chapter suggests that some castle-builders did a little of the latter and others did quite a lot of the former. The upshot was that early thirteenth-century Ireland saw old-fashioned castles being built alongside castles which, though modest in scale, were conceptually in the vanguard of contemporary north-west European architecture.

Working out the sequence of new, forward-looking, building-projects in Ireland during the reigns of Richard I and John is difficult because the only fixed dates available pertain to a few royal works. The earliest work of the new architectural modernism in Ireland was apparently baronial, not royal. That should not be a surprise. The English crown showed no real interest in fortifying Ireland with its own money until John's reign started, by which stage ideas had started flowing freely across the Channel and even the Irish Sea. Even then, one of John's earliest works in Ireland – the polygonal enclosure at Dungarvan (Waterford) – was distinctly archaic, suggesting that the crown was not focused on producing up-to-date work in the Irish lordship.[13] For the architectural historian seeking to understand the trajectory of castle development, knitting the baronial works in and out of the chronology of royal work during John's reign is not easy. That is a testimony to just how quickly ideas moved around.

Trim

Hugh de Lacy's castle at Trim was unfinished when he was killed in 1186. It is possible to work out exactly what he had built of the outer enclosure by then (Fig. 45).[14] The north-western curtain was built, apart from a tower at its west end, which was the point at which the curtain would have returned to the south-east. The eastern curtain, running alongside the river, was also his work, and it was nearly finished: the towers overlooking the river were evenly spaced, and three of them were built, but a fourth, at the southernmost point of the wall, was not built. That was the point at which the curtain wall would have returned to the south-west. The two mid-wall river-side towers were actually more up-to-date than the donjon which stood behind them. Rectangular towers for archers – one can identify them because windows for archers were in recesses, and not simply splayed – appeared in English curtain walls from the mid-1160s, possibly first in royal work, as at Orford and Bamburgh (Northumberland), and they enjoyed some popularity right to the end of the century.[15]

him from his account of 'the [earlier] Gothic castle' in England, placing him instead alongside Henry II in a chapter entitled 'The Early Angevin Castle'. **13** See Guy 2018–19, 21–2. Although not a 'shell-keep' as rigidly defined by Robert Higham because it was not built on a motte, it was certainly in that earlier twelfth-century tradition (see Higham 2015, 22). **14** Hayden 2011, 188–9. **15** For Orford's lost curtain wall (built between 1165 and 1173) see Guy et al. 2011–12, 63, 70; for Bamburgh's towers (built c.1170) see Goodall 2011, 132, 134. The identification of the east curtain at Trim as Hugh de Lacy's work secures a date in the later 1170s

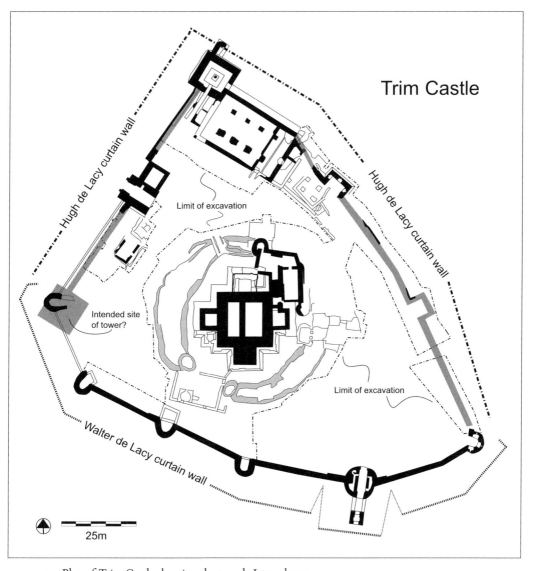

Trim Castle

Hugh de Lacy curtain wall

Hugh de Lacy curtain wall

Limit of excavation

Intended site
of tower?

Walter de Lacy curtain wall

Limit of excavation

25m

45 Plan of Trim Castle showing the two de Lacy phases.

Hugh's son, Walter, was a minor in 1186, so it is unlikely that any work was carried out on the castle during the three years of his wardship. Walter actually only came into possession of the lordship of Meath in 1194. It has been suggested by Seán Duffy that Walter probably did not have the resources to engage in substantial building work at Trim in the second half of that decade, but that he would have been able to work on the castle between 1201 and 1207 when he was resident in Meath.[16] By this chronology,

or 1180s for the earliest phase of Carlingford (Louth), *pace* McNeill, who assigns it an early thirteenth-century date (1997, Fig. 26 caption).   **16** S. Duffy 2011, 11.

46 The Dublin Gate, Trim Castle, viewed from the roof of the donjon.

47 The Dublin Gate and adjacent curtain wall at Trim Castle. Slight changes in fabric and/or alignment of the curtain wall indicate that the barbicaned gate-tower (with adjacent short stretches of walling) was built first, followed by the tower to the south (on the right-hand side in the photograph), followed by the curtain wall between them.

the castle was left unfinished and therefore vulnerable for at least fifteen years. Duffy's analysis is difficult to square with the National Monuments Service official account of the chronology of the donjon.[17] There, it is suggested that during these very years the donjon was raised in two separate phases to its present, four-storeyed, height. Publication of the detailed survey of the donjon is badly needed, and not only for the sake of that building's comprehension: clarity on its chronology might also bring greater clarity to the chronology of the castle's enclosure. It seems unlikely to me that the donjon was heightened while the enclosure around it was left so unfinished.

The original plan for a full-curtained enclosure around the donjon is not known, but stretches of straight wall were probably intended to produce a large four-sided

17 Hayden 2011, 107–12.

48 The interior of the Dublin Gate of Trim Castle, showing the round arch at first-floor level, and a similar arch in the original, 1170s, part of the donjon (*opposite*).

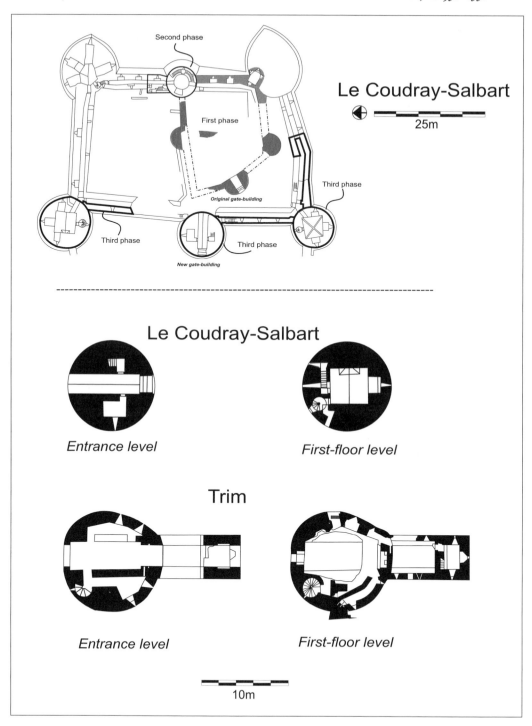

49 Plans of Le Coudray-Salbart Castle, showing its main phases, and the Dublin Gate of Trim Castle.

enclosure. Hugh's scheme was abandoned under Walter's watch in favour of something very different.[18] The first new work undertaken by Walter when he gained possession of the castle seems to have been the so-called Dublin Gate, the cylindrical tower punctured by a passageway and protected by a small square barbican (Fig. 46). Short stretches of curtain wall were built on either side of this tower, indicating that building work proceeded outwards from it in both directions. This gate-tower is, I suggest, the first important work in Ireland of the new era of architectural experimentation, the era of 'medieval modernism'.

Work on the completion of the curtain wall around Trim's donjon seems to have stopped after this gate-tower was built, leaving it free-standing for a period of, perhaps, no more than a few years. The curtain wall which was eventually built to enclose the donjon did not outline the area envisaged for enclosure when that cylindrical gate-tower was built. I would argue that the gate-tower was the first building to be erected in pursuit of an ambitious plan to develop the space south-east of the donjon – note its passage's orientation – but that this plan was abandoned for some reason, with a decision then made to finish the enclosing of the castle ward by simply connecting the two unfinished ends of Hugh de Lacy's original curtain wall with a new, thinner curtain running outwards in both directions from the circular gate-tower (Fig. 47).

The date of the gate-tower's construction is not known, but, *pace* Duffy's suggestion about Walter's financial incapacity for substantial architectural work, it might have been built in the later 1190s, with the remainder of the curtain wall built in the 1201–7 period.[19] There is one hint in the gate-tower's fabric that it is late twelfth-century work. This is the arch over the portcullis slot. It is a moulded round arch framed by rubble voussoirs, identical to arches in the *first*, 1170s, phase of the donjon (Fig. 48). The presence of that arch compels us to bring the date of the gate-tower as far back in time as possible during Walter's lordship, which basically means 1195–1200. Such a date would put it slightly earlier than the parallel most often cited for it: the gate-tower of the Angevin castle of Le Coudray-Salbart (Deux-Sèvres).[20]

Work on that great Poitevin castle began after 1202, and it was far enough advanced for King John to visit in 1206. In the first building campaign there, a much smaller castle was laid out, with a D-shaped gate-tower, solid apart from a short through-passage. The castle was quickly enlarged and a new gate-tower, perfectly circular in plan, was built on the same principle as the smaller original one (Fig. 49). This new tower had a drawbridge which rested on an external pier, and there might have been a barbican beyond that (although it is unlikely, based on the evidence of other French castles which had drawbridge piers). Although Coudray-Salbart was an Angevin

---

18 For the argument that there was a change of plan see O'Keeffe 2013b; 2017a; 2018b. **19** Alan Hayden, Trim's more recent excavator, allowed that a late twelfth-century date for the gate-tower is a 'remote' possibility, noting similarities between its masonry and that of the plinth (claimed to have been) added to the donjon in the 1190s (2011, 189–90).   **20** Baudry 1991. For the Trim parallel see Knight 1987, 78–9. McNeill describes the Trim tower as 'an imitation' of the Coudray-Salbart tower (1997, 24).

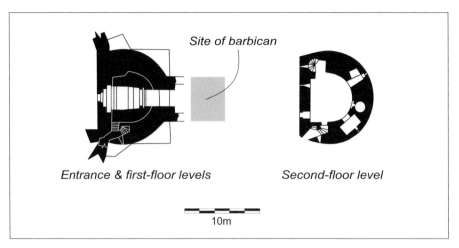

Site of barbican

Entrance & first-floor levels   Second-floor level

10m

50 Plan of the gate-tower in the town wall of Thouars.

property, there is no reason to think that any architectural ideas moved between it and Trim (or, rather, between Trim and it). The towers at the two castles should be regarded as parallel versions of a common concept: the perforated round or near-round gate-tower.[21]

This concept might first have entered Angevin castle-building culture in Poitou, the region in which Coudray-Salbart is located.[22] The first examples there seem to date from the late twelfth century when it was an Angevin territory. The well-preserved town gate at Thouars (Deux-Sèvres), for which Marie-Pierre Baudry has now suggested a possible date at the end of the twelfth century,[23] was outwardly not unlike Trim's Dublin Gate (Fig. 50). It had a barbican, the loss of which is unfortunate because it might have been of the same design as that at Trim. There are other parallels for the Trim gate-tower in the region, though none is exact. A gate-tower with a flattened external face at Harcourt (Vienne) was possibly also built before the end of the twelfth century.[24] Other than Trim, examples outside Poitou appear to be post-1200 in date, including the very simple example at Dunamase.[25]

The curtain wall which connected the barbicaned gate-tower with Hugh de Lacy's original curtain wall at Trim featured smaller, simpler, open-backed towers, their curving outer faces signifying that they too belong to a new 'modernist' architecture. Only one of them – that at the junction of the two curtain walls at the south end of the castle – had loops for archers, making it effectively a curved version of the open-

---

21 While Trim was unique, there was a tower in the de Lacy territory which resembled it a little: the remarkable 'Butter Gate' at Drogheda was an octagonal gate-tower on the town wall. Its loss is to be lamented: photographs showing similarities with work of *c.*1200 at Trim (the upper part of Hugh de Lacy's original gate-building) and Carlingford (the tops of the corner towers) suggest that it was built by Hugh II de Lacy, Walter's brother.   **22** See Mesqui 1991, 312, for the possibility of a Poitevin origin.   **23** Baudry 2001, 270.   **24** Ibid., 179–80.   **25** See, for example, Langeuin 2002, 366; Curnow and Kenyon 2000; McNeill 1993. A similar tower at Dover is dated to *c.*1200 (Goodall 2011, 174).

backed, flat-faced towers of Hugh's curtain wall. That tower thus embodied the transition between two architectural styles. It is possible that there was a conscious decision to give this particular tower such a transitional character. At very least, one can identify this tower as the first of the new curtain wall towers to have been built by Walter. The other towers on the new wall were windowless, as were the stretches of curtain wall between them.

The contrast at Trim between Walter de Lacy's curtain wall and his father's earlier curtain wall is striking. The former was entirely devoid of arrow loops, except in that 'transitional' tower; the latter was punctured by no less than twenty-seven of them. The great, almost undisciplined, sweep of the new curtain wall recalls work found in Capetian and Angevin territories in twelfth- and thirteenth-century France. The closest relevant formal parallels for the small open-backed towers in Walter's wall are probably to be found in pre-1200 Angevin work in France, as at Falaise (Calvados), where radiocarbon dating points to the last two decades of the twelfth century, and Gisors (Eure), where they are dated to before 1193.[26] It is conceivable that the masons who built Trim's barbicaned Dublin Gate in (I suggest) 1195–1201 were given the task of completing the curtain wall, and that they, or their master mason, had previously worked on Angevin projects in France. There is no evidence that they, or he, had worked in England.

To conclude, the great de Lacy castle at Trim was in the vanguard of the changes at the end of the twelfth century in these islands, and it was probably the actual place where the new 'modernist' architectural ideas were first put into practice in Ireland. But, while it might have enjoyed chronological primacy, Trim Castle ended up as a cul-de-sac. The changes made to the castle enclosure from the mid-1190s to about 1210 were spectacular by Irish standards, but they inspired no obvious imitation. Recognizing that it is generally difficult to identify lines of influence from specific castles in an age like that discussed here, simply because ideas moved very briskly, it does still seem that Walter de Lacy's master mason at Trim – assuming there was just one – returned whence he came after the work was done, or that he disappeared into anonymity on less high-profile jobs.

NEW 'MODERNIST' DONJONS

During the twelfth century in Norman, Capetian and Angevin territories, some new types of focal building emerged as alternatives to the rectangular donjon, ensuring that by the end of that century, when Walter held Trim, the rectangular form was effectively passé in the most elevated social-political circles of north-west Europe. Every well-connected master mason in England and France in the 1190s would have known that there was an expanded menu of designs. That menu had expanded most rapidly in the middle decades of the twelfth century on French soil. Hugh de Lacy's

---

26 Fichet de Clairfontaine et al. 2016, 244; Mesqui and Toussaint 1990, 291; the open-backed tower might first have been developed in the earlier twelfth century: see Blary 2012, 42.

master mason at Trim would certainly have known that shapes other than the rectangular were being used in the planning of donjons in France, even though he did not use one of those shapes himself at Trim. Alterations made by Walter's mason to the Trim donjon in the late twelfth and early thirteenth centuries were limited by the template of Hugh de Lacy's original structure.

Three of the new donjon designs which developed in mid-twelfth-century France were used in Ireland in the early period of Anglo-Norman lordship: the polygonal, the cylindrical and the 'turreted'. A section is devoted below to each of these designs. As will be shown, all of the examples were built after 1200, with the exception of Castleknock. The identities of the patrons of these donjons, many of whom can be identified, suggest that the menu of designs actually had a fairly limited circulation. Between them, King John (as both a patron in his own right and a granter of land to castle-builders) and William Marshal the elder account directly or indirectly for a good number of the new works. Add the fitz Geralds and, in a final bow for their family, the de Lacy brothers, and one accounts for almost all the new 'modernist' donjons in early thirteenth-century Ireland.

POLYGONAL DONJONS

The polygonal (multi-sided, or multi-angled) donjon was a Norman or, more likely, Angevin invention on French soil. The octagonal donjon with pilasters at Gisors has been identified as Norman and attributed to Henry I,[27] but an alternative reading attributes it to Henry II.[28] There are two royal donjons of polygonal plan in England, at Chilham (Kent) and Tickhill (Yorkshire), or three, if Orford is counted. Chilham, dated 1171–4, is a three-storeyed octagonal donjon to which is attached an original square stair-turret. It stands on a motte.[29] Tickhill, dated 1179–82, is eleven-sided, with pilasters at the junctions of its short faces. It also stands on a motte.[30] An octagonal donjon with Tickhill-type pilasters at Odiham (Hampshire) occupies a flat-ground site fortified by King John between 1207 and 1212. The donjon was long attributed to him, but excavation has suggested that it post-dates a French siege of 1216.[31] This is a small corpus of examples; it was not a popular design in the period in England. It was not popular in Ireland at the time either: only three certain examples were built on the island.

Athlone

Of the three Irish donjons, Athlone alone has an actual historical date, so it is appropriate to discuss it first. This donjon is ten-sided. It was lowered and heavily altered after the Middle Ages, so little can be said about its original form (Fig. 51). It crowns the summit of a motte which was encased in a retaining wall, the plan of which was a (symmetrical?) polygon.

---

27 Mesqui and Toussaint 1990; Ludlow 2018–19, 215, citing Christian Corvisier. **28** Most recently by Pamela Marshall, quoted by Higham 2015, 45. **29** Brown et al. 1976, 613. **30** Ibid., pp 844–7. **31** Ibid., pp 766–78; Allen and Stoodley 2010.

51 The much-altered donjon at Athlone.

The motte has been identified as part of the pre-Norman castle of Athlone (see above, pp 41–3). The site was refortified by the crown in 1210 under the justiciar, Bishop John de Grey.[32] The exact nature of that refortification is not known. Goddard Orpen, hostile to the possibility that the pre-invasion Irish were motte-builders, opined that the mound was Anglo-Norman and pre-1210 in date, and that the work recorded in 1210 was the building of a new tower on its summit by the justiciar. In 1211 a stone tower of the castle collapsed, killing Richard Tuite and eight others.[33] Orpen believed this to be the 1210 tower, that the present donjon was built to replace it, and that the motte was also encased in stone to ensure no further collapse.[34] But there is no indication in the sources that the tower which collapsed in 1211 was on top of the motte, or that it was completely beyond salvation afterwards and needed complete rebuilding. There is no particular reason, then, to doubt that the ten-sided donjon seen today is John de Grey's work.[35] But even if it is not, and if Orpen was correct in thinking it a rebuilding, it can still be assigned to John's reign.

---

32 ALC 1210.13; MIA 1210.3.   **33** AT 1211.4; AClon., p. 224.   **34** Orpen 1907b, 264–5. See also Leask 1951, 42. Building towers on mottes which had not yet settled was indeed unwise: see Mesqui 1991, 18.   **35** O'Keeffe 2019a, 123.

Castleknock

The castle at Castleknock sits on the top of a small, oval-shaped, hillock which, as a site of ancient royal assembly, was trimmed to dramatic effect in late prehistoric or early medieval times by scarping and ramparting.[36] Less than half the stone structure still stands. The missing part is the entire south side. We are very fortunate that Francis Place's depiction in 1698, conveniently redrawn by Harold Leask (Fig. 52), shows us what is now missing.[37]

52 Harold Leask's copy of Francis Place's late seventeenth-century depiction of Castleknock from the south-east. Part of the inner (pre-Norman) rampart, formed on the down-slope of the hillock on which the castle stands, is visible on the far left.

There is no obvious evidence that the Anglo-Normans made any change to the earthwork,[38] but the donjon sits on a very low rise at the east end of the summit so it is conceivable that the summit was altered to allow the donjon have that extra elevation. A towerless wall ran along the perimeter of the oval-shaped top of the earthwork, interrupted by the donjon at one end. Where it survives, one can see that this wall was irregularly polygonal. An original toilet chute on the north side, combined with the depiction by Francis Place of windows (of admittedly uncertain date) at two storey levels on the south side, allows one to classify this as a shell-keep according to Robert Higham's definition.[39] The chronological relationship of the donjon to the wall of the shell-keep is not clear, although they appear to be contemporary, but the short parapet with battlements captured by Place is of later medieval form which suggests that the shell-keep was heightened later in its history.

36 Herity 1993, 143–44.   **37** Leask 1951, Fig. 26. We are fortunate that anything survived to the late seventeenth century. Exerting his authority of rendability (see Coulson 1973), the king mandated the archbishop of Dublin in 1214 'to cause' it 'to be prostrated' (CDI I, no. 515). Four years later it still stood, so the justiciar was ordered to level it (CDI I, no. 841, 844). This too came to nothing, and eventually, after five years of negotiation, it was allowed stand after its owner gave his son as a hostage as collateral for his 'safe custody' of the castle (CDI I, nos 874, 1047, 1139).   **38** The original ramparts are largely gone from the south side of the site, and this might have been done by the Anglo-Normans to make the summit more accessible when building work was going on.   **39** Higham 2015.

53 The donjon at Castleknock from the opposite end of the courtyard. The space on top of the earthwork was so restricted that the enclosing wall was probably lined with buildings on one side (the right-hand side, as viewed here) only.

54 The two black lines mark the edges of the buttress which projected slightly at the entrance at Castleknock.

The donjon was three-storeyed. The lower storey might have been a demi-basement, its exterior marked by the high, vertical plinth which was depicted by Francis Place. The building was entered at first-floor level through a round-arched doorway facing into the small courtyard (Fig. 53). Now largely destroyed, there was an angled pilaster of very shallow projection on the north side of the doorway (Fig. 54). It is a curious feature. Although the parallel is a little inexact, there is at Chilham a pilaster of similar shape (though wider) in a comparable position relative to its doorway.

The Castleknock pilaster invites some speculation. Its position relative to the entrance – its line, projected downwards from the small fragment which survives, would have run across the width of the doorway – suggests that there was a fore-building, entered from the south. Given the limited space on the site, such a fore-building might well have been incorporated in the wall of the shell-keep. Interestingly, Place depicted a low wall outside the donjon on this very side, and while he showed no doorway behind it, one wonders if this wall survived from an outer fore-building. How else did one enter the castle originally? There appears to have been access to the courtyard via a small structure on the north side of the donjon, but it could not have been the main access because it was too confined and because the pre-Norman ramparts were steep at that point.

The entry-level room in Castleknock was exceptionally well fenestrated. Place showed externally recessed windows in the middle of each of the polygon's faces; part of one internal embrasure still survives. There was similar fenestration at Odiham. The wall above this register of windows at Castleknock was set-back externally, narrowing the upper part of the donjon. This was unique in Ireland: no other donjon has a graded

55 The interior of the donjon at Castleknock, viewed from the down-slope of the earthwork.

exterior. If the space between the top of the plinth and the set-back was the exterior of the entry-level room, Place's depiction is a little inaccurate in scale. The upper storey at Castleknock had what appears today to have been a round-flued chimney overlooking the small courtyard, and there was also a mural passage running around the north side (Fig. 55). Place depicted small slit windows at this level, one in each polygon face. For an upper chamber, one would expect more generous fenestration. It is possible that a mural passage circled most of the upper storey and that these windows illuminated that; the cylindrical donjon at Dundrum (Down) offers a possible parallel (see p. 144 below). Place also showed a slightly projecting parapet at the top of the Castleknock donjon, but this would have been an addition of the late Middle Ages.

In outward appearance, for which we have Francis Place to thank, Castleknock's donjon resembled very closely each of the towers added in the later thirteenth century or early fourteenth century to the shell-keep at Lewes (Sussex). But Castleknock's few

56 The fragmentary donjon and ring-wall on the motte at Shanid.

surviving features cannot be that late, especially if it is contemporary with the shell-keep to which it was attached. The historical evidence suggests it is a much earlier building. Its builder can be identified very confidently as Hugh Tyrel, who held the manor – the first of the Tyrels to do so – for about a quarter of a century. He probably came to Ireland with Hugh de Lacy, who granted him Castleknock at some date in the 1170s, possibly as early as 1172. Henry II revised the grant in 1177, making Castleknock a royal tenure.[40] This tenurial history is a good indication of how highly regarded was Hugh, but especially how valued strategically was Castleknock itself, at the birth of the lordship. It is likely, then, that castle-building at the site began early, and that by 1180 the stone castle was at least under construction. Given that polygonal Chilham and Tickhill were Henrician donjons of the same period, Henry's intervention in the

40 St John Brooks 1933.

tenurial arrangement for Castleknock in 1177 must be relevant to the understanding of Hugh Tyrel's choice of donjon design. Was there an instruction from England that Tyrel's new tenurial arrangement be reflected in the design of his donjon? The master mason responsible for the designs of Trim and Maynooth was probably still in Ireland in 1177; if correctly identified above (pp 87–8) as a mason from a royal workshop (whatever about his suggested identification as Maurice, the master mason at Dover), he might well have also overseen the work at Castleknock.

Shanid

The polygonal donjon at Shanid sits, like the other two, on the summit of a great earthwork (Fig. 56). The large hill-top motte seems to be largely artificial, and it overlooks a bailey. The remains of the stone castle are confined to the top of the mound, where space was limited. The donjon was apparently free-standing but at one end of an oval ring-wall, and when it had its base-batter – it has been completely quarried away – it could conceivably have been attached to the ring-wall. Higham excluded Shanid, probably correctly, from his enumeration of shell-keeps, placing it instead in the category of 'mottes with ring-walls and central donjons', examples of which are found in England and Wales but not in Scotland, and in France and Germany.[41]

The donjon was polygonal on the outside but round on the inside. A little less than half of it still stands, but it does at least survive to parapet level, so we can determine its full original height. It was only two storeys high, with a basement below an entry-level room. There are traces at first-floor level of a single window embrasure with a segmental arch over it. The likelihood is that there was one other window at this level – part of it is preserved in a large chunk of fallen masonry near the donjon – as well as the main doorway. Access to the parapet was in the missing section of walling. The wall-walk was wide, and the crenellated wall outside it was pierced by arrow slits; these were at the junctions of the polygon faces, which was unlike the positions of the slits at Castleknock. Sockets for beams reveal the presence of wooden hoarding.

There is no record of the building of this small donjon. The cantred of Shanid was held by William de Burgh in the 1190s, and briefly by Meiler fitz Henry. Thomas fitz Maurice obtained the cantred no later than 1205,[42] and it remained a possession of the fitz Geralds thereafter. The earthwork is a fairly classic motte-and-bailey, but it is not known who among those men was responsible for it. The reasonable assumption that a newly raised mound would have been unable to take the weight of a stone tower – as Orpen and Leask assumed of Athlone – would naturally lead one to postulate a gap of a good number of years between the motte and the donjon. That would tend to support the attribution of the stone castle by Ken Nicholls and Paul MacCotter to Thomas's son, John, in the 1220s or later.[43] But this date is too late for a donjon of Shanid's type. A date in the 1210s would make more sense; it would also allow Shanid be identified as a product of influence from (royal) Athlone or (quasi-royal) Castleknock, before the fashion for such donjons quickly dissipated. Basically, the later

41 Higham 2015, 49–50.   **42** Nicholls and MacCotter 2009, 50–1.   **43** Ibid.

one dates Shanid, the more difficult it is to explain why no other examples of such donjons seem to have been built in Ireland. To argue for an earlier date, and perhaps for Thomas fitz Maurice being its builder, requires one to move the earthwork castle back to the start of the century or even back into the late twelfth century. The history of the locality would allow one to imagine that William de Burgh built the motte-and-bailey castle in the 1190s as both a frontier marker and a monumental statement of intent to colonize the area. In pre-invasion times, as the Anglo-Normans surely knew, Shanid (after *seanaid*, 'synod') was a place of assembly on royal land, important enough to attract Vikings (who suffered defeat there in 834).[44] The place of assembly is probably the slightly embanked enclosure of nearly three hectares that is wrapped around the low hill on which the castle stands. This big enclosure is overlooked externally by an extraordinary ringfort-like monument, which, uniquely in Ireland, is divided, *trelleborg*-like, into four quadrants by banks which run close to the cardinal directions. Shanid was an obvious location for the Anglo-Normans to appropriate symbolically, and at their earliest convenience.

Shanid was an important locus in the fitz Gerald polity, but I think that its greatest value was symbolic. The effort required to raise a motte of Shanid's size suggests that there was an early ambition within Anglo-Norman seigneurial circles to settle the area, and William de Burgh – if indeed it was he who erected it – might have encastellated the land with a fitz Gerald grant in mind. But nothing much happened on the ground at Shanid as the thirteenth century unfolded. There was no Anglo-Norman settlement, even a church, at the site or in the locality. The donjon offered a commanding view of the countryside and was itself visible for many miles in all directions, mainly from the east, but it seems that – unless there is *a lot* of lost archaeology – there was little at Shanid to support a permanent seigneurial presence: a small circular room over a basement, inside in a tiny courtyard, on top of a high mound, located on top of a hill, did not cut the mustard as a centre of lordship. I suggest that the donjon was built to show that ancient Shanid was appropriated, memorialized and venerated in the fitz Gerald cosmos, but from a practical perspective it was too far west to do much more than mark territory.

CYLINDRICAL DONJONS

The importance of the Loire valley and the Île de France in the history of castle-building in north-west Europe is underscored by evidence that the cylindrical donjon originated there before 1150. The earliest known examples are in that region. Christian Corvisier's analysis of the royal donjon at Compiègne (Oise), for which he argues a start-of-construction date late in the reign of Louis VI (†1137), points to the French royal domain – the Île de France – as the incubation chamber; his suggested redating of the baronial donjon at Fréteval (Eure-et-Loir) to *c.*1150 confirms the importance of neighbouring Blois in the type's early diffusion.[45] The attribution of New Buckenham

44 MacCotter 2009, 43.   **45** Corvisier 2001, 44 n60.

(Norfolk) to William d'Albini and to a date between 1138 and 1146[46] indicates that there was knowledge of the type in England at a very early date, but that particular donjon seems to be an outlier, however, because a couple of decades passed before the type was used again in England, and even then it remained unpopular in Britain until the thirteenth century.[47]

Although it was adopted by Henry II and Richard I in their French territories, the cylindrical donjon was not favoured for royal castles in England. By the time Philip II had started building examples – the so-called *tours philippiennes*[48] – the form was firmly established at royal and senior-baronial levels within the two competing polities on the soil of modern-day France. When the cylindrical donjon was adopted as a viable alternative to the rectangular 'Romanesque' donjon in these islands in the early thirteenth century, it was mainly among the barons.[49]

The number of cylindrical donjons built in Ireland is uncertain. Those regarded by all writers as examples of the type are, in alphabetical order, Ardfinnan (Tipperary), Clogh Oughter (Cavan), Dundrum, Dunmore (Waterford), Inchiquin (Cork), Kiltinan (Tipperary), Leixlip (Kildare), Mannin (Mayo), Mocollop (Waterford) and Nenagh (Tipperary). I argue below that Dublin should be added to this list, *contra* the views of two senior Irish castellologists.[50] Towers in Kilkenny and Waterford cities should be added to the list also, bringing the number to thirteen. This is a minimum enumeration. There are probably others, but arriving at adjudications is difficult for two reasons.

First, in the late Middle Ages, in the southern half of Ireland mainly, cylindrical tower-houses were built in small numbers. Most of these are easily identifiable as late medieval. But in some cases, heavy ruination, the absence of diagnostic original features, or concealment by vegetation, leaves one uncertain as to whether a tower is thirteenth century or fifteenth century in date. Four examples illustrate the problem in different ways. A very small fragment of a circular tower remains at Latteragh (Tipperary). Its wall was reasonably thick (2.5m), suggesting an Anglo-Norman date; it is a documented Anglo-Norman castle-site,[51] but insufficient remains for it to be classified as a certain example of a cylindrical donjon. On balance, it probably was one. A second tower which probably qualifies as well is at Derrinlaur (Waterford). Undocumented before the end of the Middle Ages, this is a fairly substantial tower, externally more than 10m in diameter with walls about 3m thick and a base-batter. It also has late medieval features. Now very ruined, heavy vegetation prevents one assessing whether those features are original or not. Derrinlaur's scale certainly suggests that it began life as an Anglo-Norman donjon, but the absence of documentation to suggest it was in a manor capable of financing such a tower is an issue. Two other towers are a little more suspect. At Parkavonear (Kerry) is another undocumented circular tower, two storeys high and probably no more than that originally. The absence of an original ground-floor entrance points to a thirteenth-century date but

46 Hislop 2016, 113–14.   **47** A mid-twelfth-century date is now being proposed for the donjon at Longtown (Herefordshire): see http://longtowncastles.com/ index.php/dating-stone-castle/. The evidence is not (yet, anyway) convincing.   **48** Mesqui 2018.   **49** Ludlow 2018–19, 213. **50** McNeill 1997, 46; Sweetman 1999, 52; O'Conor 2014a, 342.   **51** Cunningham 1987, 147.

there are no architectural features to encourage conviction, and, for what it is worth, its crude masonry, comprised of field boulders placed in irregular courses, would lead one to wonder whether this was an idiosyncratic building completely unconnected to the donjon tradition. Newtownlow (Westmeath) is similarly puzzling. Also undocumented, the lower storey survives of a ruined circular tower. The doorway is late medieval and seems to be an insertion into what was a big but crudely built cylinder with a (now robbed) base-batter. That feature, combined with its siting on a natural elevation which resembles a motte from certain directions, raises the possibility of a thirteenth-century date.

The second problem pertains to big thirteenth-century towers attached to curtain walls. Were these merely big corner towers or did they serve as donjons? Two Irish castle-towers illustrate the problem. Buttevant (Cork) is not generally regarded as a donjon, but it was the only cylindrical tower in that castle and it had a first-floor entrance facing the courtyard. I regard it as one.[52] At Dungarvan, attached to the early polygonal enclosure is a curtain-walled enclosure of the early thirteenth century with one cylindrical corner tower. Did the polygonal enclosure continue to act as the castle's focal point in that century, or was that corner tower a new donjon? I regard it as an example because I think that its architecture is consistent with the label (see below, p. 147), but Sweetman dismissed it as a donjon, regarding it instead as simply a tower for flanking fire, while McNeill was ambivalent, excluding it from a map of such towers in one context but describing it in another as 'a round great tower'.[53]

So, to the thirteen cylindrical donjons listed above we should probably add Buttevant, Derrinlaur and Dungarvan, and, a little less confidently, Latteragh, Newtownlow and Parkavonear.[54] None of these twenty towers pre-dates 1200. The earliest *documented* cylindrical donjon – not necessarily the first to have been built – is probably in Dublin, so it is appropriate to begin there.

Dublin

The history of this castle is fairly well documented.[55] In 1204, King John mandated his justiciar, Meiler fitz Henry, to build a new castle in Dublin. The justiciar had communicated to the king the need for a *fortilicium* and was duly instructed to erect a *castellum* in a place which would be suitable for the administration of justice and, if necessary, for the defence of the city also. The instruction was to make it strong, 'with good ditches and strong walls'. The justiciar was specifically instructed to build a *turris* first, to which a *castellum* and *baluum* could then be added. There is no record of the early progress of building, and the fact that a debt – 300 marks (about £200) from Geoffrey fitz Robert – needed to be called in would suggest that commencement was delayed, if only briefly, by a shortage of finance. Geoffrey's 300 marks was less than was needed to build a tower, even frills-free. Timber was brought to the site from Wicklow in 1212. Compensation paid in 1218 to the archbishop of Dublin for losses

52 O'Keeffe 2009, 290–1; Cotter 2013, 9–10; Guy 2018–19, 85.   **53** O'Keeffe 2009, 288–9; Sweetman 1999, 57; McNeill 1997, 240; 2003, Fig. 1.   **54** Dromana (Waterford) was erroneously included in O'Keeffe 2009.   **55** For all the relevant references see Clarke 2002, 22.

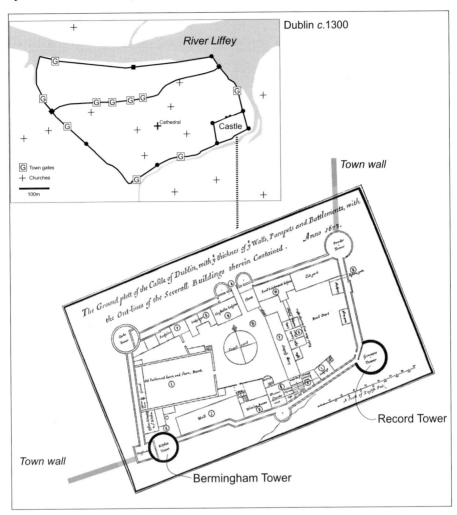

57 Plan of Dublin Castle by William Robinson (1673), and the castle's location relative to the medieval walled town.

sustained by building work is a good indication that the *castellum* and *baluum* were being developed at that time. Holy Trinity Priory was in receipt of compensation for the same reason in 1226, as was Dublin's archbishop-elect in 1230. The entire castle was nearing completion around then, because the guttering was being added.

The present castle contains only parts of the early thirteenth-century royal castle but it retains its basic courtyard form. The missing parts are known from early surveys, the accuracy of one of which – that by William Robinson in 1673 – can be trusted (Fig. 57).[56] As noted above, it has been asserted by some scholars that no donjon was

56 Reproduced here from Maguire 1974, Fig. 3. The plan of medieval Dublin, *c.*1300, is based on Clarke 2002, Fig. 5 (the towers of town gateways have been changed to circular from square).

58 The Bermingham Tower, from the south (*left*), and the Record Tower, from the north-east (*right*).

built, but the functional and morphological diversity of donjons, as documented by Pamela Marshall, leads one to conclude that the original *turris* commissioned in 1204 was no less a donjon than any other *turris* of the era. It must have been one of the cylindrical corner towers.

Con Manning suggests that the 1204 tower can be identified as that known since the Middle Ages as the Bermingham Tower, located at the south-west corner of the fortress (Fig. 58 left).[57] Originally four storeys high, this substantially rebuilt tower had an external diameter of 15m and an internal diameter of 8.6m. Manning's argument is strong. The Bermingham Tower is the odd-man-odd tower in the quadrangle, both in its positioning relative to the curtain walls and in its possession of a rectangular turret on one side. He also points out that a drawn survey of 1767 of one floor level within the tower shows it as a fully circular building, consistent with it being a lone tower to which later walls were attached (although it has to be said that its depiction as a complete circle is surely a convention, as its exterior on the north side could not have been seen at the time because of other buildings). Late medieval and early modern sources suggest that it was the principal tower of the castle at that stage.[58]

---

57 Manning 1998; 2017–18. See also Tietzsch-Tyler 2018, 115. **58** The 1767 plan does not state whether it depicts ground level or first-floor level, but the sizes of the windows suggest the latter. If that is the case, the tower had two doorways, one opening towards the western curtain

I have suggested that the 1204 *turris* should be identified as the so-called Record Tower (Fig. 58 right).[59] It is true that the Bermingham Tower 'looks' like the donjon on the site's plan. I find it difficult, instinctively, to dispute Con Manning's reading, and instinct should carry some weigh when it is informed by knowledge. But the evidence seems to favour the Record Tower, although some of it is admittedly circumstantial.

First, once it was decided, presumably by the justiciar, that the castle was to occupy the south-east corner of the walled town, its south and east curtains running flush with the town boundary, a corner position for the donjon within the castle would have made more sense, visually and strategically, than the particular position occupied by the Bermingham Tower. A parallel here, perhaps, is John's (undated) donjon in Waterford, Reginald's Tower, located at the most prominent corner of that city's wall. Second, the justiciar was mandated to attach the rest of the castle to the *turris*, so it is easier to envisage the castle growing outwards into the town-space from the corner than to envisage it growing towards the corner from the position occupied by the Bermingham Tower; indeed, compensation paid to the Church in 1218 would be consistent, perhaps, with the castle sneaking onto the archbishop's land as it grew to the north and west from the original corner *turris*. Third, the entire castle was laid out in the corner of the town as a quadrangle with a general 1:1.6 proportion, approximating to the Golden Section. This might be a co-incidence, but, if it was planned in that way, one would have to take it as evidence of the primacy of the Record Tower; the alternative is to posit that, using a proportional system, the Bermingham Tower's position was determined relative to the corner to the town, which seems improbable. Fourth, turning to the design of the building itself, the Record Tower had a first-floor entry facing into the courtyard; this is a feature of the Bermingham Tower too, but the point here is that the Record Tower possesses the prerequisite first-floor entry for a donjon. Fifth, the Record Tower compares in size with the donjon at Pembroke (discussed below), and its spiral stairs is in the same position relative to the first-floor entry: the stairwell opened onto the middle of the floor, a little to the right-hand side as one entered. This is an important parallel: it shows that the Record Tower was at least *conceived* as a donjon in how its internal space was organized. And finally, there is a curious, full-height, indentation or recess where the tower faced into the courtyard, so its ground plan was not fully circular. Manning

wall (via the small square turret) and one opening into the courtyard. In line with Manning's interpretation, such double entries are common in those French cylindrical donjons which were built in the early thirteenth century by Philip II and which were attached to curtain walls. Examples from the first decade of that century include Falaise, Gisors, Rouen (Seine-Maritime), and Verneuil (Eure). However, the same floor plan presents evidence that this was not the donjon: there is no access between the floor level and the spiral stairs. In the French donjons, such as those just listed, there was always access to stairs, whether it was a little passage off the entrance itself (as at Gisors and Falaise, for example), or a doorway in the middle of the wall (as at Rouen and Verneuil, for example). Manning does note this as a problem and suggests that the entry to the stairwell might have been blocked when the tower was used to contain a kitchen, but this seems a contrived explanation.   **59** O'Keeffe 2009. For a survey of this tower see Manning 2003.

59 The donjon at Nenagh from inside the former enclosure. The gate-building is on the right-hand side.

has pointed out that the Record Tower makes an unlikely donjon because this feature suggests that the tower was built to be a corner bastion. That is true, but I would suggest that the indent is also evidence of its antiquity relative to the other towers. Judging by William Robinson's survey of 1673, *none* of the three other corner towers had this feature. That would suggest that the Record Tower was built separately from the rest. Indeed, the visual effect of the indentation when the castle was complete might have been the highlighting of the tower's special status when viewed from the courtyard, anticipating perhaps how fosses were used in some French castles (Nesles-en-Tardenois (Aisne) and Dourdan (Essonne), for example) to set-off their cylindrical donjons.

I would suggest, then, that the Record Tower was the *turris* commissioned by John through his justiciar, that it was built with now-indeterminate lengths of the curtain wall to its north and west, and that these two lengths of curtain walling were joined

60 The donjon at Dundrum.

together (with timber from Wicklow?) to give the tower some protection while work on the full quadrangular castle was underway in the 1210s.

Nenagh, Dundrum and Leixlip

Despite a lack of explicit documentation, only two baronial castles in Ireland are certain to have had cylindrical donjons erected in the first decade of the thirteenth century: Nenagh (Fig. 59) and Dundrum (Fig. 60). The former was unquestionably begun by Theobald Walter [Butler], known to have been in the area from around 1200.[60] It was probably three storeys high and regarded as complete by the time of his death in 1206, with a further storey then added by his son after 1221.[61] By this reckoning, construction work at Nenagh started a few years before John commissioned the *turris* in Dublin, with work overlapping briefly at the two sites before Nenagh was completed. The donjon at Dundrum is confidently and convincingly attributed to

60 Gleeson and Leask 1936, 248.   **61** McNeill 1997, 28, 31.

Hugh II de Lacy between 1205 and 1210, when he was earl of Ulster.[62] It is interesting that the windows of opportunity for both men to build their donjons lasted five years at most. This indicates that donjons of this type could be erected within three or four years. Thus, the Dublin *turris* could have been completed by 1208.

One other cylindrical donjon in Ireland might also pre-date 1210: Leixlip. This plain, (now?) thin-walled cylinder has a low base-batter similar to that at Dundrum. Unfortunately, it is otherwise too heavily modernized for comment. I suggest it is early because Adam de Hereford, given a generous grant by Strongbow before 1176, retained possession of Leixlip when subinfeudating, and had a castle there in 1212.[63] De Hereford was not of the same rank as Theobald Walter or Hugh II de Lacy, but was at least of the same stature as Hugh Tyrel of Castleknock and similarly well-connected, so why should one doubt that he, like Hugh Tyrel, had a donjon in his caput at an early date? A pre-1200 date for the Leixlip tower is not impossible but is most unlikely given the chronology of the type, but a date in the decade before 1212 is entirely conceivable. The Dublin *turris*, less than ten miles to the east along the river Liffey, might have inspired him to choose a cylindrical form.

Entry to Nenagh was at first-floor level, probably protected by a fore-building (there is an otherwise inexplicable toilet chute in the adjacent curtain wall). There was also an exit onto the wall-walk of the curtain at second-floor level. Ascent through the donjon was via spiral stairs leading off the entrance passage, and then, at the level of the added storey, by mural stairs. The donjon's architecture was shaped to a degree by its attachment to a curtain wall in two places. Its fore-building was presumably designed to allow access to the curtain's wall-walk on one side, an arrangement not unlike that at Castleknock. The curtain also determined what part of the donjon was inside the castle and what part was outside, and that then determined the position of the toilet with its machicolated outlet.

Dundrum has relatively little in common with Nenagh. It is smaller in girth and lower in height. Its basement had slit windows and was accessible by spiral stairs from above. It had a first-floor entrance, as normal, and a second doorway which led, via a wooden bridge originally, onto the curtain wall. The spiral stairs giving access to the second-floor level opened off the floor (rather than off the entrance passage). The entry-level room also had a fireplace. Late medieval fabric at second-floor level has complicated its interpretation, but current thinking[64] allows that the series of mural chambers which runs around three-quarters of its circumference could be original. Although the evidence of the joist-sockets does not particularly support it, one might wonder whether the donjon was originally only two storeys high, with the mural features of the supposed upper storey being 'outside' the roof.

The comparisons between these two donjons and William Marshal's donjon in Pembroke, started in 1201, are revealing. Nenagh and Pembroke were built simultaneously but have almost nothing in common, whereas Dundrum has some features found in the Welsh donjon. Pembroke and Dundrum were free-standing;

---

62 McNeill 2003, 98.   **63** St J. Brooks 1950, 203, 207, 208 n5; Gilbert 1889, 143.   **64** McDonald 2014–15, 48–9.

61 The donjon at Dourdan.

Nenagh was attached to a curtain wall. At Pembroke and Dundrum the basement was accessible by spiral stairs; Nenagh's basement was reached through a trap-door. Entry level at Pembroke and Dundrum had a second doorway (leading to a possible balcony at the former and onto the curtain at the latter); Nenagh's second doorway (onto the curtain) was at the next floor level up. The stairs that ascended through Pembroke and Dundrum opened from the middle of their entry-level rooms so one had to enter those rooms to ascend the donjons. The equivalent stairs in Nenagh opened off the doorway passage itself, so one could ascend to the upper room without entering the first-floor room. One must conclude that Nenagh and Pembroke were built without cognisance of each other's interiors, but that the influence of William Marshal's donjon can be seen in de Lacy's donjon.

These three donjons represent variations on the cylindrical donjon as developed in France, in both Capetian and Angevin territories, some thirty or forty years earlier. The form had been available for adoption by Angevin barons in Britain for decades during the twelfth century but, with the exceptions of New Buckenham and Conisbrough (Yorkshire), it had been eschewed by them as an option. So, why did the form suddenly 'take off' around 1200 in these islands? The answer might be the *tour philippienne*, the type of donjon associated with the French king, Philip II (Fig. 61).

It is not possible to recognize with certainty any formal influence from these royal French donjons on contemporary Angevin donjons across the Channel.[65] Having said that, the earliest *tours philippiennes*, built shortly before Nenagh and Pembroke, no longer survive,[66] so a certain caution is required. Some of the plan details found in Philip's post-1200 towers are found in Angevin donjons in these islands, so there may have been a connection. For example, as at Pembroke and Dundrum, the donjons of Rouen, Lillebonne (Seine Maritime) and Verneuil each have two entrances facing each other at the same floor level, and spiral stairs ascending from the floor rather than from the entrance passage. The Nenagh placement of the main stairs is paralleled at other *tours philippiennes* such as Falaise and Gisors. Whatever about formal influence, one cannot rule out the possibility that it was the very appearance of the spectacular royal donjons in Capetian France which spurred the Angevin castle-builders into action.

Lines of descent

Can one trace a line of descent in Ireland from these pre-1210 cylindrical donjons to post-1210 castles? There are really two questions here. First, did the masons who designed the early donjons go on to other commissions in Ireland, bringing the template with them, but perhaps making some changes? Briefly, there is no clear evidence that this happened. Second, did other patrons see the type at these places and instruct their masons to build similar donjons? This is incapable of being answered, but it is a question worth some reflection. How, after all, does one spot a 'copy'? There is a third question which is worth bringing to the analysis of the later, post-1210, donjons. Could the cylindrical form have been brought to Ireland by other patrons or masons and executed without reference to, or even cognisance of, places like Nenagh and Dublin? It is possible.

Neither Nenagh nor Dundrum (nor Leixlip) had any obvious imitators. Hugh II de Lacy's brother, Walter, built Clogh Oughter around 1220, but not as an imitation of Dundrum. The first-floor room, which was the level of entry, had two windows and,

---

65 Ludlow 2018–19. For example, the complex internal rib-vaulting, one of the most striking features of the French donjons, did not cross the Channel.   **66** Jean Mesqui regards the now-lost towers at Bourges (Cher) and the Palais de Paris as the first two in the *philippienne* sequence; the former was completed in 1190 and the latter, the *turris Parisius*, was possibly built around the same time but was certainly extant in 1202–3 (Mesqui 2011, 311); for Bourges see Châtelain 1991, 120–1; for the identification of *turris Parisius* as the Palais de Paris tower rather than Philip's new cylindrical donjon in Louvre, see Guerout 1953, 138–42; Cohen 2015, 239 n46. The date of construction of the Louvre tower is not recorded, but it is probably the building described as *turris nostre de Louvre* in 1204 (Hayot 2013, 9 n4).

unusually, two additional doorways, one leading to a now-destroyed stairs and the other to a parapet on a wall attached to the donjon. There was no upper room, even though the tower was tall enough. Similarities with Dundrum – two windows at each of the two lower-floor levels, for example – are insufficient to suggest a direct link.[67] When William Marshal proceeded to build a new castle in Kilkenny, probably in 1207,[68] he chose not to repeat the format of his Pembroke donjon, thus denying that great Welsh building any direct influence in Ireland, except perhaps in the Hook lighthouse of the 1240s.[69] Instead, he built at Kilkenny a five-sided enclosure castle with four round corner towers, one of which was huge and must have served as the donjon.[70] Knowledge of Dublin and its (supposed) corner donjon might have influenced him. Whatever the case, he was open to being influenced. He was certainly not committed to creating a personal style for his castles, unlike Philip II. In Wales, for example, he followed Pembroke with Usk, a castle of very different plan;[71] in Ireland he followed Kilkenny with Carlow and Lea, two towers of pre-*philippienne* Capetian design (see below, pp 150–7).

King John himself was responsible for one major building project after Dublin and Waterford: Limerick Castle. The £700 recorded in the pipe roll of 1211–12 paid for the gate-house (see below, p. 166) and the cylindrical north-east tower.[72] The latter might have been envisaged as a donjon. Dan Tietzsch-Tyler, despite noting its size relative to the Record Tower in Dublin, concluded that it was 'never intended to be any more than one of several mural towers'.[73] The argument is reasonable, but evidence that the tower functioned in tandem with a timber-framed hall might qualify it as a donjon.

Post-1215 towers

The cylindrical donjons that are left to be discussed were all products, directly or indirectly, of grants made by King John in 1215.[74] Although the number is small, we can divide them according to patronage, date and design.

On its own is Inchiquin, which can be attributed to Maurice fitz Gerald, second baron of Offaly (†1257).[75] There were only two habitable storeys, the upper one having a fireplace and toilet. Although strongly built, it was a relatively low tower, closer in original appearance to Dundrum than to Nenagh. It was probably built by 1220.

Next is a group of three, defined by morphological similarities. The cylindrical tower on the curtain wall at Dungarvan should be classified as a donjon (see above, p. 138). The evidence supporting this claim is the presence of a small, half-round, stair-turret bulging from its side. Similar turrets are found on cylindrical donjons elsewhere, as at early thirteenth-century Skenfrith (Monmouthshire), for example, or Philip II's Montlhéry (Essonne). Comparable stairs turrets are also found in the other two towers: Ardfinnan, a three-storeyed tower, and Kiltinan, probably two-storeyed originally but

67 Manning 2013.   **68** Bradley and Murtagh 2017, 222.   **69** Dan Tietzsch-Tyler has suggested that Mocollop had a Pembroke-like upper vault (Ludlow 2018–19, 247–8), but, pending accurate survey and fabric analysis someday, the theory is rejected in O'Keeffe and Whelan 2019–20. For Hook see Murtagh 2016.   **70** See Murtagh 2017.   **71** Knight 2008.   **72** Tietzsch-Tyler 2013, 145.   **73** Tietzsch-Tyler 2013, 145.   **74** For details of the grants see Empey 1981. **75** O'Keeffe 2004b.

62 The donjon at Mocollop. The upper part of the tower dates from the late Middle Ages. Note the large window. The gate-tower, which had a counter-weighted drawbridge, seems to have been added to the enclosure around the donjon, but is possibly later in date than the donjon's first phase.

heightened in the late Middle Ages. Dungarvan is probably the work of Thomas fitz Anthony, who in 1215 secured a hereditary grant from John of all the royal lands in the counties of Waterford and Desmond, including the castle of Dungarvan.[76] The manors of Ardfinnan and Kiltinan were granted by John to Philip of Worcester in 1215. He died in 1218.[77] These three donjons were probably built, therefore, between 1215 and 1220.

This little group of donjons has an outlier in Co. Mayo, at Mannin. The last-dated of the cylindrical donjons of Anglo-Norman Ireland, this extremely fragmentary structure is probably of the late 1230s or 1240s. Tom McNeill assigned it to John fitz Thomas, son-in-law of Thomas fitz Anthony of Dungarvan.[78] It had a pair of semi-round turrets distributed as if to make room for an equidistant third, the space of which was occupied by a small fore-building; Longtown, a distant cousin of the group, had three evenly-spaced turrets.

Thomas fitz Anthony can be identified as the builder of the final two donjons to be discussed: Dunmore and Mocollop. These have nothing in common other than

---

76 Beresford n.d. [a].   **77** Beresford n.d. [b].   **78** McNeill 1997, 94; Knox 1911.

their patron. Dunmore is dated to the early thirteenth century by its plank-centred arches and a mural stairs.[79] It is a modest ruin. Mocollop, in contrast, was one of the biggest and finest cylindrical towers in Ireland (Fig. 62).[80] Free-standing, it was built inside (and necessitated changes to) an older enclosure; there are parallels for this sequence elsewhere in the Angevin world, as at Châtillon-sur-Indre (Indre), where the cylindrical donjon was built in the 1180s, or Tretower (Breconshire), where the comparable donjon was built about half a century later.[81] Mocollop had an unusual clockwise/counter-clockwise stairs system: the stairs ascended clockwise outside the tower as far as the first-floor entrance, which is a feature paralleled in the 1230s at the native Welsh castle of Dolbadarn (Caernarvonshire),[82] but it then ascended anti-clockwise within the wall-thickness. Philip II's donjon at Chinon (Indre-et-Loire) might have the first example of the arrangement. The large pointed window at second-floor level at Mocollop cannot be paralleled in any of the Irish donjons, but can be paralleled in Wales, as at Pembroke and Cilgerran (Pembrokeshire), as well as in some *tours philippiennes*.

To conclude, all the Irish cylindrical donjons were started, and a number of them completed, in the first two decades of the thirteenth century, except for Clogh Oughter, after 1220, and Mannin, after 1235, both of them (co-incidentally?) built on lacustrine crannogs. The type had been known in Angevin culture from the mid-twelfth century, but Philip II's promotion of the type in France at the end of that century might have been a catalyst for its appearance in Ireland at Nenagh (between 1201 and 1206) and Dublin (after 1204). It is possible, though incapable of proof either way, that those two early donjons inspired other castle-owners in Ireland to shift from the rectangular donjon. The Irish donjons betray no direct French influence, with the possible exception of Mocollop. The waning of the type's popularity in Ireland mirrors that elsewhere, although it seems to have happened a little faster in Ireland. There is no obvious explanation for its waning. Its possible identification as a type associated with certain families, not to mention the crown, might for reasons of politics have dissuaded some other castle-builders from adopting it. But a better explanation is that the shape was simply unwieldly for a chamber tower, allowing the simple two-storeyed rectangular tower to remain the go-to design.

TURRETED DONJONS

The third group of donjons is the one for which the Irish evidence is of greatest European interest, and so I discuss its constituent buildings in some detail. The donjons in question are rectangular blocks with cylindrical towers at their corners, and so they appear like towered enceintes scaled down to the size of donjons. Leask, the first to identify them as a group, called them 'towered or turreted keeps'.[83] In France, the

---

79 Although located within the territory granted to fitz Anthony, the place is not documented after 1203 when John confirmed grants by Henry II to an Irish chieftain of Dunmore (CDI I, no. 190). **80** O'Keeffe and Whelan 2019–20. **81** Robinson 2010; Corvisier 2010, 321. **82** Goodall 2011, 221, 227; Avent 2004. **83** Leask 1951, Ch. 5.

corner towers of comparable buildings are called *tourelles*, turrets. Accordingly, I describe them here as 'turreted donjons'.

Carlow

The donjon at Carlow was fairly complete until the early nineteenth century when one half of it was blown up. Fortunately, there are earlier depictions which are demonstrably accurate, including one published by Francis Grose in 1791 (Fig. 63).[84] There is no record of its construction, so, while nobody would assign it to any family other than the Marshals, there is no consensus on whether it was built by the elder William in the 1210s or by his son, also William, in the 1220s.[85] My own view is that the father built it (see below, p. 155). Whatever its exact date, Carlow's donjon is an intriguing monument. Robbing of the masonry from the inner face of the surviving west wall throughout the entire height of the building, effectively slicing open vertically the donjon's walls, makes interpretation difficult, but there is sufficient left today (Fig. 64) for some informed speculation.

Entry was at first-floor level in the short north wall. The doorway led straight into a room illuminated by windows in both short walls and, presumably, the now-lost long east wall. There were two toilets at either end of the west wall at first-floor level. Both were accessible by short dog-legged passages beside the turrets, and neither alerted visitors in the main floor space to their presence; that at the south end of the wall was slightly lower and would have been reached by some descending steps.

Two doorways opened into mural stairs in the west wall. The first doorway was immediately inside the main door on the right-hand side, and was encountered before one entered the main floor space. Stairs ascended in a southerly direction from there to a point at second-floor level about halfway along the length of the building. As it rose through the height of the first-floor room, the stair-passage had a barrel-vaulted roof; beyond that, the nature of its roof is uncertain. A second doorway, now fully gone because the inner face of the wall was quarried away, was a little north of halfway along the west wall of the first-floor room, and it opened into stairs which descended to the basement. At the point at which it reached the basement it led through a doorway into the lower part of the south-west turret; one imagines that there was also, at this point, another doorway opening into the main floor space of the basement, and that this was the only means of access to that level. The lower part of the north-west turret was accessible from this level originally, so it was conceivably a prison.

In having two mural stairs, then, with one going down and one going up, and with the start point of the former almost directly below the end destination of the latter, Carlow was conceptually divided latitudinally in two parts, each roughly square. Such a division could have manifested itself in a physical partition – even just a screen – running cross the width of the room at first-floor level, immediately south of the doorway which gave access to the basement; such a partition would have been

84 Grose 1791, 74.   **85** For the elder Marshal see O'Conor 1997, 15–16, and Tietzsch-Tyler 2018a, 121; for the younger Marshal see Ludow 2018–19, 252.

63 Carlow Castle in the late eighteenth century, about twenty-five years before half the structure was blown up. Sixteenth-century alterations, captured here, are still visible in the surviving ruin.

mirrored in the basement, probably with a solid wall. One's natural tendency when looking at donjons is to assume that, if there were cross-walls to begin with, they were longitudinal, but latitudinal partitions in donjons are not unknown, and there is one in stone in the basement of Terryglass, another donjon in this small group.

The key question at Carlow is whether the level above the entry level was an actual *floor* level or simply constituted the roof space. The evidence tends to favour the latter. If the only stairs in the building were the ones for which there is evidence today, the stairs giving access from an upper room – a private room by definition – to a first-floor reception room would probably not have exited right beside the main entrance into the tower. Carlow's master mason was imaginative and skilled enough to design a different system if the choreography of lordly descent demanded it. So, I think Con Manning was correct in his speculation that Carlow had a 'low-level' (or counter-sunk) roof.[86] In this scenario, the ascending stairs in the west wall gave access to the parapet, from where the tops of the turrets were accessible by wall-walks. The point at which the stairs exited at parapet level was half-way along the wall, raising the possibility that the counter-sunk roof was actually two roofs parallel to each other, their ridges running across the short axis of the building, with the gutter-valley between them.

Lea

Although regarded as later than Carlow, there is no actual record of the construction of the donjon at Lea. All writers agree that it was built in either two phases within a

64 Carlow donjon interior. The truncated north wall with the entrance at first-floor level (*above*); the long west wall, with the ascending scar of the now-destroyed vaulted stairs-passage (*opposite top*); the south end of the west wall, with traces of the vaulted stairs-passage which descended into the basement, and the truncated south wall (*opposite bottom*).

65 Part of the exterior of Lea Castle, showing the top of the only intact corner turret and (partly hidden by vegetation) the twin-light window to which all writers on the castle have drawn attention for dating purposes. One can see a slight change in the fabric of the turret, corresponding to the level at which the tower was extended upwards by a single storey in the third quarter of the thirteenth century.

fairly continuous sequence or in two periods with an interval, but none of them presents cast-iron cases for any specific dates. Leask suggested that the donjon – or at least the top part of it – was built early in the third quarter of the century.[87] Kieran O'Conor tentatively suggested a date of *c.*1220 for its earliest part and 'after 1225–1230' for its later part.[88] Karen Dempsey gives a pre-1257 (but still mid-century) date for the earlier part and a pre-1268 date for the later part.[89] Excavation might actually help to resolve the issue. It has the potential to establish whether there was originally an earth-and-timber castle on the site, to reveal how long (approximately) such a castle

86 Manning 2002, 139.   **87** See respectively 1941, 50–1; 1943, 143.   **88** O'Conor 1999, 187–9.
89 Dempsey 2016b, 247.

functioned, and to determine whether there was a stone-walled enclosure before the donjon was started.

The key question from the chronological perspective is whether the donjon was a Marshal work or a fitz Gerald work. The current consensus is firmly the latter, which puts it post-1216, when Lea became a Geraldine possession.[90] But the attribution of the donjon to the post-Marshal period has clearly been influenced unduly by the only architectural feature for which an approximate date can be suggested: a twin-trefoil window, assignable to the middle decades of the thirteenth century. Critically, this is in the upper, second-phase or second-period, section of the donjon, so it does not date the donjon's first phase (Fig. 65). Yet, it has dragged the suggested date of the *entire* building away from the first quarter of the century – its natural home chronologically – towards its middle. I will show below that, unless one engages in special pleading, the laying out and earliest building phase at Lea must be assigned to the same master mason who designed Carlow for the Marshal family. Although that would not be proof, it would certainly suggest that Lea, in its first phase at any rate, was also a Marshal work. It would date, then, from the eight years after 1208 when the teenaged Richard Marshal – William the elder's son – was given possession by royal order of the district, previously held by Meiler fitz Henry.[91] Dating the first phase of Lea to the period 1208–16 does not resolve the question of Carlow's date, but it does strengthen the case for identifying Carlow as a work of the elder Marshal.

The most important point of comparison between Lea and Carlow is at first-floor level. This was the entry level. The format at Lea was very similar to that at Carlow. The door was at the end of a short wall, right beside a turret. In the side of the doorway passage and beside the entry to the turret was a dog-legged opening onto stairs which rose through the thickness of the wall to roof level; one difference is that Lea had no toilet there. The basement of the turret beside the entry was not accessible originally from the basement of the main block, so it too, like that at Carlow, might have been a prison. The only known access to the basement of the donjon was via another mural stairs which led directly into the basement of another turret. This differed from the Carlow arrangement only in the sense that entry to the stairs at Lea was in a window embrasure and in a different wall from the other stairs; the principle was the same.

Lea, however, did have an original second floor, which Carlow seems not to have had. The long mural stairs by-passed it, so it is not known how the second-floor room was accessed from below. The large opening in the north-west wall at second-floor level (Fig. 66) is identified by Dempsey as the original 'formal access route or primary entrance of the donjon', and she further identifies the (now-inaccessible) room at this floor level within the northern turret as a private chapel with a sedilia and an east-facing window.[92] Both identifications are problematic. The latter is most unlikely. A sedilia is a group of three seats, the middle for an officiating priest, flanked on each side by assistants. There was no room for three seats, and castle chaplains seem not to

---

90 McNeill 1997, 144; O'Conor 1999, 187–9; Sweetman 1999, 78; Dempsey 2016b.   **91** CDI I, 375, 378.   **92** Dempsey 2016b, 242.

66 The interior of the donjon at Lea, photographed from first-floor level. The chapel recess is visible in the end wall, above the original first-floor entrance with its round-arched doorway.

have had assistants, unlike some parochial and most monastic priests. The room in the turret seems to be just that: a room, albeit one with big window embrasures. The feature identified by Dempsey as a doorway is better interpreted as a chapel recess. First, it is part-splayed. Second, the sockets do not make sense as door features but could be explained as having held altar or reredos fittings. Third, it is east-facing. And fourth, it is above the entrance, which is the normal position for a chapel in a castle. So, this entire second-floor level at Lea is best explained, then, as a private space from which the lord descended – at the end opposite the suggested chapel – into the reception room below, his point of descent being faced by those who entered the donjon directly from outside.

The third-floor at Lea was added later, as all writers have observed. That is most apparent in how the mural passage containing the stairs was extended, its roofing changing from barrel-vaulted to lintelled. Although there is no way of knowing, the basement of the donjon might have received its parallel (plank-centred) vaults at the time this upper floor was added. The question is whether the upper floor represents a second phase of building, simply following an original intention, or a second period of building. Dempsey opts for the former, concluding that what we see today is the completion, following a short pause, of a scheme which was envisaged when the tower was first laid out.[93] On that basis, she allows the trefoil-headed twin-light on the third floor be the fixed chronological point from which she then back-dates by no more than a couple of decades the original building. But I think that the upper floor represents work of a different period, not of a different phase. I agree with Dempsey that the upper part of the donjon is best attributed to the third baron of Offaly, Maurice fitz Gerald (†1268), and his wife, Agnes de Valence.[94] The de Valence connection will bring us presently to another donjon, Ferns.

Dempsey describes as 'over-cautious' – she really means 'too early' – Kieran O'Conor's suggested chronology for the donjon.[95] But I argue above for an alternative chronology, going in the other direction: Lea is older than O'Conor suggested, not younger. It and Carlow were both Marshal castles, and they were started around 1210, give or take a few years. They were designed on the same principles, and so they form a unique pairing, even within the larger group of Marshal commissions in these islands.[96]

Terryglass

Few Irish castles of demonstrable architectural-historical importance are as puzzling as Terryglass. Again, here is a castle of immense interest for which there is no documentation pertaining to construction. Leask believed it to be as early as Carlow, which is almost the same size as it.[97] He was probably correct.

All that remains today is the latitudinally-partitioned basement of a main block, rectangular in plan but not perfectly so, and four turrets, two of them being more or less equal in diameter (Fig. 67). It is a grim ruin today, but some roll-moulded external window jambs – could they possibly have been taken from an earlier church? – suggest it was an attractive building in its day. The walls stand to a consistent height most of the way around, which suggests that the tower was not finished or that it was carefully lowered at some stage and for some reason which is not easily fathomed. Its original height cannot be determined now, but the manner in which it was truncated suggests

---

93 Dempsey 2016b, 247.   94 Ibid.   95 Ibid., 246.   96 Knight described them, and Ferns, as 'quite unlike any other Marshal work' (1987, 81).   97 Leask 1943, 143.

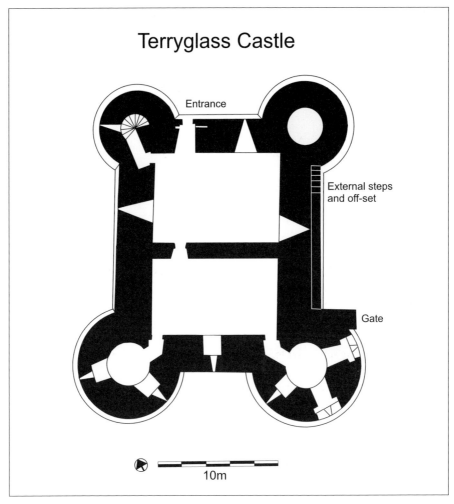

67 Plan of the donjon at Terryglass.

there was only one storey above the basement, even though its thick walls would have been able to carry two storeys.

In common with Carlow and Lea, there was an entrance in a short wall beside a turret. However, this entrance was into the basement. The turret in question contains spiral stairs too narrow to have been the main artery linking the courtyard outside the tower to the first-floor room. The first-floor level in one of the turrets also had a doorway, accessed by a narrow flight of steps built into the outside of one of the long walls. The opening in the turret was still visible in 1833.[98] The likelihood is that these steps led to the room above a prison, as there was apparently no access from the turret

98 'B' 1833.

to the main block at that level. The presence of a prison in a turret attached to the entrance façade is another point of comparison with Carlow and Lea.

Ferns

One of the grandest seigneurial buildings of the thirteenth century in Ireland, the complex tower at Ferns had a three-storeyed main block flanked by large turrets which rose an additional storey (Fig. 68). The ground plan was irregular but roughly trapezoidal. The interior was too large to have been floored or roofed without partitions. McNeill suggested that there may have been a central light well to support the floors,[99] but it was probably not big enough as a building to necessitate such a sophisticated arrangement. However it was partitioned, the lack of physical traces suggests that timber was used. One cannot say whether a partition ran along its length or width, but if it was the latter it could not have been medial because of the position of a mid-wall fireplace. The fenestration on the surviving long wall suggests instead that there was a partition across the width of the building at first- and second-floor levels, which in turn allows one to speculate that there was a reception room inside the entrance, a barrier separating it from a great chamber to which the chapel was attached, and an entire upper floor of private space. The only stairs to survive ascends as a spiral in the corner of the only turret to remain fairly intact. But it cannot have been the only means of moving through a building of this size. The entrance does not survive but was at the end of the surviving long wall and was probably at first-floor level.

As with the other buildings discussed above, there is no record of its construction. David Sweetman, who conducted some excavations on the site in the 1970s, is alone in giving Ferns an early thirteenth-century date.[100] The architecture does not allow it. Leask claimed the donjon to be no earlier than the mid-thirteenth century, when (in 1247) it became a possession of William de Valence.[101] Roger Stalley dated its chapel to the second half of the thirteenth century.[102] McNeill allowed a similar date, assigning it to William de Valence (†1296) or Aymer de Valence (†1324).[103] More recently, mid-century parallels have been identified for some of the details of its chapel, while some of its other features have been compared with ones found in the three late thirteenth-century castles in Carlow (especially Clonmore), and in the de Valence work of the 1280s at Goodrich (Herefordshire).[104] So, although no exact date can be established for Ferns, there can be little doubt that the castle was the work of William de Valence. A date in the 1270s or 1280s would be consistent with the evidence. Lea might well have been the main inspiration for the design of Ferns.

The French connection?

These four donjons differed from others in thirteenth-century Ireland in having corner turrets. They exerted no obvious influence, except perhaps on the design of Tullowmacjames (Tipperary) where a small chamber tower of the later thirteenth

---

99 McNeill 1997, 124.   **100** Sweetman 1979, 218; 1992, 326; 1999, 78.   **101** Leask 1951, 49. He dated it elsewhere to *c.*1260 (1943, 143).   **102** Stalley 1971, caption to Pl. 11.   **103** McNeill 1997, 144.   **104** O'Keeffe and Coughlan 2003, 146–7.

68 The exterior of Ferns Castle. The surviving turret on the right-hand side contains the vaulted chapel.

century has a single corner turret (Frontispiece). So, do the four donjons constitute a group, as Leask maintained? Carlow and Lea certainly deserve to be paired. They are the only donjons in Ireland in which straight mural stairs ascended past the entry-level room to roof level or, in the case of Lea's second phase, an upper storey. Each had descending mural stairs linking the entry level to the basement, and that was unusual in Ireland but not unique (it was a feature of Ballyderown, for example). It is difficult to speak confidently of either innovation or imitation in how the stairs-systems worked at these two donjons. One can see in Lea in particular the trickle-down across a span of two centuries of the genius of Loches: there, on the right-hand side of the point of entry into the donjon, a mural passage leads to stairs which descend into the basement, while on the left-hand side near the entrance, mural stairs ascend into the body of the tower. Lea had essentially the same arrangement, but reversed. The Loches comparison is made here only to support the point that Lea was as carefully thought-out as any of the rectangular donjons built up to the final quarter of the twelfth century in England or France. Arguably, Carlow was even more carefully thought-out, and was more unusual in how its two stairs were in the same wall.

Terryglass is slightly different, but there is enough evidence to suggest that it was a relative of both, particularly Carlow. But the inclusion of Ferns in the group is a little more problematic. It merits discussion alongside Lea especially, because of the de Valence connection, but to describe it as a descendent of the early thirteenth-century

69 The donjon at Nemours.

towers is to risk underestimating the importance of the ways in which it differed from
them. It was palatial in the way that no post-1200 focal building of an Anglo-Norman
castle in Ireland could be described as such. To describe it as a chamber tower is not
inaccurate but it downplays its relative showiness.

Leask was of the view that these turreted donjons were an invention of the Anglo-
Normans in Ireland. While that claim is no longer made in print, my own
identification of near-contemporary French parallels, first made in 1990, has not been
cited by other writers until very recently.[105] Yet, these Irish donjons cannot be
understood otherwise. Those French parallels fall into two groups, possibly reflecting
slightly different conceptual origins. On the one hand, there are some donjons in
which the corner turrets are solid for at least half their height but contain upper-floor
rooms, or at least stairs. The examples are mainly in the west of France, and the dates
are worth noting. Romefort (Indre), for example, was built between 1180 and 1190,[106]
and Noirmoutier (Vendée) was built between 1189 and 1206.[107] Further east, in the Île
de France, the donjon of Mez-le-Maréchal (Loiret) was either built between 1148 and
1181, or between 1191 and 1214.[108] The smaller and shallower that the corner turrets

105 O'Keeffe 1990, 22; Ludlow 2018–19, 251.   106 Mesqui 1987.   107 Baudry 2019.
108 Châtelain 1983, 257.

are in these donjons, the more pilaster-like they appear, suggesting that they might have been developed out of those square and rectangular donjons in western France in which the conventional corner pilasters were round-sectioned. In the other group in France, the turrets were not solid, except perhaps at basement level, but contained rooms for much of their height. Examples are more widespread geographically, but their dates compare with those of the first group. Ambleny (Aisne), for example, dates from either 1150–85 (according to Jean Mesqui) or *c.*1200 (according to Pierre Héliot); Nemours (Seine-et-Marne), dates from either 1150–80 (according to André Châtelain) or *c.*1200 (according to Jean Mesqui) (Fig. 69); the *fort des Tourelles* at Vernon (Eure) was extant in 1202/3.[109] Related to these are donjons with just two turrets on the same elevation: the *tour Manassès* at Meung-sur-Loire (Loiret), dating from the 1160s, and the donjon at Vic-sur-Aisne (Aisne), undated but built in the twelfth or thirteenth century.[110] The point of this run-through the French evidence is to demonstrate that, by the start of the thirteenth century at the latest, there were models available for copying in Ireland.

Visual similarities are difficult to assess comparatively, especially when the visual concept – the rectangular block flanked by turrets in the manner of a larger enclosure-castle – is relatively simple. But that might be the clue. William Marshal or knights in his company did not necessarily see inside the castles which they encountered, so conscious imitation might have been confined to external appearance. Carlow's intact wall makes it the one Irish donjon in the category to give us an impression of what a complete donjon of the type was like, and the French castle which one immediately thinks of as a comparator is Nemours, which is similar in height and proportions. I would not suggest that Nemours *was* the model, but one could not rule it out. William Marshal the elder could have seen it. Neil Ludlow raised that possibility but then dismissed it because he followed Jean Mesqui's date of *c.*1200 for Nemours.[111] However, its probable construction by Gauthier de Villebéon, suggested by André Châtelain, allows it an earlier date. Gauthier was the grand chamberlain of France under Louis VII and Philip II. Living close to Paris, it does not stretch the imagination too far to think that William Marshal not only met him but also saw his castle.

A PARADIGM SHIFT?

In the traditionally deterministic narrative of medieval castle-building, the 'keep' slipped out of fashion in north-western Europe when castle-builders came to realize, first, that its functions could be distributed among other structures, and second, that its stonework could be better employed in strengthening the enclosure wall, which

109 Mesqui 1977, 145 n97; Héliot 1969, 166. For Nemours, see Mesqui 1991, 128; Châtelain 1983, 265. For Vernon see Mesqui 2011, 303–8. The motte-summit donjon at Montfort-sur-Meu (Ille-et-Vilaine), demolished in 1848, was apparently square with four corner towers; Christophe Amiot has dated it on comparative grounds to the second half of the twelfth century (1992, 45–8). **110** Mesqui 2014, 19. For Vic-sur-Aisne, see Salch 1979, 1219; it is not late eleventh-century, as implied by Denis Rolland 1984, 141.   **111** Ludlow 2018–19, 251.

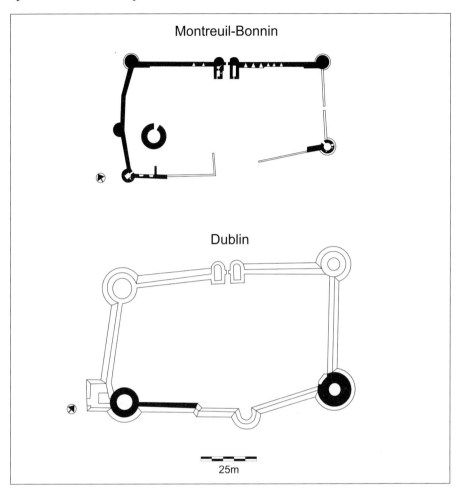

70 Plans of Montreuil-Bonnin Castle and Dublin Castle.

could itself be made more efficient by being given a symmetrical footprint and circular corner towers.

Whatever the validity of its supposed cause-and-effect relationship with the general decline in donjon-building, the move towards mirror-image symmetry or at least orthogonal regularity in the design of castle enclosures started in north-western Europe in the later twelfth century and rapidly picked up pace after 1200. The earliest surviving fully symmetrical castle of the new 'modernist' age in north-western Europe seems to be Druyes-les-Belles-Fontaines (Yonne), with a large square courtyard, round corner towers and two square interval towers. Its date is uncertain, but it had been built by 1188, if not before 1162.[112] The first fully symmetrical castle enclosure to feature only round or D-shaped towers was probably Philip II's Louvre in Paris, started in the

112 Héliot 1965, 1966, 240–2; Mesqui 1991, 41.

last decade of the twelfth century. Now gone, it had the elements which were later to appear consistently in combination in new fortresses: pairs of towers flanking the entrances, round corner towers and D-plan interval towers. The Louvre's plan was exact in its symmetry. Other early works simply approximated towards symmetry. Philip II's castle at Guainville (Eure-et-Loir), for example, his first castle built on the Franco-Norman border in 1190–4, had a small quadrangular court with small round corner towers, and, although it was not quite symmetrical, each stretch of curtain wall had a single window arranged symmetrically.[113]

The first Angevin castles to combine symmetrical planning and round corner towers were on French soil. In Angevin Poitou, Montreuil-Bonnin (Vienne), a cylindrical donjon sits inside a fairly symmetrical enclosure with quite small corner towers and a twin-towered gate-building in the centre of one of the long walls. It has been identified as the work of Richard I, which places it in the 1190s.[114] This is an interesting castle from an Irish perspective, because the morphological distance between its enclosure, a royal work, and the *castellum* and *baluum* in Dublin, also a royal work, is quite short (Fig. 70). Dublin was not completed until about 1230, but work on the enclosure beyond the *turris* was sufficiently well advanced by 1218 for compensation to be owed to the archbishop of Dublin. An obvious difference between the two castles is the placement of their donjons, but between them they illustrate the change in the positioning of such donjons over two decades: Montreuil-Bonnin typifies the off-centre placement of cylindrical great towers within enclosures in the later twelfth century and in the first decade of the thirteenth, as found at Pembroke and Philip II's Louvre in Paris for example, whereas Dublin is in the tradition of French castles like Dourdan. The important point here is that the similarity between their enclosures tells us that John's castle in Ireland conformed closely to a type with which the Angevins were familiar, not in England but in France.

Dublin was among the first castles in these islands to have been provided with a twin-towered gate-building, perhaps *the* classic individual feature of the new architecture which emerged around 1200.[115] Unfortunately, little is known about its design, except that the passage between the towers was short. Although very early, probably of the 1210s, it was not necessarily the first of the type in Ireland. Tom McNeill would seem to argue that such a distinction belongs to the Carrickfergus gate-building. He originally dated this to the second quarter of the thirteenth century and to the patronage of Hugh II de Lacy after his return from exile in 1227; Paul Duffy continues to favour that date.[116] Motivated by the new date of *c.*1189 suggested for the gate-building at Chepstow (Monmouthshire),[117] McNeill now argues for a date for Carrickfergus between 1205, when de Lacy acceded to the earldom of Ulster, and 1210, when he was expelled by King John.[118] He argues that the original structure – two

113 Mesqui 2016.   114 Baudry 2001, 270.   115 For the early example at Dover see Goodall 2011, 159.   116 Duffy 2015; 2018, 316–20.   117 Avent and Miles 2006; Tietzsch-Tyler 2018, 122–3. The date of *c.*1189 is based on the dendrochronology of the wooden gateway (Avent and Miles 2006, 51–62, 81–90). Neil Guy has made a good counter-argument for a date in the 1230s (Guy 2015–16, 193–201; see also Tietzsch-Tyler 2018a, 99).   118 McNeill 2014–15, 20–4; Gormley and McNeill 2016–17, 229–33. For the original date see McNeill 1981, 44–5.

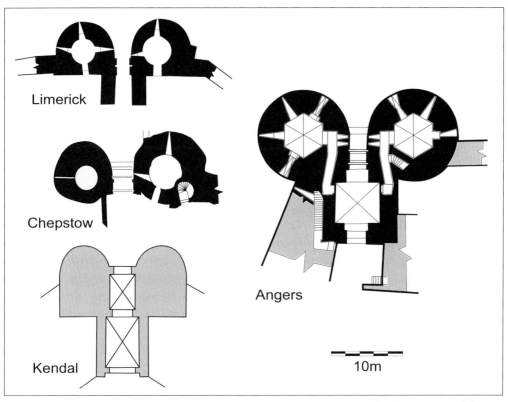

71 Plans of twin-towered gate-buildings with rear projections, at Limerick, Chepstow, Kendal and Angers.

circular towers, each probably of three storeys, with a wooden-roofed gate passage between them – stood free of the rest of the castle until a new curtain wall was brought out to meet it in the later 1220s. One piece of architectural evidence is now cited in support of this early date: he originally regarded the twin-light window at first-floor level in the east tower as an insertion, having been taken from some other context, but now regards it as primary. Is the new date he suggests for Carrickfergus acceptable? It is, but it is not convincing. First, Chepstow is an inexact parallel, whatever its date: unlike at Carrickfergus, its towers are neither of equal size nor properly circular. Second, between 1215 and 1223 some work was carried out by the crown on the defences of Carrickfergus, and McNeill identified this work as the wall immediately in front of the small donjon-dominated courtyard.[119] The classic archers' tower built at one end of this wall is unquestionably of this date; Angevin France provides

119 McNeill 1997, 54–5.   **120** There are very similar windows in Niort (Deux Sèvres) from the late twelfth century. The comparable windows in the town wall at Vernon also have shouldered arches similar to those at Carrickfergus. The Vernon wall is of uncertain date, and Jean Mesqui has suggested the paired loops are later thirteenth century and Capetian (Mesqui 2011, 310–11), but they could be Angevin work pre-dating Philip II's capture of the town in 1196.

contemporary comparanda for the manner in which its arrow loops were part-straight-sided.[120] It does seem unlikely, though, that the crown would have spent money on a new screen-wall (including this tower) in front of the donjon but left isolated the two cylindrical towers flanking the main gate leading towards the donjon. The relationship of the twin-light window to its host tower is clearly critical to dating the Carrickfergus gate-building. Stylistically, the window can be dated fairly accurately to between 1190 and 1210.[121] I think McNeill was correct originally in identifying it as an insertion. There is some merit to Dan Tietzsch-Tyler's suggestion that it originated in a chapel above an early gate passage, to which the two towers were later added.[122] I favour the later date in the later 1220s which was originally suggested by McNeill for Carrickfergus.

A better candidate than Carrickfergus for the first twin-towered gate-building in Ireland is that at Limerick, built with the money accounted for in the pipe roll of 1211–12.[123] It is a structure with interesting parallels (Fig. 71). Outwardly it may have resembled Dublin, but it was different in plan in at least one respect: it had a rectangular block projecting into its courtyard from the rear.[124] The feature was possibly paralleled in Ireland at the gate-building at Nenagh.[125] There are remains of such a feature in the outer twin-towered gate-building at Chepstow.[126] Another example of the feature once existed at Kendal (Cumberland), significantly a castle possessed by King John in 1216.[127] An advanced version of it is found in Angers (Maine-et-Loire), in the *Port des Champs*, after 1220.[128] One feature of the pair of Limerick towers which might help us to identify the source of the entire composition is the flat rear wall behind each tower. Being flush with the insides of the adjoining curtains, the towers only flanked the front of the passage. This is an unusual arrangement in Ireland, repeated only – and independently – at Ballymote (Sligo) at the very end of the century; the norm was for the flanking towers to project back into the courtyard. It is an early arrangement. It is found in England at Helmsley (Yorkshire) in work dated to between 1190 and 1227.[129] But it is more common in France. For example, it was used before 1210 at Goulancourt (Oise), and possibly around the same time at Yèvre-le-Chatel (Loiret),[130] after 1214 at Mez-le-Maréchal,[131] and in 1226 at Nesles-en-Tardenois.[132] The angled passages into the two towers at Limerick can be paralleled early in the thirteenth century at Charny (Côte-d'Or).[133] One should be cautious in highlighting French parallels for a single gate-building that conformed to a type popular in these islands throughout the thirteenth century, but transmissions directly to Ireland from France in the early thirteenth century cannot be ruled out. The turreted donjons are evidence of that.

121 Its round arches, square-section rear arches, and its square-shaped capital imposts, are firmly Romanesque, but its capitals and, especially, both the bands (or rings) on the shafts and the base-forms are classic early Gothic.   122 Tietzsch-Tyler 2018a, 103.   123 McNeill 1997, 47. 124 Dan Tietzsch-Tyler, who describes the plan-type as 'T-shaped', has speculated that the two side walls of the rectangle might survive from an earlier gate-building (2013, 121). 125 Hodkinson 1999, 163–4; Tietzsch-Tyler 2013, 123.   126 Avent and Miles 2006; Tietzsch-Tyler 2018, 122–3.   127 Curwen 1913, 416–19.   128 Chauveau et al. 2013, 251.   129 Goodall 2011, 184.   130 Châtelain 1983, 361–2.   131 Mesqui 1981, 208; Châtelain 1983, 369–70. 132 Mesqui 1991, 44.   133 Salch 1979, 290.

The first two twin-towered gate-buildings in Ireland, therefore, were probably in the royal castles of Limerick and Dublin. The chronology of the other examples in Ireland can be established with some accuracy. Roughly contemporary with Limerick and Dublin might be the pair of towers at Nenagh, as there cannot have been a long interval between the building of its donjon and its curtain wall, as well as the demolished example at Kilkenny. The next gate-building in chronological sequence in Ireland might be that at Dungarvan, probably part of the work carried out on that castle between 1215 and 1220 (see above, p. 147). From the late 1220s is Carrickfergus, as argued above, and Dundrum, also built by Hugh II de Lacy.[134] From the mid-1230s is Castleroche (Louth), discussed below. There is then a small group of examples which can probably be dated to the 1240s. Ballylahan (Mayo) was probably built by Jordan d'Exeter, who was granted the land in 1240.[135] Kiltartan (Galway) and Lea are sufficiently similar to be considered contemporary; Lea is difficult to date because its host castle was built in many phases, but Kiltartan Castle in its entirety probably dates from the 1240s, the decade after the settlement of Connacht began. In all three, Ballylahan, Kiltartan and Lea, the walls of the towers are thinnest where they flank the central passages, an idiosyncrasy which can be paralleled at Tonbridge (Kent), dated to the middle of the century, and Leybourne (Kent), dated 1266.[136] No more examples of twin-towered gate-buildings are known in Ireland until the last quarter of the century, starting with Roscommon, built 1275–7, followed by Ballymote, shortly before 1300, Ballintober (Roscommon), of around the same date, and Greencastle (Donegal), built in 1305. These castles are discussed below. There is, finally, the example at Ballyloughan (Carlow) from the end of the thirteenth century; there, the gate-building is actually a rectangular block with towers at the front corners.[137]

Castleroche

Of all the castles erected in Ireland in the middle decades of the thirteenth century, Castleroche, the great rock-top fortress of the de Verdun family, is arguably the most important from an architectural-historical viewpoint (Fig. 72).[138] In 1233, Roesia de Verdun came into the secure possession of the land inherited from her father, and two years later she and Hugh II de Lacy resolved a long standing dispute between the two families.[139] In 1236, Roesia boasted that she had 'built a good castle strongly in her land against the Irish', something which 'none of her predecessors was able to do'. Her boast about Castleroche needs to be treated with a little caution. The source is the royal record, to which Roesia herself must have provided the information, but there is no evidence that she was ever in Ireland. Also, three years – from 1233 to 1236 – is a fairly short span for a baronial fortress of its size, especially given evidence of slight changes in design during construction.

134 McNeill 1980, 22; 1997, 91–2.   **135** Brown 2016, 256.   **136** Martin and Martin 2013 (Tonbridge); Salter 2000, 54 (Leybourne).   **137** O'Keeffe 2001b.   **138** For a detailed discussion of what follows here, see O'Keeffe 2014–15.   **139** For the family's history see Hagger 2001.

72 Castleroche – literally, the castle on the rock – viewed from the south.

The gate-building, two storeys high above the now-destroyed passageway, was the first structure to have been built.[140] It contained private rooms at upper-floor levels. Construction work on the castle seems then to have proceeded in an anti-clockwise direction around the top of the rock, ending with the building of the great hall which adjoins the gate-building on one side (Fig. 73). That hall was at first-floor level and must have been three-aisled. It pre-dates the three-aisled hall which was built in Dublin Castle under royal instruction in 1243 and modelled on the hall of Canterbury.[141] It also pre-dates the aisled hall built (to emulate the Dublin hall?) in Trim Castle by Geoffrey de Geneville after 1254.[142] The gate-building and hall at Castleroche together constituted a form of hall-and-chamber block, although that would not have been apparent to those who viewed it from the outside.

140 Similarities between it and the barbican towers of St Laurence's Gate in Drogheda, probably built on foot of a 1234 murage grant, suggest the sharing of a master mason in the aftermath of the negotiated peace between the de Verduns and de Lacys in 1235.   **141** CDI, I, nos 2612, 2793; see O'Keeffe 2015, 215.   **142** Hayden 2011, 196–7.

73 The gate-building and hall at Castleroche. The former was completed before the latter was started.

A construction date for the Castleroche gate-building of the mid-1230s gives it considerable importance. Conceptually and chronologically, its closest parallel seems to be the gate-building at the de Clare castle of Tonbridge. In both cases, the towers projecting to the front do not contain separate rooms above ground-floor level. They are not so much towers, in other words, as boldly curving façade bays attached to rectangular blocks, the first- and second-floor rooms within which offered high-status accommodation (Fig. 74). Tonbridge was built in the middle of the century.[143] Its model is likely to have been Henry III's great twin-towered gate-building of the late 1230s at London (now gone).[144] Castleroche might have been an early experiment, if not the earliest, in the design. It might even have influenced London and, through it, Tonbridge and Caerphilly (Glamorgan). After all, Roesia was known personally to Henry III. He had agitated personally for her marriage to Theobald Butler.

SYMMETRICAL DESIGNS OF THE LATE THIRTEENTH CENTURY

The near-symmetrical quadrangular plans at Dublin and Limerick were not copied in Ireland. The next time the plan-type appeared was in middle of the century, at

143 Martin and Martin 2013, 271, 274–5. **144** Goodall 2011, 191.

74 The interior of the gate-building and hall at Castleroche. Note how the former was rectangular on the inside, although seemingly twin-towered on the outside. Note also how it was elevated high above the hall. Although the two structures worked as a unit, it was an uneasy marriage, thanks in part to the topography of the site, although changes made to the design of the castle as it was being built might also account for this.

Greencastle (Down), where its use was independent of the two royal castles decades earlier; Tom McNeill has drawn attention to its similarity with that at Skenfrith.[145] After *c.*1270, however, regular quadrangular plans appeared again in Ireland. The examples fall into two groups, one in the northern half of Ireland, and one in the southern half.

The southern castles are quite generic. None has a particular feature or characteristic to allow one trace a pedigree. They are simply enclosure castles with (some or all) corners marked by towers, and no central buildings. Liscarroll and Kilbolane (both Cork), the former with its four corner towers extant and the latter with two of a presumed four extant, can be dated by historical inference to between the later 1260s and the mid-1270s.[146] The smaller castle at Quin (Clare) had towers at each of its corners. Building work started in 1279 or 1280, and it was probably still ongoing when the castle was burned down around 1285.[147] Castlegrace (Tipperary) might be included,

145 McNeill 1997, 88–91.   **146** O'Keeffe, 2013d.   **147** Hodkinson 2004.

75 The (early fourteenth-century?) corner tower at Clonamicklon. A domestic block was built alongside this tower, but its character is uncertain thanks to later obstruction. The corresponding tower at the other end of the wall (not shown here) seems to be a late medieval rebuild. The gabled building in the background is a thirteenth-century donjon to which substantial alterations were made in the sixteenth century.

but it appears always to have had only two towers fronting a regular courtyard in front of a residential block.[148] It is not dated; its details suggest only that it is post-1250 in date. Brittas (Limerick) might have been similar in plan to Castlegrace. It was possibly completed by 1288.[149] Clonamicklon (Tipperary) also had two towers fronting a courtyard, at the back of which was an older chamber donjon. One of the circular towers was attached to a residential block (Fig. 75). There is no recorded date of construction, but historical evidence suggests Clonamicklon is the latest of the southern Irish series, with a date in the early 1300s.[150]

There are four castles in the northern group. Richard de Burgh, 2nd earl of Ulster, was responsible for three of them, of which two had near-symmetrical plans. Tom McNeill has discussed all three in detail, highlighting their parallels outside Ireland.[151] I have relatively little to add here.

Ballintober, first, is a large rectangle, extensive in area. Reading an *inquisition post mortem* description (1333) in the light of the recent discovery of evidence for internal buildings, it seems that its walls were built to enclose an older (unfortified?) settlement which had a hall, a chamber-block, a kitchen, and other buildings, all arranged around a smaller courtyard.[152] Its polygonal towers reflect influence from Edwardian

148 McNeill 1997, 139–40.   **149** O'Keeffe 2015, 245.   **150** Ibid., 2015, 246.   **151** McNeill 1997, 101–6.   **152** O'Keeffe 2015, 247. For the geophysics see Brady 2012.

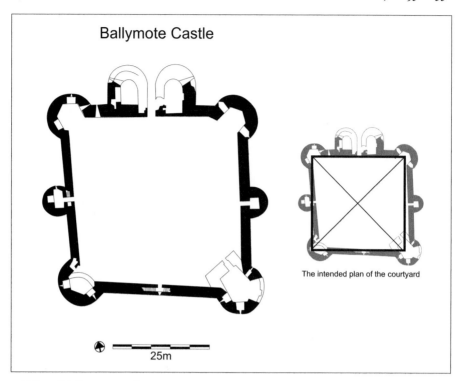

76 Plan of Ballymote Castle.

Caernarfon (Caernarvonshire), so building work could not have started before 1283 at the very earliest. It was probably built around 1300.

Ballymote, second, was started in 1299 and was built to the design principle seen at Edwardian Harlech (Merionethshire) and (especially) Beaumaris (Anglesey). It was conceived with considerable geometrical regularity, but something went seriously awry when it was being built: none of the angles is a right-angle (Fig. 76). In the temptation to scoff at it, the significance of the error at Ballymote for our understanding of the process of castle-building can be overlooked. Had this castle been planned in its entirety on the ground using ropes, the error would have been identified. So, that is not how it was planned. It is apparent that building work started on the entrance façade, but that the angles of the returns at the two corner towers were incorrectly calculated. The error became more obvious as the work progressed towards the rear wall across the courtyard, but it was too late by then to fix it. It is very likely that the builders were working off an actual plan – a drawing of some description – which had been provided to them, and so they felt empowered to start at one end without first marking out the full extent of the castle on the ground.

Greencastle (Donegal), third, started in 1305, famously has features which connect it to both Harlech and, especially, Caernarfon, as McNeill has discussed. Not generally recognized, however, is that its plan also resembles somewhat that of the small inner

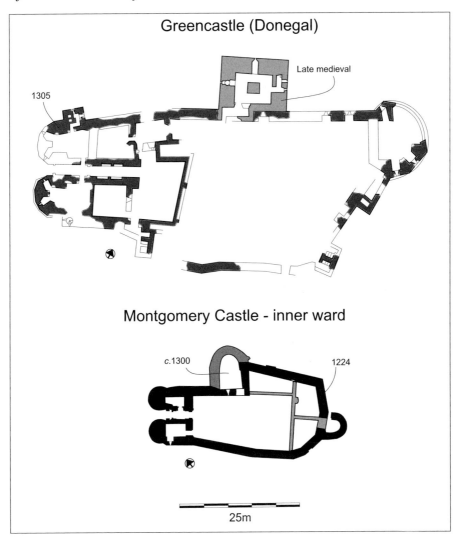

77 Plans of Greencastle (Donegal) and Montgomery Castle. Rubble and vegetation obscures many of the details of the former.

ward at Montgomery, a royal castle on the Welsh border which was held by Hubert de Burgh between 1228 and 1232, and which had the 2nd earl of Ulster's uncle as its constable in the 1240s (Fig. 77).[153]

The fourth castle of the northern group is Roscommon (Fig. 78). It has good documentation.[154] The site of the castle was chosen in 1262 but work only started in 1269.[155] The annalists complained that in 1267 much of Connacht was 'despoiled and

153 Remfry 2005. The plan of Greencastle is based on that published in Lacy 1983, 366.
154 Murphy and O'Conor 2008; O'Keeffe 2018d.   **155** AC 1162.4; ALC 1262.2.

78 Roscommon Castle, viewed from what was the edge of the lake when it was built. The small projecting tower of rectangular plan on the left-hand side is the only feature which breaks the symmetry of the fortress (see Fig. 81). The late sixteenth-century alterations to the castle are visible.

harried for the building of that castle',[156] but this is presumably not the full explanation for the delay. Lords who built castles on land owned by the Church sometimes had to pay compensation retrospectively,[157] but some advance consideration of proprietorial rights might be part of the explanation for the gap in time between the choosing of the site of Roscommon Castle in 1262 and the start of construction seven years later.[158] Compensation of 15 marks was paid in 1276 to Brother Maurice, bishop of Elphin, 'for his fee for the site of the castle'.[159] This was paid at the time when the original 1269 castle was being rebuilt (see below), so it seems to reflect a negotiated compensation.

The decision to build a castle in Roscommon, hatched under Henry III, has long been explained in terms of the extension and maintenance of colonial power in the heartland of Gaelic Ireland, an explanation buttressed by the fact that the present fortress was built in the 1270s by Edward I, notorious for castle-building exploits against the Welsh.[160] Whether that is the principal explanation is open to question. Five of Roscommon's cantreds had been retained by the Gaelic-Irish in a tenurial arrangement with the crown. The royal castle was built just inside the largest and most southern of those cantreds, arguably less to impose royal authority on the native inhabitants of central Roscommon – how effective could it possibly have been at such a task? – than to give physical manifestation to the crown's claim to ultimate ownership

156 AU 1267.1.   **157** See, for example, the case of Dublin in 1218 (CDI I, no. 848).   **158** The trend towards litigation by the Church when its land was alienated in the earlier thirteenth century might explain why greater care seems to have been taken by the Anglo-Normans later in the century to come to some advance agreement with the Church in respect of the encastellation of ecclesiastical land, as in the case of Annaghdown (Co. Galway) in 1252 (CDI 2, nos 76, 77; CDI 2, nos 274, 459).   **159** CDI 2, no. 1294.   **160** See, for example, Murphy and O'Conor 2008; O'Conor 2014b. The theory that Co. Roscommon was a frontier has its clearest articulation in Tom Finan's important book (2016).

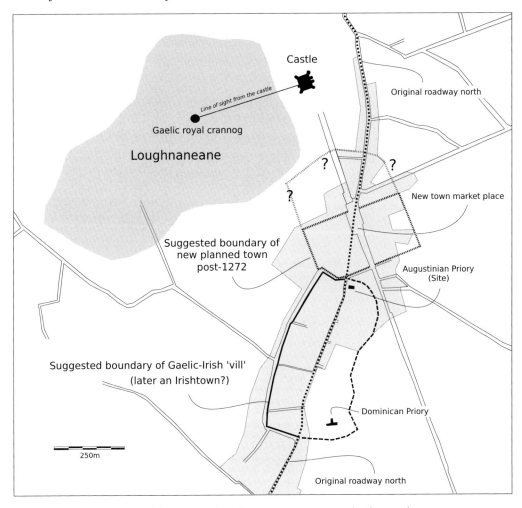

79 A reconstruction of the topography of Roscommon town in the thirteenth century.

of this land. As evidence that the intent at Roscommon was less aggressive than has been assumed, one can turn to an inspeximus of 1282 of a charter issued by the Anglo-Normans some time around 1270. That charter granted to the prior and convent of St Coman, a native foundation of regular canons, permission to continue 'their weekly free market on Saturdays in their Irish vill, between their house and that of the Dominicans in the same vill', and 'to water all their animals in the lake under the K.'s castle of Roscommon'.[161] The original native settlement at Roscommon was obviously retained, and the topographical analysis of the modern town allows its extent to be suggested (Fig. 79).[162]

161 For a slightly more nuanced reading of the evidence for the entire Roscommon region see O'Keeffe 2018c; 2018d.   **162** O'Keeffe 2018d, 195.

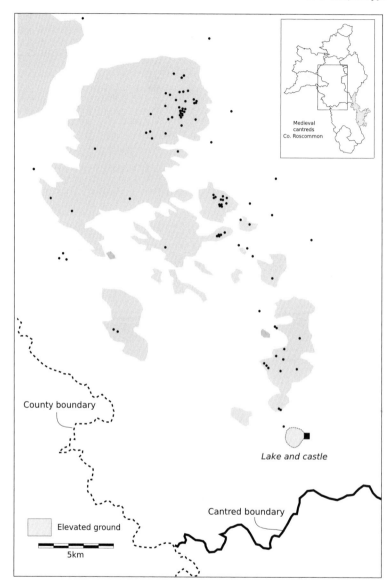

80 The location of Roscommon Castle relative to the prehistoric and early historic ritual landscape of Co. Roscommon. The dots represent ritual monuments, most of them barrows and mounds.

The actual site chosen for the castle is of considerable interest, both in terms of the local landscape and the wider regional landscape (Fig. 80).[163] It straddles a lake in low-lying ground,[164] and commands no view of the surrounding landscape. But the lake in

163 For what follows see O'Keeffe 2018c; 2018d.　　**164** Its boundaries were altered so that the edge of the lake ran parallel to the castle. In this regard, it resembled the lakes at places like

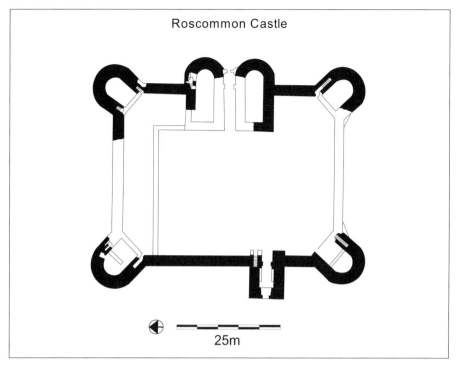

81 Plan of Roscommon Castle.

question, Loughnaneane, *Loch na nÉn*, the lake of the birds, was no ordinary lake. A crannog in its centre at the time of the castle's construction had been a royal site, and it was possibly the place where a fragment of the True Cross was enshrined in the so-called Cross of Cong in the early 1120s. The castle looked out at it (Fig. 79). The lake had earlier associations. Buried on its shore was Fergus Mac Róich, the one-time king of Ulster who, according to *Táin Bó Cúailgne*, marched on Ulster with the Connacht army led by Queen Medb and her husband Ailill. According to tradition, Fergus appeared from the grave to recount the story of that great cattle raid on Ulster. *Loch na nÉn* was also place of entry to the Otherworld. It was the watery portal through which, according to a tale of ninth-century origin, Laeghaire Mac Crimhthainn, 'the noblest youth there had been among the men of Connacht', entered the world of 'the fairy people', eventually deciding to stay. The Otherworld was not just a place of sub-lacustrine fantasy. The lake marked the southern boundary of a region of ancient 'otherness': the prehistoric and early historic ritual landscape of central Roscommon, marked by barrows and various ceremonial monuments, reached southwards as far as the lake. It seems, then, that the site for the castle was chosen on Henry III's watch in the full knowledge of the importance of the location in the mental cartography of the native Irish, and that the great stone castle was then built by Edward I, a man whose fascination with history and folklore is well documented.[165]

Kenilworth (Warickshire) and Caerphilly. **165** For further evidence of Edward's interest in

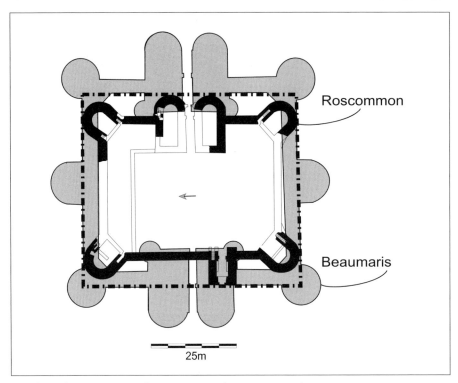

82 Plans of Roscommon and Beaumaris Castles superimposed.

The first castle, begun in 1269, was wrecked by the local king, Aedh Ua Conchobhair, whose father, Feidlim, had managed to keep the peace through reasonably good relations with Henry III. Expenditure of about £3,500 between 1275 and 1285, most of it in 1277–8, accounts for the present castle, a classic Edwardian 'keepless' castle with four rounded towers and a twin-towered gate-building (Fig. 81).[166] Planning for the stone castle probably began around 1275, the year after the ever-hostile Aedh Ua Conchobhair died, and the ground plan would have been marked out on the ground by 1277 at the very latest. The chronology is significant. In 1277, Edward was engaged in the first phase of encastellation in north Wales, but the fortresses of that campaign do not compare with Roscommon in design, except at Aberystwyth, where there is a Roscommon-like twin-towered gate-building. But the Roscommon design appears in Edward's second campaign of building in Wales, which started in 1283. It is, therefore, the first outing in these islands for the perfectly quadrangular Edwardian plan-type. Roscommon's metrical 'fit' inside Beaumaris, the last of the great Welsh castles, suggests a common template (Fig. 82). Master James of St George, the Savoyard master mason most associated with the second campaign castles in Wales, did not arrive in north Wales until spring or, more likely, early

myth and legend see Rachel Swallow's important analysis of Caernarfon Castle and its location (2019).   **166** McNeill 1997, 96.

summer 1278.[167] The template could not have been his, because it had already been used in Ireland.[168]

Roscommon differs from its two closest parallels from that second campaign, Harlech and Beaumaris, in having D-shaped corner towers. That shape was not unusual in gate-buildings but it was rarely used otherwise, so it requires explanation. Bordering the Welsh lands, Henry III's new castle at Montgomery, started in 1223, had a tower of that plan at an early date and a larger tower of the same plan added many decades later (see Fig. 77).[169] The plan-type was also used for major towers during the thirteenth century in the irregularly planned castles of Caergwrle (Flintshire), Carndochan and Castel y Bere (Merionethshire), Dinas Brân (Denbighshire), and Ewloe (Flintshire), all castles of the princes of Gwynedd.[170] Is it possible that knowledge of these castles – fortresses of the Welsh, in opposition to which Edward built his own northern Welsh castles – informed what was built in Roscommon?

How important is Roscommon Castle in the history of castle-building in north-western Europe? To answer that question, it is important to reflect on how the adjective 'scientific' has been used in the scholarly literature to describe the architecture of castles like Roscommon in which towers were arranged, normally with some symmetry, to maximize flanking fire.[171] 'Scientific' presupposes a rigorous process of testing options in a quest to find an optimal design. It presupposes, by extension, that earlier architectural schemes were not quite so rational. A belief that contemporary masons were involved in a quest to create the optimal castle design has traditionally driven the narrative of thirteenth-century castle development. It explains, for example, the preoccupation with the typology of gate-buildings.[172]

Admittedly impressive, the royal castles of north Wales enjoy an extraordinary level of veneration because of this narrative. 'The apogee of the English castle in its military and defensive form', wrote Andrew Saunders, 'is seen in the castles erected on the orders of Edward I and largely to the design of Savoyard engineer Master James of St George: Conwy (Caernarfonshire), Caernarvon, Harlech, and Beaumaris'.[173] The evidence of Roscommon shows us that Saunders was wrong to attribute the design to Master James of St George, but the more interesting point here is that his description of Master James of St George as an engineer – master masons equally are associated with churches – is in lockstep with the unconsciously-biased promotion of these castles as monuments of ur-masculinity. Yet, for all their fame, three of the four castles of Edward's second castle-building campaign – the exception is Caernarvon – were essentially just variations on designs which had been in circulation for some decades. In fact, the essence of the design of Beaumaris – the most perfectly designed of all the Edwardian castles – first appeared half a century or more earlier, in the little-known Montaiguillon Castle (Seine-et-Marne), built between 1215 and 1220 according to Jean Guerout, or in the 1230s according to Jean Mesqui (Fig. 83).[174]

---

167 Coldstream 2010, 37. **168** O'Keeffe 2011b, 61–54; ibid., 2015, 248–9. **169** Butler and Knight 2004. **170** Butler 2012. **171** See, for example, Saunders 2017, 164. **172** See, for example, Mesqui 1981. **173** Saunders 2017, 164. **174** Guerout 1966, 57–80; Mesqui 1980, 241–2.

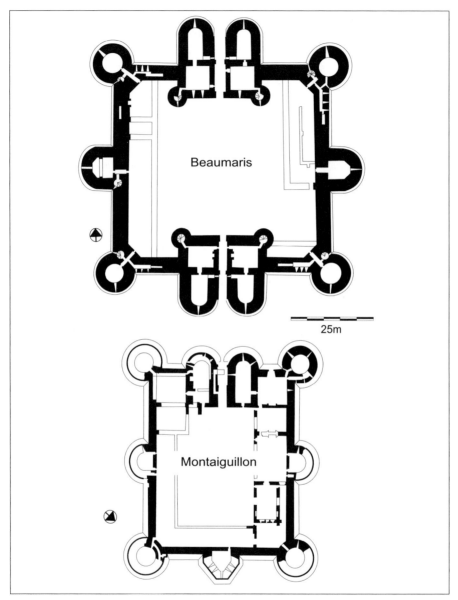

83 Plans of Montaiguillon and Beaumaris Castles compared.

Every road needs a destination;[175] every story a climax. The story of the 'scientific' approach to castle design had in north Wales a perfect climax in a group of royal castles built, with symbolic happenchance, right at the end of a century which started with feverish experimentation. Now, to query the adjective 'scientific' is not to deny that

175 Note the title of Jeremy Knight's important paper, 'The road to Harlech' (1987).

castle-builders were interested in symmetry but, rather, to query the rigour with which they pursued it, and to query their motivation – problem-solving? – for doing so. Still, for as long as the great northern Welsh castles are allowed the insinuation that they are the most superior examples of military architecture from the Middle Ages, Roscommon Castle deserves international recognition.

CONCLUSION

King John is a key figure in the history of castle-building in Ireland. Before 1199, the year he was crowned, the area of English lordship had been largely restricted to the east and part of the south of the island. The colonial landscape had been dominated by mottes, with only a few stone castles. By the time John died in 1216, the area of the lordship had expanded, especially in Munster. Unlike his brother or his father, he engaged in the process of encastellating Ireland, building motte-castles in strategic locations and building some reasonably large stone fortresses in urban centres. The men to whom he gave grants were also castle-builders.

To be clear, John was not directly responsible for the importation of every new design that appeared in Ireland immediately after 1200. One might even argue, first, that his reign simply coincided with a period of experimentation, and second, that a more capable and less capricious king might have created in Ireland an environment in which castle-builders would have been able to embrace an even greater range of the new French developments. But there is no gainsaying John's importance: the seventeen years of his reign saw Ireland's encastellated landscape transformed, and he was central to that process.

That transformation brought castle-building culture in Ireland fully into the north-west European mainstream. The thirteenth century is the one century of the Middle Ages in which Ireland was in that mainstream. The expansion and stabilization of the Anglo-Norman lordship occurred at a time when the design-ideas developed in France in the later twelfth century became orthodox, and Ireland, as a new Angevin possession, was well-positioned to play host to them. And it did, but only to a degree. Dublin, Limerick, Kilkenny, Carlow and Lea were among the few castles in Ireland which were up-to-date by the standards of the period from 1200 to 1220. Such castles had one key thing in common: they were built by men whose possessions were not confined to Ireland. Men like King John and William Marshal travelled, so they were exposed directly to new trends in architecture overseas.

Innovative designs were few and far between in Ireland after that initial flurry of activity. The demise of the de Lacy family might well have contributed to that. No major aristocratic family in late twelfth- or early thirteenth-century Ireland had been as in tune with contemporary architectural developments elsewhere, but Hugh's untimely death in 1186, Walter's wardship, and Hugh II's expulsion from Ulster in 1210, leaves one wondering what might have been built had the family not drifted off the national stage so rapidly.

We should, of course, be careful not to make innovation the sole criterion for evaluating castles in the thirteenth century, even if the trajectory of castle architecture had been shaped at an early date by innovation. Anglo-Norman lords in Ireland were probably not hugely concerned with experimentation and innovation anyway. Why would we expect them to have been? In any case, had they been, they might have struggled to afford it. The lordship was not a wealthy place. The land was good but the population was small, so less money circulated in its economy than circulated in any area of equivalent size in England or France.

During the middle decades of the thirteenth century few castles of international interest were built in Ireland. Castleroche is probably the most noteworthy. Late in the century the towered enclosure of symmetrical plan was introduced into Ireland. By any criterion, the one great work of that type in that era is Roscommon Castle. An Edwardian royal work, it is a geographical outlier of the famous Welsh castles, and it pre-dates those which Edward had built to a quadrangular plan. Whether the Welsh castles deserve to be regarded as climactic within the trajectory of European castle-building is open to debate, but for as long as they enjoy their exalted status Roscommon deserves to share that glory.

Some centuries are regarded by historians as 'long', like Europe's twelfth century, the character of which was shaped in the middle of the eleventh century. For the Irish castellologist, the thirteenth century lasted a century, with half a decade added on at each end. It started with Walter de Lacy's work at Trim in the later 1190s. Thanks to the war and famine which followed, it ended with the earl of Ulster's Greencastle (Donegal) in the first decade of the fourteenth century (although Clonamicklon might be a little younger). The quarry sites and the masons' yards fell idle for most of the rest of that century.

CHAPTER 5

The long tail of European influence: a late medieval epilogue

The late medieval period in Ireland has ill-defined chronological boundaries. A start-date of 1350 would not be particularly contentious. An end date is more difficult to select because the end of the late medieval period is the end of the Middle Ages itself. Different aspects of medieval culture survived for decades long after any one of the various events which historians would select as transformative.[1] The question, then, is whether one selects a date to mark the start of the transformation from the medieval period to early modernity or the point at which the transformation was more or less complete. Choosing the latter means a date no earlier than 1600, which would be absurdly late by European standards. Choosing the former means *c.*1550. That is the period of the dissolving of the monasteries by Henry VIII, and, as Jane Fenlon has shown, the period of the first appearance of Renaissance forms in major houses in Ireland.[2] Such a chronology for Ireland aligns well for the architectural historian with the English and European chronology. For Matthew Johnson, the mid- to late sixteenth century saw 'the construction of elite domestic architecture as a discursive object', a comment that expresses the shift in how social identity was newly constructed around how buildings were viewed and reimagined as objects of discourse.[3] Moreover, as Ethan Matt Kavaler has shown, Gothic as a style petered out between the early and mid-sixteenth century.[4]

It has long been recognized – and it is not disputed here – that the majority of Irish castles date from this late medieval period. For a book on the encastellation of medieval Ireland to treat the late Middle Ages as an epilogue, as I do here, would be perverse were the book's principal aim the description and holistic interpretation of the Irish building stock. But viewed from the perspective of external influence on Irish castle architecture, or more accurately from the perspective of the relevance of architecture outside Ireland to the understanding of those castles, the late medieval period in Ireland really is quite different from the late twelfth and thirteenth centuries. There is certainly evidence that castles of the later period in Ireland relate to, and perhaps even reflect direct influence from, contemporary castles in Britain and France, but the majority of castles beyond the initial phases in the period under review were the products of internal development.

---

1 McNeill 2007.   2 Fenlon 2011.   3 Johnson 2007, 122.   4 Kavaler 2012.

Between the mid-twelfth and mid-sixteenth centuries, some 250-odd castles are mentioned explicitly in the surviving contemporary written sources for Ireland, a number of them many times. It is a surprisingly low count. Actual construction dates are mentioned for one-fifth of that total; most of those are late twelfth- or early thirteenth-century dates, and most of those in turn pertain to earth-and-timber castles. When we calculate that figure of 250 as a percentage of the total number of castles or castle-sites known from seventeenth- to nineteenth-century sources, it represents about 5 per cent of the total. That is a tiny percentage; it is possible that no other country in western Europe has such poor documentation.

One is forced to fall back almost exclusively on the architectural-historical evidence for the purpose of dating castles in Ireland. Thankfully, that can be done with reasonable precision. For thirteenth-century stone castles, architectural dating can sometimes be accurate to within a couple of decades, allowing patrons be identified by name. For the late Middle Ages, however, accuracy by this technique to within a century is often the limit of what is possible. Stylistic dating is predicated on an assumption that certain forms or motifs had periods of currency, and that those periods are known. But the dates assigned to those periods in Ireland have often been assumptions themselves, informed by some factual knowledge but largely shaped by instinct. The dating of ogee and cusped-ogee windows is a case in point: the default date for these in the Irish literature is the fifteenth century, maybe the sixteenth if the decoration 'looks' later, but the ogee first appeared in Ireland in the early fourteenth century, and, being a form associated with English 'Decorated' architecture (see above, p. 116), it could in theory have been in Ireland from the middle of the thirteenth century.[5]

The dating of late medieval castles in Ireland over the past half-century or so owes much to how Harold Leask, in his classic *Irish castles and castellated houses*, first published in 1941, mediated his knowledge through his instinct. He correctly recognized that post-1300 castles are harder to date with accuracy than those of the previous century, in part because the written record is simply less helpful. He then alighted on some early fifteenth-century documentary references pertaining to specific castles and to castle-building in general, and he allowed them to be the starting point of his analysis of the later medieval stock. He was not unduly bothered by the relative lack of recorded construction dates thereafter, and he happily assigned castles to the fifteenth and sixteenth centuries. He did not apply the same attitude to the same relative lack of dates between 1300 and 1400. Instead, he took it that turmoil in that century – endemic warfare and the Black Death, for example – would have led to a downturn in castle-building. Thus, Leask bequeathed to subsequent generations of Irish castellologists the theory of a fourteenth-century hiatus. It was not a hiatus across the entire building industry;[6] it was a hiatus in castle-building.

---

5 O'Keeffe 2015, 43–8.   **6** Documented dates of foundation for mendicant friaries indicate that the same century was actually not devoid of any major building activity. See McNeill 1985–6.

84 Exterior views of the great tower of Barryscourt Castle, from the south (*left*) and north (*right*).

He was essentially correct about the fourteenth century. It is known that some fortresses, probably of small size, were built for local and regional protection in eastern Ireland in the middle of the century, but the number is small.[7] None survives. There is also an important native Irish fortress of the period at Dangan Iviggin (Clare). Built by Cumheadha MacNamara who died around 1370, it has a ruined great tower which was designed in the tradition of the earlier donjons, albeit with an original double vault.[8] Notwithstanding these sites, the documentation does indeed suggest that a downturn in castle-building activity started early in the fourteenth century and ended around 1400.[9] Brian Hodkinson has documented an early, pre-1402, urban castle in Limerick.[10] Emper (Westmeath) was built in 1405, Tulsk (Roscommon) in 1406, Mountgarret (Wexford) by 1409, and Kilclief (Down) in the 1410s.[11] Recently obtained radiocarbon dates from Barryscourt Castle (Cork), one of the largest castle buildings of later medieval Ireland, reveal it to have been built around 1400 (Fig. 84).[12] The number of sites here is small, but the year 1400 really does mark the start of the extended period in which new castles appear in historical records, even if those records do not pertain to their actual construction.

7 O'Keeffe 2015, 262–4.   8 Westropp 1898–1900, 351; Ua Cróinín and Breen 1986; O'Keeffe 2015, 258.   9 O'Keeffe 2015, 257.   10 Hodkinson 2005.   11 MIA, 1405.7, 1406.12; Grattan Flood 1916, 85; Jope 1966, 233. All were towers.   12 Sherlock 2017. For the dating of tower-houses using twigs from wickerwork centring see Sherlock 2013.

85 Exterior view of Ballymoon Castle. The entrance was protected by a barbican (or was intended to be so).

Ballymoon Castle: problem and prospective

Leask confidently placed one major work at the very end of the Anglo-Norman period of castle-building: Ballymoon Castle (Carlow). A courtyard structure with no flanking towers, it did not fit into his later thirteenth-century 'keepless castle' class. Equally, it had no dominant tower, so it had no visual similarity at all with the fifteenth-century tower-houses (Fig. 85). Detailed study of Ballymoon and two other castles in the same county, Ballyloughan and Clonmore, suggests that he was more-or-less correct in respect of its chronology: the architectural details which they share point to a date at the end of the thirteenth century for all three.[13] In giving Ballymoon a specific date of *c.*1310, Leask nudged it into the fourteenth century where its 'otherness' could be accommodated. He did not know who built it. The very clear evidence that it was left unfinished – the outer wall 'stops' at the same height almost all the way around, and there is a missing storey – allows one to suggest that its patron was Roger Bigod, earl of Norfolk, who died in 1306.[14] Why, then, being more or less contemporary with Greencastle (Donegal), was it not discussed in the previous chapter? The answer is given below.

Ballymoon's plan was intended to have four conjoined ranges of domestic spaces around a central courtyard. It appears that the rooms in each range were intended to be three storeys high, but with at least one exception: the great hall, placed above a (?demi-) basement, was to be the equivalent of two storeys in height (Fig. 86). The remains of toilet chutes in the wall-top all the way around the circuit of the castle suggest that the unbuilt upper floor was intended in places to match the floor beneath it. Planned patterns of movement around the castle are not known, but there is enough evidence to suggest a number of doors at first- and second-floor levels opening into

13 O'Keeffe 2001b.   **14** For the most recent analysis see O'Keeffe 2015, 237–40.

86 The great hall of Ballymoon Castle, with its double fireplace, and the principal chamber to its left. Note the sloping sills of the two hall windows: they give a good impression of how high the hall was intended to be. Ground level inside the castle is higher than on the outside, so those windows would have appeared very high off ground level when viewed from the outside.

the central courtyard, as well as step-up or step-down thresholds between conjoined rooms. Chambers – perhaps better described as lodgings – on the north-east and part of the south-east ranges were intended to have been two-storeyed above basement level (Fig. 87), so there must have been internal stairs, if only of wood. The cross-loops which line parts of three of the exterior walls speak of a martial function for Ballymoon. The windows intended for the unbuilt upper storey were going to be bigger perhaps – there is some small structural evidence that it was the plan – and more generous fenestration would have been intended for the walls on the courtyard side.

Ballymoon Castle was very unusual by the standards of *c*.1300 in the Angevin territories. It was designed with no gable-ended structures but, rather, as a continuous suite of rooms. There are no known parallels for it in Ireland at any period of the Middle Ages, and the closest parallels in England date from later in the fourteenth century. There, comparable schemes were developed within older castle enclosures, starting most systematically at Berkeley Castle (Gloucestershire) between 1326 and the

87 Small chambers, probably lodgings, inside Ballymoon Castle. The doorways lead to toilets; the chutes of toilets drop down within the wall thickness from the unbuilt upper floor, suggesting that floor was to mirror the one which survives in part today.

1340s, but the first *de novo* centrally-planned complex with a regular-plan courtyard, an upper hall, and a continuous suite of private apartments at first-floor level was at Windsor (Berkshire), built by Edward III in the third quarter of the fourteenth century.[15] Windsor's scale was very much larger and the comfort level considerably greater, but the principle was not very different from that at Ballymoon. Continuous suites of rooms around orthogonally-planned courtyards, with domestic activities starting at first-floor level, characterize a number of major new works in later fourteenth-century England, such as Bodiam (Sussex) and Wressle (Yorkshire). All of these had corner towers, giving them a rather old-fashioned and militarist gait. External appearance clearly mattered. But it mattered less at Ballymoon. It was essentially planned from the inside out: projecting toilet turrets were built where toilets were needed, denying the castle that visual symmetry on the outside which seems to have mattered to builders and patrons in England.

Of all the Irish castles discussed in this book, Ballymoon is the one which most needs excavation in order to be understood. Exposure of the buried remains of the inner wall – some are clearly there, below the grass – would illuminate to some extent the intended or permitted pattern of movement through the continuous suite, and that

15 For Berkeley see Emery 2006, 16, 58–66; for Windsor and its significance see ibid., 2016, 39.

would aid the comparison between Ballymoon and the relevant English castles. Artifacts might clarify its date – could it possibly be *later* fourteenth-century? – and illuminate the social connections and cultural affiliations of its patron. Left unfinished in a fairly isolated location, Ballymoon could not possibly have exerted any influence on any other Irish castle, but three of its features or aspects were signposts to the future. That puts it in the *conceptual* genealogy of the later medieval tower-houses, and it gives an added urgency to its excavation.

First, it is the earliest castle in Ireland in which we have evidence for accommodation for a large household (if not also guests), and the earliest to have been planned as such from the outset rather than created by accretion through time. Tower-houses – especially the large ones of southern Ireland – contained more domestic rooms than one finds in most Anglo-Norman castles in Ireland, and Ballymoon is the first castle in which we can see that multiplication of domestic spaces.

Second, the lodgings or private rooms were of consistent size in Ballymoon: some might have been longer than others, but they were all of the same width. Thus, the design of Ballymoon imposed some metrical restrictions on its domestic spaces. Tower-house designs made the same imposition. Those spaces were arranged horizontally at Ballymoon, but the ranks of the occupants, whether household members, retainers or guests, might have been reflected in their proximity to the great hall, itself bounded by the lord's chamber at one end. Such spaces were arranged vertically in tower-houses, where social rank might have been indicated by the proximity to the lord's chamber at the very top. But the principle is the same.

Third, like Ballymoon, tower-houses were generally planned from the inside out: windows, fireplaces and toilets were put where they were needed, even if they gave the towers an external asymmetry. It was not until the Elizabethan era that a desire for external symmetry, manifest in fenestration and chimneys, was allowed to shape the internal arrangements of a great residence. But castle-builders of the thirteenth century often made some attempt at symmetry, such as by placing towers at corners or in mid-wall positions. In its asymmetry, Ballymoon, despite its date, looks to the later medieval future, not to the Anglo-Norman past.

DEBATING THE ORIGINS OF TOWER-HOUSES

The upshot of a perceived century-long period of relative inactivity was, for many years, a perception of stylistic *discontinuity* between castles built before 1300 and those built after 1400. Leask treated the later castles – most of them tower-houses – as products of an indigenous tradition, unrelated to any architectural developments outside Ireland. This raised an issue which he did not address directly. If the later castles did not represent some continuity with the past, should they not therefore be products to some degree at least of external influence? How can they be explained if neither of these options is invoked? Leask had a novel solution. He identified the origins of the Irish tower-house in the so-called '£10 castle acts', early fifteenth-century acts of parliament authorizing the payment of a small amount of money to

88 The tower-house at Donore (Meath). Harold Leask described it as a 'very simple' building. This is misleading. It is a medium-sized tower-house for its region, four storeys high, with vaults over two of the storeys, all accessed by a spiral stairs in a small turret of round plan (to the right of the restored entrance doorway in the photograph). The external corners are rounded, which is not a common feature of towers in the Pale but is nonetheless found in all parts of it. To my knowledge, only two tower-houses with rounded corners within the four counties of the Pale are dated, both by inscribed stones: Athgoe (Dublin), which also has a round turret for the stairs, dates from 1579, and Blackwood (Kildare) dates from 1584. Donore's use of vaulting suggests it is not so late – vaulting seems to have gone out of fashion in Ireland after the mid-sixteenth century – but it might not be as early as Leask suggested. The tower-house at Causestown (Meath) seems to be the work of the same mason.

subjects of the crown in the English Pale who would build towers to certain dimensions.[16] The dimensions seem to have permitted only small towers of simple rectangular plan, allowing him to postulate a development of the tower-house from that simple form in the English Pale towards more complex configurations later and elsewhere. Thus, the parliamentary offer of a grant provided, in his account, both a stimulus for the start of a tradition and a template for an actual structural type. Inconveniently, none of the small number of castles documented in subsequent records of the dispersal of grants actually survives, so Leask identified a possible undocumented example in the field: Donore (Meath). This quite unexceptional tower-house then found itself garlanded with National Monument status, its broken features restored (Fig. 88). Today, the '£10 castle acts' are not regarded as particularly significant.[17] The amount of money offered was too small to allow an individual landowner to dream of building a castle if he could not afford one anyway. It was also too small to persuade any wealthy landowner intending to build a castle to make any change in design.

Leask's theory that the tower-house developed in response to parliamentary acts was inherently problematic. The acts make no reference to vaulting, for example, but almost all the surviving tower-houses of the Pale region – none of them '£10 castles' – had lower storey vaults, even though they were not needed for structural stability. Yet, Leask's core assumption that function determined form has found some support through the years. Terry Barry claimed, for example, that it is 'logical to view this phenomenon of *defensive* towers as being an *afforable* response to meet local security requirements'; he suggested the possibility of tower-houses developing independently in different places, a model which he described as one of 'multi-lateral evolution', and, as Leask had done implicitly, he rejected the possibility of external influence in that process.[18] Conrad Cairns, Barry's former student, had previously expressed a rather similar view on the matter of external influence, writing that 'discussion about where people in Ireland got the idea of tower houses... is rather unnecessary, because the small tower is so obvious a device, and occurs so often in areas where there was a lack of security and small-scale war, that it must have been invented independently in many countries'.[19]

In the 1990s, the identification of the thirteenth-century 'hall-house' changed how the origin of the tower-house as a type was understood. In a short paper in 1992, Tom McNeill discussed the case for identifying the tower-house as an indigenous type, as Leask had viewed it, and he claimed that the case depended on the identification of the 'hall-house'.[20] Ultimately, he left the question of tower-house origins unanswered, despite the title of his paper, but he reduced the solution to two options: the tower-houses either 'developed out of the stone hall houses of the lesser thirteenth-century lords', or they were 'introductions of the fourteenth century, chamber towers without

---

16 Leask 1951, 76–7. Bradley and Murtagh 2003, 212.   **17** Although see Sweetman 1999, 137.
18 Barry 1995, 223; emphasis added.   **19** Cairns 1987, 9–10; for a restatement of the view that the development of the tower-house needs to be understood in the context of endemic warfare in later medieval Ireland see Barry 2004.   **20** McNeill 1992, 13.

the accompanying halls'. He did not deal with the apparent contradiction here: how could the tower-house, if it was a *chamber* tower, evolve out of the '*hall*-house'? He then framed as a question the two options which he had laid out: 'do [the tower-houses] represent simply the way of life of the thirteenth-century gentry in hall houses carrying on and becoming widespread [in the late Middle Ages] or are they something new, a new life for new lords?'[21]

McNeill's paper was a short contribution to the debate, but it heavily influenced later commentaries by persuading those interested in tower-house origins that they needed to address the role of the 'hall-house' in some way. It took a decade for some suggestions to emerge. David Sweetman suggested in 2003 that the 'hall-house' had diffused eastwards from Connacht, which he believed to be its place of origin, into Leinster, where it developed into the tower-house and from where it began to diffuse back to the west.[22] Prehistorians once engaged in such flights of diffusionary fancy about types of tomb, but it is strange to see such an interpretation offered in recent times for documented monuments of medieval culture. More recently, Rory Sherlock, citing an example of the complex-plan, early fifteenth-century, tower-house of Claregalway (Galway) as evidence, used the 'hall-house' to offer some support to Terry Barry's earlier theory of 'multi-lateral evolution': believing an early fifteenth-century date to be an 'early' date for a tower-house in western Ireland, he wrote that the date 'seems to indicate that large, early tower houses in the west evolved directly from earlier hall houses in that region and may owe little or nothing to smaller, contemporary tower houses in the Pale'.[23]

For many scholars today, the early speculations of McNeill, Sweetman and Barry would now mainly be of historiographic interest, because in the past decade the Royal Irish Academy, no less, has twice given its imprimatur to Rory Sherlock's interpretation of domestic space in tower-houses, and that interpretation gives a place to the 'hall-house' in the story of tower-house origins.[24] The central premise of Sherlock's work, basically, is that tower-houses contained halls, and that the towers represent continuity with the earlier 'hall-houses', which he believes to have contained halls also. 'We can argue very strongly', he wrote, 'that Irish tower houses were a largely Insular development that sprung *in some way* from earlier hall houses and which were designed to facilitate more complex social environments than the simpler hall houses could accommodate'.[25] In some tower-houses, he argues, the hall was retained at first-floor level, where he and others believe it to have been in the 'hall-houses', but with private rooms arranged above. But in medium and larger towers, he argues, the hall was moved to the top storey, to the room which was open to the roof, and that the private rooms were placed underneath the hall (Fig. 89): 'the builders of Irish tower houses in the fifteenth century prioritized the central hearth and open roof space as critical elements of hall design and so, when building tower houses that were taller and had more rooms than the hall houses that preceded them, Irish builders facilitated these

---

21 Ibid., 14.   22 Sweetman 2003, 131–2. Tom Finan has suggested that the 'hall house' at Kilteasheen (Roscommon) is in the tower-house ancestry (2015, 27).   23 Sherlock 2015, 87. 24 Sherlock 2011a; 2014b.   25 Sherlock 2015, 87; emphasis added.

89 The tower-house in Garbally (Galway) was extant in 1504, so it dates from the fifteenth century; it is probably post-1450 to judge by its architectural detailing. Note the large room at the top, above the vault.

priorities by locating the extra chambers *beneath* the hall'.[26] Elsewhere, he expresses the distinction between first-floor and upper-floor halls in tower-houses as having a geographical basis: 'typically, western tower houses had a top-floor hall carried on a vault with private accommodation below it, while eastern tower houses often had a first- or second-floor hall with private accommodation above it. In this way, tower

26 Sherlock 2011a, 133; emphasis added. See also O'Conor 2014a, 343: in tower-houses 'the hall tended to be located on the uppermost level'.

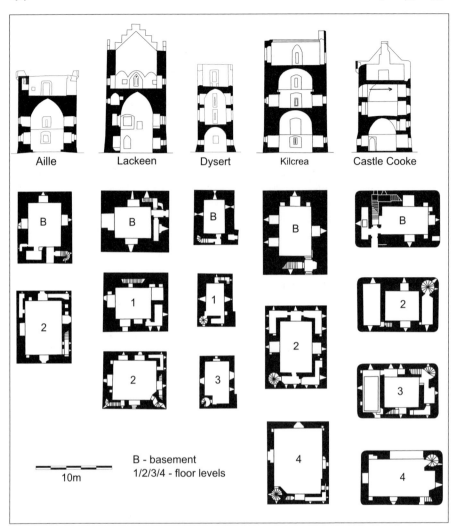

90 Cross-sections and plans of the tower-houses at Aille, Lackeen, Dysert, Kilcrea, and Castle Cooke.

houses in the east of Ireland are comparable to Scottish examples, while those in western areas appear to represent a distinctly Irish form.'[27]

I suggest respectfully that this interpretation is incorrect. My view is that the tower-houses were entirely chamber towers, and that they never contained halls in the sense that *aula* had a specific meaning in the Middle Ages. The top-floor rooms were not halls but principal chambers. They were elevated to positions of maximum privacy. With their larger-than-average windows, they allowed the best views of the landscape.

[27] Sherlock 2014b, 355.

They were, themselves, visible from afar, rising above the roofs of the other castle buildings.[28]

Five towers out of the many hundreds which survive are used here as examples to illustrate the point. Two of them are three-storeyed (Aille and Lackeen), one of them is four-storeyed (Dysert), and two of them are five-storeyed (Kilcrea and Castle Cooke) (Fig. 90).[29] In each of these cases, the upper floor has a vault beneath it and was open to the roof, so each of these would be regarded as having a top-floor hall in the Sherlock model. There are three reasons to reject that interpretation for these towers, and for others like them. First, the top-floor rooms were at the ends of spiral or dog-legged stairs, often narrow and poorly lit, which made them unsuitable for the public functions of halls.[30] Second, in Angevin culture the hall was normally a ground-floor space, and while the first-floor hall was not unknown between the late eleventh and fifteenth centuries,[31] it was never at third- or fourth-floor level. Third, and most decisively, nowhere in medieval architectural culture, Angevin or otherwise, were the private rooms of a household ever layered *under* a public room, requiring them to be by-passed by those going to the hall. As a final comment, one of the pillars of the arguments that tower-houses had halls was the thesis that Scottish tower-houses contained halls, but Scottish castellologists no longer think this is the case and now regard their tower-houses as residential structures.[32] With that buttress removed, the Sherlock model is left as a proposition of Irish exceptionalism, and there is no need for that. Ironically, Sherlock is correct in positing that the upper room of the 'hall-house' migrated to the top of the tower-house. But it migrated upwards *as a chamber*. That was not exceptional; that was normal.

THE ASCENT OF THE TOWER-HOUSE

There is variation in tower-house design, but within a fairly narrow spectrum of options. Two common (though by no means universal) patterns within that variability help to illuminate the ancestry of these towers in thirteenth-century architecture.

First, it is not unusual to find, especially in Munster, that the stairs ascends as a straight flight immediately to the left of the entrance, before turning into a (clockwise) spiral at first-floor level (as at Dysert and Kilcrea, for example). The first floor thus marked the 'start' of the building. One can see it on the outside of tower-houses, without even entering. At Gortmakellis (Tipperary), for example, built in the sixteenth

---

28 As Dixon and Lott have written of the northern English chamber towers, 'the emphasis [was] on the signalling out of the lord's apartments above the roofs of an adjacent range of buildings' (1993, 95). **29** Eadie 2010; O'Keeffe 2013–14; 2014c; the documentary evidence is laid out in O'Keeffe 2015, 262–72. The cross-sections are adapted from Salter 2004a; 2004b; 2004c. **30** Gillian Eadie has noted that kitchens are generally absent from tower-houses (Eadie 2015a, 10), whereas they normally accompanied halls for prandial convenience, making the carriage of food from outside the tower to the top floor of the tower even more unlikely. **31** Hill and Gardiner 2018; Emery 2016, 39. **32** The seminal work is Tabraham 1988; see also Stell 2011, 19–24; Oram 2012; 2015a.

91 Gortmakellis Castle (Tipperary). The round-arched windows and the manner in which the gables are flush with the walls (rather than concealed behind parapets) indicate a sixteenth-century date.

century, the doorway is on the right-hand side of the entrance wall, thus creating a 'run-up' to the corner where the spiral stairs begins at first-floor level, as indicated on the outside by the stack of small windows on the left-hand side of the tower (Fig. 91).

Second, and encountered far more commonly, three features or parts of tower-houses – the entrances to the towers, the stairs giving access upwards, and the small rooms which were ancillary to the big rooms – are frequently contained within notional structural units of their own, rising through the heights of the towers. In towers where this is the case, each floor is divided into two spaces in a 2+:1 ratio, with the larger part being the main floor space. This scheme is found most often in towers where the stairs ascend to the left of the main entrance, as in the towers of Dysert and Kilcrea, but it is also common to towers where one finds the stairs to the right of the main door, as at Aille and Lackeen, or (as is actually very rare) directly in front of the doorway, as at Castle Cooke. In earlier donjons, a fore-building or a flight of external steps provided the access to the habitable spaces. Tower-houses did not have fore-buildings, but one could say that the fore-building's equivalent in the late Middle Ages was effectively *inside* the tower-house: it was the narrow space in the 2+:1 ratio.

In the tower-houses of the east coast of Ireland, especially in the English Pale, the arrangement is slightly different. The stairs are generally spiral-form from ground level up, and are commonly in projecting turrets. There is, therefore, no sense of an internal fore-building in any of these towers, nor is there any change in the character of the stairs to suggest that the habitational zone started at first-floor level. But one can still argue that the first-floor level had a particular status in these east coast towers. A recurring feature of Pale tower-houses in particular is the vaulted basement, which gives the first-floor room a stone floor. That vault was often the only vault in one of these buildings. The basement did not need to be vaulted for structural reasons, so it was a design option. The important point is that, despite differences in how their stairs and vaults were arranged relative to elsewhere on the island, the tower-houses of the Pale and other parts of eastern Ireland maintained the first-floor level as an important horizontal register, and so they, like the towers in southern Ireland, continued the tradition established in the thirteenth century.

There are, of course, important differences between the rectangular Anglo-Norman donjons of the thirteenth century and the later tower-houses. First, the tower-house basements were accessible at ground level, whereas in the earlier buildings they were normally only accessible from above. Second, there were no doors to bar progression upwards at first-floor level in the tower-houses, whereas in the earlier buildings the doors which controlled all movement were at that very level. Finally, there were no strong external indications in tower-houses that their first-floor levels had any special significance, whereas in the earlier buildings the foreworks or external steps communicated that very point. Nevertheless, the principle was the same: the habitational spaces in all the buildings being discussed here, regardless of date, began at the first floor.

FORMAL SOURCES

The suggestion that the Irish tower-house contained private space and was therefore an elaboration of the earlier chamber provision does not answer questions of formal origin. Where did the idea of building multi-storeyed chamber towers come from? Where did the actual designs come from?

One can see a line of descent – 'ascent', more accurately – from the two-storeyed chamber tower of the thirteenth century to the tower-house, as was discussed above.

But this is not an explanation. In any case, some features in the tower-houses were not developed from earlier, thirteenth-century, features. For example, long spiral stairs were infrequent, and original vaulting was extremely rare, in the thirteenth-century towers. Now, one might trace features such as these back to ecclesiastical architecture in Ireland, to monuments such as the crossing tower in the early fourteenth-century Carmelite priory church in Castlelyons (Cork), for example, which has both spiral stairs and vaulting. But to do so would be to relocate the problem of the origins of such features to a context where the castellologist does not need to deal with it. It would not resolve the issue of when or why such features were then used in castles.

The critical observation we should make is that the tower-house appeared fully formed in Ireland around 1400. The date of *c*.1400 for Barryscourt in particular, but also the early fifteenth-century date for Claregalway, both from radiocarbon dating (see above, pp 185, 192), are sufficient to show that the type did not evolve from simple to complex. That is not to say that there was no internal, insular, development or innovation thereafter. But the genesis of the tower-house as a type must surely have owed *some* debt to buildings outside Ireland. This is a critical point: it is only by postulating some external influence that the appearance of 'mature' tower-houses around 1400 in Ireland – towers erected by builders with the requisite skills for patrons who knew what they wanted – can be reconciled with the evidence for a hiatus in the previous century in Ireland.

Tower-building was universal in later medieval Europe, so those Irish-born who travelled abroad would have encountered towers almost everywhere. In the absence of evidence for significant in-migration from overseas, that outside influence was carried to Ireland by those who travelled from Ireland and returned, as elites or as merchants, or it was brought to Ireland by overseas merchants and was first manifest in coastal locations.[33] Speculation of such vagueness is frustrating but unavoidable.

Those who were of English descent in Ireland are the most likely to have understood how towers 'worked' as residential spaces, having come from a culture in which towers already featured as chamber accommodation. That would lead one to suspect that tower-houses first appeared in areas dominated by the descendants of the invaders. The distribution of the towers probably bears that out: tower-houses are found in every part of Ireland, but the heaviest concentrations are in the counties of south Leinster (Wexford and Kilkenny), east and north Munster (Cork, Tipperary, and Limerick), and south Connacht (Galway), all contiguous and all within the area of the former Anglo-Norman lordship. Northern Leinster (the former English Pale counties of Kildare, Dublin, Meath and Louth) also has high numbers, but areas of mountain and bog detach the north Leinster cluster from the more expansive tower-house zone further south. The only part of Gaelic Ireland where tower-houses had a high density is Co. Clare, which was contiguous with the former lordship areas of Limerick,

---

33 McAlister (2019) shows how later medieval Ireland was connected economically to a wider world, and she discusses the role of tower-houses in the economic network, but does not address – in fairness, her book is not an architectural history – the evidence for and against outside influence on the architecture.

Tipperary and Galway. This national distribution pattern – tower-houses are most common in southern Ireland – has implications for the tracing of sources outside Ireland.

Of the places geographically close to Ireland, England is perhaps the most unlikely to have played a direct role in the very earliest history of the Irish tower-house, given both the relative infrequency of towers there and the differences between many of them and many of the Irish towers. There are certainly some northern English towers, as at the two Northumbrian castles of Edlingham and Etal,[34] in which one can identify (often earlier) variations on what one encounters in Ireland, and one could argue that they should be considered relevant to Ireland because the circumstances of their construction compare to some degree with the tower-houses of the English Pale. But a link is unlikely. The comparisons are not so strong that one feels obligated to identify possible processes of transmission: there was no obvious agent – the crown, or any great family – to carry ideas from one border region to another.

Scotland is the other candidate across the Irish Sea. There, the tower-house tradition started in the fourteenth century. The Scottish tower-houses compare quite well with the Irish tower-houses, and some compare better than others. A small number of examples suffices to make the point. A good example is the tower at Smailholm (Roxburghshire).[35] Its stepped gables and small flat-topped windows are distinctively Scottish, but the essence of its plan can be paralleled in Ireland. It is unmistakeably a chamber tower, with the castle's more public (and prandial) functions being accommodated in external buildings on the site. Also capable of being paralleled in Ireland in some regards is the tower at Cardoness (Kirkcudbrightshire).[36] This is five storeys high with a vault over the two lower storeys. The entrance is in a long wall, whereas in Ireland it was normally in a short wall, but there was an entrance lobby, with the stairs on one side and a small guardroom on the other.[37] Less comparable in its internal layout with anything encountered in Ireland is the tower at Lochleven (Kinrossshire).[38] Here, the residential space starts at first-floor level, above a vaulted basement, but the mode of access from the outside to the first-floor level is unparalleled in Ireland. That first-floor room is also vaulted; consecutive vaults over consecutive rooms is not a feature found in Ireland, but it is found elsewhere in Scotland, as at Castle Campbell (Clackmannanshire).[39] That room at Lochleven was apparently a kitchen. Food could be served to the room above – accessible by a corner spiral stairs, as one finds in Ireland – through a hatch, suggesting that it was a room used for eating, even if it was not a hall as conventionally understood. The room above that again at Lochleven was clearly private (complete with a small oratory) and is the equivalent of the upper-storey chamber in Ireland. A small kitchen is found in the upper level of a projecting tower at Craigmillar (Edinburgh), indicating another room used for eating.[40]

Despite some of the positive comparisons just outlined, there is one very good reason why Scotland should not be regarded as pivotal to the development of the Irish

---

34 Dixon 1992, 89–90; Nelson 1998.   **35** Tabraham 1993b.   **36** Grove 1996.   **37** Grove 1996.
38 Tabraham 1994.   **39** Cruden 1999.   **40** Pringle 1996.

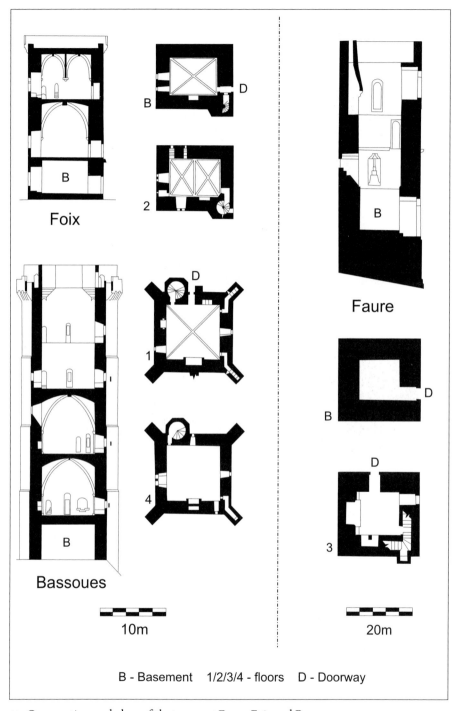

92 Cross-sections and plans of the towers at Faure, Foix and Bassoues.

93 The tower at Fouras.

tower-house. Its historical connections were with Ulster, a part of Ireland with relatively low numbers of towers, few of them complex structures. It is barely conceivable, both for historical and geographical reasons, that the complex designs of tower-houses in southern Ireland from early in the fifteenth century came from Scotland, or even developed from ideas that were first developed in Scotland.

So, if not from England or Scotland, could a formative inspiration for the Irish tower-house sequence have come from France, directly south of the part of Ireland where the number of towers in Ireland is greatest? Jean Mesqui argued that the third quarter of the fourteenth century, especially the peaceful decade-long (1360–70) interruption of the wars, was transformative in the history of the *tour-résidence* in France. He described the great royal tower of Vincennes (Val-de-Marne) from 1361 as the first complex, inclusive, *tour-résidence* to have been built in France in a long time.[41] Initially the preserve of the royal house, tower-building trickled down to lower social

41 Mesqui 1991, 145. Dixon and Lott mention Pierrefonds (Oise) as another example of a great tower of *c*.1360 (1993, 95), but see now Mesqui 2008, 203–4.

levels in France as the fourteenth century gave way to the fifteenth. From the end of the fourteenth century, towers comparable to some degree with those in Ireland were not uncommon (Fig. 92).[42]

We might pay special attention to the fourteenth- and fifteenth-century towers of south-west France, a region long connected with Ireland. The tower at Fouras (Charente-Maritime), for example, with two lower vaulted rooms (Fig. 93), was on the coast, which was precisely the sort of location where it would be seen by merchants or aristocrats travelling to France from Ireland. Moving inland, the tower of Larrouquette in Plieux (Gers), for example, dated by Salch to the fourteenth century but by Séraphin to the thirteenth,[43] has its main residential room at the top of a stack of plainer rooms. It is not unlike what one finds in Ireland. It is also one of many French towers with dual entrances, a feature known in southern Ireland.[44] To cite another example, the tower in the castle of Herrebouc in St-Jean-Poudge (Gers), first mentioned in 1344, has a vaulted lower storey, and stairs and small rooms are partitioned off to create a 2:1 ratio of spaces on the inside;[45] the vaulting arrangement is not common in southern Ireland, but the partitioning of the rooms and stairs in a 2:1 ratio recalls larger southern Irish tower-houses. The case for French influence in the genesis of the tower-house in southern Ireland is moderately strong.

WHY? FROM OBSERVATION TO EXPLANATION

The narrative in which the simple, single-pile, two-storeyed chamber tower of the thirteenth century elongated vertically to become the tower-house of the late Middle Ages is not unique to Ireland in its basic storyline, even if it is unique in its details. But a narrative is not an explanation. *Why* did the nature and positioning of the chamber change?

Chamber accommodation in the castles of Angevin culture had been fairly restricted in a spatial sense for most of the period into the fourteenth century. Ireland was no different from England in that regard. The residential footprint increased in some royal works in England during the reigns of Henry III and Edward I, particularly in the palaces, but it generally remained restricted otherwise. In mid-to-late thirteenth-century Ireland, the royal castles, whether new (Roscommon) or long-founded (Dublin), probably had above-average residential provisions by the national standard, but none was exceptionally well-provided with chamber space, probably because the kings were not planning to visit. The baronial castles in Ireland – the unfinished Ballymoon excepted – were not designed to provide much residential space, at least in stone.

A change in the treatment of chamber space can be detected in England in the fourteenth century, both in new works built at older castles and in brand new castles.

---

42 For Faure (Lot) see Séraphin 2006. For Foix (Ariège) and Bassoues (Gers) see Mesqui 1992, 146, 149.   **43** Salch 1979, 910; Séraphin 1999, 14.   **44** Sherlock 2006, 74–8.   **45** Gardelles 1970.

94 Baldongan Castle in the late eighteenth century. The end-buildings are clearly late medieval, but features depicted in the building between them suggest a thirteenth-century hall.

The chamber enlarged from what it had been, even into the reign of Edward I. That enlargement took many forms, but, as Matthew Johnson observed, 'underlying [the] apparent diversity there is a common spatial ordering'.[46]

The enlargement most often involved changes on the horizontal plane: chamber-blocks were extended laterally or, in more ambitious plans, new buildings were built to line new courtyards and were given over entirely to private, residential, use. Sometimes, however, the enlargement involved the building of towers to contain the chambers. In some instances, as at Wardour (Wiltshire) and Warkworth

46 Johnson 2007, 68.

(Northumberland), the courtyard plan was essentially compressed to give the impression of a massive tower.[47] The preferred option in northern England from the mid-fourteenth century was the free-standing residential tower, as at Etal (Northumberland), dated 1341.[48] Towers were also built further south in England in more secure settings, such as the five-storeyed tower-house of Tattershal Castle (Lincolnshire), built in the 1440s by Ralph, Lord Cromwell.[49] Speaking of Tattershal, Anthony Emery has noted how it was a private space into which the family could retreat directly from the adjacent great hall, whereas in the same Lord Cromwell's residence at Wingfield, the tower of *c*.1450, also five storeys high, was beside two ranges of lodgings but separate from the hall.[50] Here is a simple example of variability in the residences of a single powerful individual.

In Ireland, the tower-house was also the favoured setting for accommodating private space in castles from around 1400, and there was also a clear preference for keeping the tower physically separate from the hall in the manner seen at Wingfield. But it should be noted that there are some exceptions to this in Ireland. Occasionally a hall block was adjacent to a tower, in the manner seen in some fourteenth-century Scottish castles, such as Doune (Stirlingshire),[51] and in some instances the hall was flanked by residential and service structures in the H-plan arrangement found in English houses.[52] The example most English in character is Athcarne (Meath), but the first-floor hall and the transverse wing, both now demolished, were late sixteenth-century additions to a tower-house. At Baldongan, now demolished but best known from two late eighteenth-century drawings,[53] a first-floor hall of possible thirteenth-century date was flanked in the late Middle Ages by a transverse wing at one end and by a pair of towers at the other (Fig. 94). The fifteenth-century hall-and-chamber blocks at Killeen and Dunsany (both Meath) are heavily modernized but seem to have been of related form. As a final example, the neglected Liscartan (Meath) had a hall flanked by complex towers of different dates within the later Middle Ages. On the whole, though, as I have discussed at length elsewhere, as soon as these tall chamber towers appeared in Irish castles in the fifteenth century, the (mainly detached) halls diminished in size.[54]

The explanation for the transformation of the chamber in the fourteenth and fifteenth centuries lies mainly in the enlargement of the medieval household. In brief, in Angevin culture the great household comprised two groups.[55] The first group was the permanent staff. This had three senior officerships: the stewart, who had oversight of the entire domestic aparatus, the treasurer, who kept the accounts, and the chamberlain, who took responsibility for the lord's private chamber as both a physical

47 Dixon and Lott 1993, 95.   **48** Emery 1996a, 91–2, 159. The popularity of the tower-house in the north was probably linked to the dangers inherent in a border with Scotland, but it was also a signifier of wealth and status for those who had fought against the Scots and wanted their architecture to be a reminder of their military achievements and of their determination to remain domiciled in the border region (King 2007).   **49** For a description see Emery 1996b, 308–16. For a discussion see Johnson 2007, 55–67.   **50** Emery 1996b, 351.   **51** See Oram 2012.   **52** See, for example, Cooper 1999, 76, 82, 98.   **53** Grose 1791, between 8 and 9.   **54** O'Keeffe 2014c.   **55** The literature is extensive. See, for example, Herlihy 1985, and Woolgar 1999.

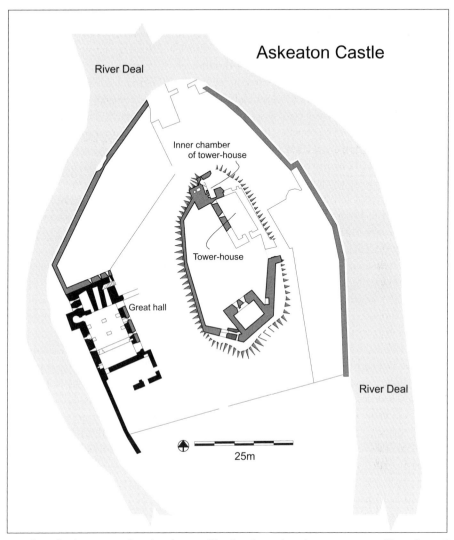

95 Plan of Askeaton Castle. The phasing, like the plan, is based on Tom McNeill's reading of the ruins, but I think that the walling of the inner courtyard, which is on a low rock, is partly thirteenth-century in date, giving the layout of the castle a resemblance to Adare (see Fig. 38), which in turn might point to Askeaton having pre-Norman origins. Whatever the case, in the late Middle Ages this castle was unusually well-provided with accommodation by the standards of the period in Ireland.

space and an institutional concept. The permanent staff would include the chaplain, wardrober, valets, pages, manual servants, and so on. The second group was the retainers. These were generally men of lower authority who were heads of household in their own right. Their presence as supporters enhanced the lord's own authority. Retainers could also be men whose training or experience was of some practical or political value in certain contexts. Retainers resided more temporarily, but their status demanded high-quality residential space, and so they tended to be provided with individual lodgings with separate entrances (which is possibly what we observe at Ballymoon). The documentary record provides evidence that household size increased to its largest in England in the first half of the fourteenth century – not coincidentally, a period of diminished royal authority under Edward II (†1327) – before falling back after the Black Death.[56] That increase in household size coincides with the enlargement of the footprint of residential, or chamber, space. A reduction in the number of properties held by and maintained by powerful lords was also a factor in the expansion of the chamber: power concentrated in individual places rather than dispersed among multiple properties increased the need for households to be accommodated in the one location.

The circumstances which explain the increase in chamber space in England are not documented explicitly in Ireland. There is, anyway, a scarcity of information on households in Ireland before the early modern period. But the great seigneurial castles of the late Middle Ages – the ones which were central to the great earldom and lordship hegemonies – do seem to have had fairly complex and hierarchical households, comparable perhaps with those of contemporary Scotland, where the evidence is better.[57] The largest and most complex single structure in the stock of late medieval castles in Ireland, early fifteenth-century Bunratty (Clare), was evidently designed for multiple occupancies. Analysis of its layout, based on Rory Sherlock's detailed account, suggests that its main floor space (commonly identified as the great hall) was courtyard-like: the upper parts of the four corner towers were accessed from it, with two of the four designed internally to be small tower-houses in their own right.[58] The late sixteenth-century evidence from the later medieval earldom of Desmond, in Munster, is also especially valuable. Askeaton, for example, had two courtyards and 'a large hall, a great chamber, 3 cellars, a kitchen and other necessary places and bedrooms'.[59] The 'large hall' was in the outer courtyard and was a remodelled thirteenth-century structure. The 'great chamber' was the large, now broken, tower-house in the middle of the castle (Fig. 95), its main upper floor serving as some form of audience chamber or presence chamber, akin to that which occupies the second-storey level at Barryscourt (Fig. 96).[60] Askeaton was a large residential complex evidently equipped for a large household. The same can be said of Castleisland (Kerry). Almost completely destroyed, this had two courtyards, two chambers over the main gateway, a hall, a parlour with 'low' chambers above it and another chamber at one end of it, a great dining chamber, a buttery and pantry and various cellars, and a chapel with chambers

---

56 Woolgar 1999, 15.   **57** See Oram 2015b, 233–6.   **58** Sherlock 2011b; O'Keeffe 2015, 85–6.
59 CELT: The Desmond Survey 1598: 156, ¶418.   **60** McNeill 2010, 180; O'Keeffe 2015, 273; 2017, 234–5. To my mind, the building history of Barryscourt is still not resolved, *contra* Pollock and Manning 2017 (see originally Monk and Tobin 1991; O'Keeffe 1997b). The wall between the northern tower and the main block at first-floor level has a curious arrangement of mural passages that requires explanation rather than just noting, and the need for a first-floor entrance (later blocked) into the former is not explained. The running of the first-floor chimney flue out the side wall of the tower is unusual for a feature purported to be original, and the doorway off the main stair into that same level sits awkwardly relative to the steps and robs the stairway of an uninterrupted run from ground level to the great reception room at second-floor level.

96 The room at second-floor level in the tower of Barryscourt Castle. Although it has the features of a great hall, it is higher within the building than was normal for halls, and the castle has an external hall anyway.

and lodging above.[61] Newcastle West (Limerick) had a courtyard with 'a round tower at every angle with divers places and rooms in every tower' and inside the courtyard there was 'a great hall, large chamber, very good rooms'. Some of the buildings survive.[62] A final example is Mallow (Cork), where, prior to destruction, there were two courtyards, a tower, and a hall to which was attached a smaller tower with rooms for lodgings.[63]

Although these records mention courtyards, these enclosed spaces seem to have been walled areas within which (and sometimes against the walls of which) were various structures. They were not formally planned courts, in other words. The English surveyors who observed these complexes seem to have been rather unfamiliar with the patterns, because they deployed a more limited vocabulary than they presumably had from their own experiences of elite domestic architecture at home. But the descriptions do provide one useful hint: the surveyors did not perceive these complexes to be dominated by single towers. The description of Mallow is the exception. Askeaton *had* a dominant tower of complex plan, but the surveyors did not describe it as a tower. The sense one gets, in other words, is of residential complexes in which the social topography was organized on the horizontal level as much as the vertical.

61 NLI MS 7861, fols 175v, 176; see Fenlon 2011, 144.   **62** Tietzsch-Tyler 2011.   **63** Berry 1893.

The Munster complexes might well have been indigenous creations, in the sense that the builders simply put the buildings they needed for their large households in the places that seemed most convenient. That would seem the most likely explanation. But it is not inconceivable that they had some knowledge of residential complexes outside Ireland. Medieval Scottish royal residences, for example, such as Dunfermline (Fife), Falkland (Fife) and Stirling (Stirlingshire), provide interesting parallels in the sense that they, as John Dunbar noted, had 'no particular building type or layout' prescribed.[64] But we might again look from Munster to France rather than to Scotland, for it was far more accessible from the south coast of Ireland. In some regions of south-west France, the lords' most private lodgings were usually kept separate from the towers which, though private too, offered some communal hospitality, while in other regions of the south-west the lodgings and towers were combined in single units.[65] The late sixteenth-century descriptions of some Munster castles suggest a similar diversity of combinations of towers and lodgings, so it is possible that some knowledge of French architectural practice filtered into the Desmond world through the south coast ports.

Castles like Askeaton and Mallow were apparently exceptional in late medieval Ireland. Their households were big, reflecting the scale of the authority of their owners. But the great majority of castles in post-1400 Ireland were far less complex. They presented a simple binary distinction between the *aula* and the *camera*: the hall and chamber were separate buildings in those castles, and there were no other residential spaces. Many of those who built these less complex castles after 1400 must have come from families which had never owned castles previously. Many of the tower-house builders had, therefore, no inherited households, nor any direct experience of the composition of a household in contemporary English society. So, those collectives which formed *de facto* households in Ireland's late medieval castles did not include the types of officer, or retainer, or even servant, which would have been found in an elite English residence of the same period. Rather, they were almost certainly, as Gillian Eadie has suggested, familial collectives:[66] the family was the household. Such intimacy reduced the need for the types of barriers and valves which, in domestic English architecture, controlled the interaction between grades of officers, servants and retainers, and gave that architecture its complexity.

CONCLUSION

The one period of the Middle Ages in which Ireland's encastellated landscape most resembled that of contemporary Europe was the fifteenth century: it was the century when free-standing domestic towers proliferated. The Irish towers conform to a general European type, and some influence from Europe – from France specifically – is likely to explain both their emergence in the first instance (around 1400) and their internal planning, although the latter appears to have been shaped to a considerable degree by the influence of the organization of space in earlier, thirteenth-century,

64 Dunbar 2002.   **65** Séraphin 1999.   **66** Eadie 2015b.

donjons in Ireland. Whatever the original source(s), once established in the early fifteenth century the tower-house became 'Irish'; it is difficult to identify evidence that the tower-house tradition remained actively shaped by tower-building traditions outside Ireland before the mid-sixteenth century at the earliest. Later towers, not discussed in this book, might sometimes reflect the influence of Renaissance military architecture in their use of, say, diagonally opposed corner turrets, and some reflect (in the decoration of their fireplace-surrounds, for example) a more aesthetic input from the Renaissance, but there is a striking insularity to the tower-building tradition for the 150 or so years before that happens.

It has long been popular to think of the encastellation of Ireland with tower-houses as evidence of endemic late medieval turmoil. But the historical record does not support any claim that Ireland was an especially dangerous place in the late Middle Ages, even if competing polities sometimes took up arms against each other, and even if parts of the island were at times hotbeds of general, essentially apolitical, lawlessness. The architecture of the later castles undermines any claim that encastellation was motivated by fear. Few later castles in Ireland would have withstood any sustained attack; fewer were ever faced with the prospect. On the contrary, the towers indicate relative wealth. Their very existence is testimony to that: families hitherto unable to afford to build residences in stone began to invest in substantial buildings. A question for the future, to be addressed by social historians and archaeologists together, is whether the emergence of the tower-house brought about a change in how the household was conceptualized and organized in Ireland. Was the tower as a residential type adopted so readily after 1400 because changes in the constitution of households were then underway? Or did the emergence of the tower-house effect changes in domestic life at elite levels?

CHAPTER 6

Conclusion

Castellology has been flourishing in Ireland since the 1980s. Its maturing as a discipline was marked by the appearance of the major works of synthesis by Tom McNeill and David Sweetman in the late 1990s. Recent years have seen a significant increase in the number of publications on castles in Ireland, and noticeably by a larger cohort of individual researchers, many of them former students of castellologists working in the Irish university sector. After several decades mainly outside the loop, the enrolment of Ireland in the pan-European conversation on castles is indicated by the inclusion of many Irish researchers in the biennial Château Gaillard conference on castellology.

But discussion of the international context of castles in Ireland has been consistently missing from most of the literature generated in Ireland in the past few decades. Among the archaeologists whose principal focus is the archaeology of castles, Tom McNeill has really been alone in seeking to explain Irish evidence by reference to non-Irish evidence. My book has attempted a more systematic pursuit of the relationships between castle-building in Ireland and overseas. It has presented a map of the ebb and flow of influence into Ireland from outside, and I have plotted on that map the very few occasions when castle-building in Ireland *might* itself have been influential beyond the island.

The book started and finished with uncertainty. Prior to 1169, when experienced castle-builders from a land of heavy encastellation arrived in Ireland, the only firm evidence for castles on the island is provided by the annalists who documented a small number of sites between the 1120s and 1160s. We can be thankful that those annalists used the word 'castle'. However, we do not know if they could have chosen to use that word in other instances and with respect to other monuments. Rather than allow the annalists the only voice on the matter, I have used a combination of indirect, circumstantial and comparative evidence to make the case for more extensive pre-Norman encastellation than any other researchers have allowed. Scholars of a conservative disposition will perhaps – almost certainly? – reject the lengthy argument that I made. To my mind, there are really only two ways of addressing the question of native pre-1169 encastellation. One is to stick firmly to the evidence and to draw from the testimony of the annalists the conclusion that, apart from a few western outliers, the Irish did not know much about castles before the Anglo-Normans gave them a dramatic crash-course. The other, which I favour, is to think contextually, even imaginatively, but to do so informed by knowledge of evidence and its interpretation outside Ireland.

A different type of uncertainty pervades the end of the story presented here. Castle-building was widespread in the late Middle Ages in Ireland. The island's encastellated landscape from the start of the fifteenth century until deep into the sixteenth resembled that in many parts of Europe. And that is the very source of the uncertainty. It can be no coincidence that towers are found almost everywhere in medieval Europe, but what were the processes by which many different fourteenth-century European societies, following a sustained period of experimentation with other forms, converged on the tower as both the preferred domestic form and the preferred signifier of seigneurial power?

In Ireland, there is a narrative in which the tower-house of the late Middle Ages evolved or developed, *independently of outside influence*, from the donjon of the thirteenth century. It is the narrative, now well established in Irish castellology, which ties the 'hall-house' to the tower-house. But it is a story, not an explanation. Medieval buildings were inanimate objects; they neither evolved nor developed. As a type, the Irish tower-house was the product of decisions made by masons with technical know-how responding to patrons with ideas about both power and domesticity. So, the challenge to understand the emergence of the tower-house in Ireland is two-fold. It is, first, to determine the degree to which such decisions were informed by knowledge of contemporary developments outside Ireland in architectural style, in domestic arrangements, and in the symbolism of power. It is, second, to identify which 'outside Ireland' place or places were decisively influential. The fact that the Irish tower-house appears as a mature form after the hiatus of the fourteenth century is a sure sign that there was some external input in its early development. The jury must remain out for now on the source or sources of that input – I think French influence might have entered Munster – but the mere acceptance of the proposition that there *was* outside influence would mark a significant step-forward for Irish castellology.

There is less uncertainty when we seek to understand Anglo-Norman castle-building between the 1170s and the early fourteenth century. The origins of designs found late in the twelfth century in Ireland can be traced to England. By the time they appeared in Ireland they had to some degree slipped out of fashion in England, even though, ironically, the archaism of the donjon of Trim was rendered up-to-date by Henry II's (deliberately archaic?) donjon at Dover. The castle architecture of the Angevin aristocracy in England in the early thirteenth century was shaped by architectural developments in both Angevin and Capetian France, and ideas from there crossed into Ireland, sometimes via the kingdom of England and sometimes directly from France. The absence of exact dates makes it difficult to map the routes along which ideas ran, but dates alone would probably not allow a detailed map anyway: ideas moved rapidly in the years in which Richard I and John reigned. The curtain wall at Trim, and turreted donjons of Carlow, Lea and Terryglass, are the best candidates for French-origin architecture transferring from France to Ireland without any corresponding work being built in England.

The story of castle-building in Ireland from the 1220s has two narratives running sequentially. That to the 1270s or thereabouts is one of insularity: few older castles were updated in response to developments outside Ireland, while new castles in Ireland generally had small donjons which, in having simple chambers above basements, adhered to a long-established tradition. In the other narrative, from *c.*1270 but featuring some earlier outliers, the geometrical castle with corner towers makes its appearance. Its source is outside Ireland, probably England, but the type is so generic in the late thirteenth century that tracing its genealogy is difficult. Masons might have left clues in the metrologies of the buildings, in which case it might some day be possible to follow the routes by which certain castle designs ended up in Ireland, but for the present such routes must remain unknown. Of these later castles, Roscommon is the stand-out work; it would be regarded as a very significant work of architecture regardless, but its relationship with the great northern Welsh castles gives it added lustre.

MISSION ACCOMPLISHED? SOME REFLECTIONS FOR THE FUTURE

This book started with a serious of questions posed in respect of the post-1169 castles and their perception when viewed from outside Ireland. Here are some of the questions again, rephrased. What castles in Ireland are typical of their periods? Were any of them innovative or radical by contemporary English or French standards? Should any divergence from contemporary English or French norms be regarded as illustrative of the general heterogeneity of medieval architectural culture? Should such divergence be seen instead as evidence of the essential insularity of architectural culture in Ireland? Each of these questions has been answered *inter alia* in the preceding chapters, some more directly than others.

I have repeated those questions here because, to conclude this book, I want to return to them and ask questions of them in themselves. The premise of this book is that international context is important. That is probably indisputable: no archaeologist of the Middle Ages – a period of documented and attestable interconnectivities across physical and political boundaries – would deny the importance of knowing material from as wide a geographical area as possible. Why, though, in the case of the Irish castles discussed here, does 'international context' matter? And for whom might it matter?

The casual visitor to a castle would probably find it intrinsically interesting to know how that castle compares with examples elsewhere. In many years of visiting Trim Castle and listening to the guided tours given to tourists and casual visitors, I have yet to hear it contextualized properly as a work of architecture. I can only guess that such visitors would actually be interested in knowing, for example, that the donjon's design can be traced back to Normandy via the Tower of London, or that the great curving sweep of curtain wall, visible from the top of the donjon, represents one of the earliest examples in these islands of a way of thinking about fortification which developed in France. As presented to visitors, Trim Castle stands in isolation, and for all they know it is unique, not in the sense that it represents a remarkable deviation from any norm but in the sense that there might as well be no other castles. Some knowledge of 'international context', if there is such knowledge, will always enhance the enjoyment of visiting a castle.

For the castellologist, by contrast, the identification of international comparanda for any castle is an actual professional task. Comparative analysis is the bread and butter of analytical castellollogy. But it creates a challenge that is rarely recognized and more rarely addressed. What exactly do comparisons *mean*? The simple answer is that comparisons are about connections and their identification, and if comparisons can be made across physical and political boundaries, so much the better. Some comparisons allow us to trace pedigrees, to identify ancestors, descendents or siblings. Trim is a case in point. Other comparisons allow us to comment more generally about trends and connections: a castellologist from England or France would regard Ballymote, for example, as intrinsically interesting as an example of a type of castle found elsewhere in the same period, even if he or she would have no particular use for specific knowledge of Ballymote. Were I, in the spirit of a castellologist's parlour game, to list and rank the Irish castles which I think should be known to every specialist outside Ireland, the two royal castles of Dublin and Roscommon, and the baronial castle of Trim, would certainly come out top. I would argue that the short stretch of walling to survive of the *l'an mil* fortress of Lotteragh Upper merits that ranking too. Not far behind all of these would be Nenagh, Carlow and Lea, and Castleroche. Of the later medieval castles, Bunratty alone would make the list, as probably the finest work of the period of greatest architectural insularity. A place on the list should be reserved for the unfinished Ballymoon. Had it been completed, we might be celebrating it today as the single most unique work of medieval architecture in Ireland.

I want to finish by highlighting a different, more elusive, answer to the question: what exactly do comparisons *mean*?

Let us connect the concept of 'meaning' to the concept of 'understanding'. Finding parallels for a castle like Trim or Roscommon certainly allows a deeper level of understanding of it, but within narrow confines. This book offers deeper understandings of a lot of castles, but does so in a restricted sense. In what way? The parallels that archaeologists can identify are formal by nature. Conceptual and experiential linkages between buildings are much more elusive. Yet, castles would have meanings within those realms too. To spend some extended time today in, say, Castleroche, watching the play of light on the walls as the day progresses, or detecting warm spots and cold spots, or *listening* to how the wind sounds as its sweeps around the walls from different directions, is to experience it properly. To identify Tonbridge in England as a formal parallel for its gate-building does not mean that Castleroche is 'understood'. Walt Whitman once said that architecture is what we 'do' to a building when we look at it, to which one might add that it is also what we 'do' to a building when we enter it and allow ourselves be conscious of its textures, its spaces, its colours and shades, as well as its silence, its elusiveness, its capacity to cause us to emote in some way. To understand a castle *deeply*, and to allow a reflexive engagement with it to inform one's understanding of the constructivist role of its surfaces and spaces in the material world of the Middle Ages, requires more than interrogating it through the lens of a body of formal-comparative information. The problem is that there is no easy methodology – no method that one can follow using a checklist of questions – to funnel one's experiential engagement with a medieval building into a narrative in which formal-comparative evidence has a place. Therein lies a challenge.

The word 'theory' makes people nervous. It makes castellologists especially nervous. Few areas within medieval archaeology have practitioners more resistant to theory than castellology. But theory's various -isms (such as post-structuralism) and -ologies (such as phenomenology) simply describe strategies, or 'awarenesses', by which historians of all stripes can interrogate historical buildings in search of their meanings.[1] I have steered clear of such strategies in this book because I set about a task that did not require me to deal with them. I have only sought to explain Ireland encastellated through the narrow window of the formal comparison. But there is a whole other conversation needed before we can claim to understand the *meanings* of the structures with which Ireland was encastellated. That is a project for the future. It is a project that I challenge the next generation of researchers to face.

1 O'Keeffe 2001a; 2018a.

Bibliography

Aarts, Bas 2012 'The origin of castles in the eastern part of the delta region (NL/D) and the rise of the principalities of Guelders and Cleves', *CG* 25, 3–16.

— 2015 'De Zeeuwse motte-burchten in een nationale en internationale context', *Nehalennia* 188, 11–19.

Allen, David and Stoodley, Nick 2010 'Odiham Castle, Hampshire: excavations 1981–85', *Proceedings of the Hampshire Field Club and Archaeological Society* 65, 23–101.

Amiot, Christophe 1992 'Les donjons quadrangulaires du duché de Bretagne avant les guerres de Succession (1050–1350)', *Mémoires de la Société d'histoire et d'archéologie de Bretagne* 69, 43–76.

Austin, David 1998 'Private and public: an archaeological consideration of things' in H. Kühnel, H. Hundsbichler, G. Jaritz and T. Kühtreiber (eds), *Die Vielfalt der Dinge: Neue Wege zur Analyse mittelalterliche Sachkultur*, 163–205. Wien.

Avent, Richard, 2004 *Dolwyddelan Castle, Dolbadarn Castle, Castell Y Bere*. Cardiff.

Avent, Richard and Miles, David 2006 'The main gatehouse' in R. Turner and A. Johnston (eds), *Chepstow Castle: its history and buildings*, 51–62. Hereford.

'B' 1833 'Tirdaglass Castle', *The Dublin Penny Journal* 2, 181.

Bachrach, Bernard S. 1975 'Early medieval fortifications in the "west" of France: a revised technical vocabulary', *Technology and Culture* 16, 4, 531–69.

— 1993 *Fulk Nerra, the Neo-Roman consul, 987–1040*. Berkeley.

Barrett, Catherine J. 2018 'Origins of the French bastides', *Journal of Urban History* 44, 3, 421–56.

Barry, Terence B. 1995 'Defence and settlement in late medieval Ireland' in Barry et al., *Colony and frontier in medieval Ireland*, 217–28.

— 2004 'Tower houses and terror: the archaeology of late medieval Munster' in Clarke et al., *Surveying Ireland's past*, 119–28.

— 2007 'The origins of Irish castles: a contribution to the debate' in C. Manning (ed.), *From ringforts to fortified houses: studies on castles and other monuments in honour of David Sweetman*, 33–9. Bray.

Barry, Terence B., Frame, Robin and Simms, Katherine (eds) 1995 *Colony and frontier in medieval Ireland: essays presented to J.F. Lydon*. London.

Barthelémy, Dominique 1992 'La mutation féodale, a-t-elle eu lieu? (note critique)', *Annales: Économies, Sociétés, Civilisations* 47 (3), 767–77.

— 1997 *La mutation de l'an mil a-t-elle eu lieu ? Servage et chevalerie dans la France des X*ᵉ *et XI*ᵉ *siècles*. Paris.

— 2009 *The serf, the knight and the historian*. Ithaca.

Baudry, M.-P. 1991 'Le château de Coudray-Salbart', *Bulletin archéologique du comité des travaux historiques et scientifiques* 23–4, 137–212.

— 2001 *Les fortifications des Plantagenêts en Poitou 1152–1242*. Paris.

— (ed.) 2001 *Les fortifications dans les domaines Plantagenêt XIIe-XIVe siècles*. Poitiers.

— 2019 *Le château de Noirmoutier*. Niort.

Baylé, Maylis (ed.) 1997 *L'architecture normande au moyen âge*, 2 vols, Paris.

Berdoy, Anne 2014 'Le lexique de la résidence aristocratique dans les Pyrénées occidentales' in Bourgeois and Rémy, *Demeurer, défendre et paraître*, 597–600.

Beresford, David n.d. [a] 'fitz Anthony, Thomas', DIB online.

— n.d. [b] 'Worcester, Philip of', DIB online.

Berry, Henry F. 1893 'The manor and castle of Mallow in the days of the Tudors', *JCHAS* 2, 21–5.

Béthus, Teddy 2019 'Château de Pouzauges', *AM* 49, 328–9.

Beuchet, Laurent 2014 'De la motte du comte à la forteresse ducale: le château de Guingamp (Côtes-d'Armor)', *AM* 44 (2014), 71–123.

Biermann, Felix 2015 'Spätmittelalterliche Turm- und Burghügel in Mecklenburg-Vorpommern' in O. Auge (ed.), *Vergessenes Burgenland Schleswig-Holstein. Die Burgenlandschaft zwischen Elbe und Königsau im Hoch- und Spätmittelalter*, 309–46. Frankfurt am Main.

Blair, John 1993 'Hall and chamber: English domestic planning 1000–1250' in Meirion-Jones and Jones (eds), *Manorial domestic buildings in England and northern France*, 1–24.

— 2018 *Building Anglo-Saxon England*. Princeton.

Boas, Adrian J. 2005 *Crusader archaeology: the material culture of the Latin East*. London.

Bocquet, Anne 2004 'Le donjon de Sainte-Suzanne: suite des études archéologiques', *BM* 162, 3, 213–15.

Bonde, Sheila 1994 *Fortress churches of Languedoc: architecture, religion, and conflict in the high Middle Ages*. Cambridge.

Bony, Jean 1939 'La technique normande du mur épais, à l'époque romane', *BM* 98, 155–88.

Bonhomme, Florian, Guillin, Sylvie, Lehner, Réne-Pierre and Mouillebouche, Hervé 2010 'Trois châteaux bourguignons du Xe siècle datés par 14C-AMS' in H. Mouillebouche (ed.), *Chastels et maisons fortes III. Actes des journées de castellologie de Bourgogne, 2008–2009*, 11–18. Chagny.

Bosworth, Joseph and Toller, T. Northcote 2010 'Castel', *An Anglo-Saxon dictionary* [online].

Bouillot, C. 2000 'Aux antipodes de beau geste: le geste laid et inconvenant dans la literature des XIIème et XIII XIIème siècles', *Le beau et le laid au Moyen Âge*, 45–56. Aix-en-Provence.

Bourgeois, Luc 2006 'Les résidences des élites et les fortifications du haut Moyen Âge en France et en Belgique dans leur cadre européen: aperçu historiographique (1955–2005)', *CCM* 49, 113–41.

— 2011 'Castrum et habitat des élites (France et ses abords, vers 880–vers 1000)' in D. Iogna-Prat et al. (eds), *Cluny, le monachisme et l'émergence d'une société seigneuriale*, 463–87. Rennes.

— (ed.) 2009 *Une résidence des comtes d'Angoulême autour de l'an mil: le castrum d'Andone (Villejoubert, Charente). Publication des fouilles d'André Debord (1971–1995)*. Turnhout.

Bourgeois, Luc and Rémy, Christian (eds) 2014 *Demeurer, défendre et paraître. Orientations récentes de l'archéologie des fortifications et des résidences aristocratiques médiévales entre Loire et Pyrénées*. Chauvigny.

Boutoulle, Frédéric 2014 'Les résidence de la petite aristocratie rurale en Gasgogne occidentale (XIe, XIIe et XIIIe siècles). Réflexions à partir d'un corpus de textes' in Bourgeois and Rémy, *Demeurer, défendre et paraître*, 601–8.

Brachet, Auguste 1873 *An etymological dictionary of the French language*. Oxford.

Bradley, John, Ó Drisceoil, Cóilín and Potterton, Michael 2017 (eds), *William Marshal and Ireland*. Dublin.

Bradley, John and Murtagh, Ben 2003 'Brady's Castle, Thomastown, Co. Kilkenny: a fourteenth-century fortified town house' in Kenyon and O'Conor (eds), *The medieval castle in Ireland and Wales*, 194–216.

— 2017 'William Marshal's charter to Kilkenny, 1207' in Bradley et al., *William Marshal and Ireland*, 201–48.

Brady, Neill 2012 *Ballintober Castle, County Roscommon*. Roscommon Heritage Poster Series, No. 7.

Brather, Sebastian 2004 'The beginnings of Slavic settlement east of the Elbe', *Antiquity* 78, 314–29.

Brewster, T.C.M. and Brewster, A. 1969 'Tote Copse Castle, Aldingbourne', *Sussex Archaeological Collections* 107, 141–80.

Brown, Daniel 2016 *Hugh de Lacy, first earl of Ulster: rising and falling in Angevin Ireland*. Woodbridge.

Brown, Elizabeth A. 1974 'The tyranny of a construct: feudalism and historians of medieval Europe', *The American Historical Review* 79, 1063–88.

Brown, R. Allen 1976 *English Castles*. London.

— 1977 'An historian's approach to the origins of the castle in England', *AJ* 126, 131–48.

Brown, R. Allen, Colvin, H.M. and Taylor, A.J. 1976 *The history of the king's works: the Middle Ages*, vol. 2. London.

Bur, Michel 1982 'Vers l'an mil, la motte, une arme pour une révolution', *L'information historique* 44, 101–8.

— 1993 'Aux *origines du second réseau* urbain. L'impact du château sur le peuplement' in M. Bur (ed.), *Les peuplements castraux dans les pays de l'Entre-Deux*, 5–13. Nancy.

Butler, Lawrence 2010 'The castles of the princes of Gwynedd' in Williams and Kenyon (eds), *The impact of the Edwardian castles in Wales*, 27–36.

Butler, Lawrence, and Knight, Jeremy K. 2004 *Dolforwyn Castle. Montgomery Castle*. Cardiff.

Cairns, C.T. 1987 *Irish tower houses. A Co. Tipperary case study*. Athlone.

Cameron, Angus F., Amos, Ashley C. and Healey, Antonette 2007 'Castel', *Dictionary of Old English: A to G* online. Toronto.

Campbell, M.W. 1971 'A pre-conquest Norman occupation of England?', *Speculum* 46, 1, 1–31.

Carey Bates, Rhiannon and O'Keeffe, Tadhg 2017 'Colonial monasticism, the politics of patronage, and the beginnings of Gothic in Ireland: the Victorine Cathedral Priory of Newtown Trim, Co. Meath', *Journal of Medieval Monastic Studies* 6, 51–76.

Cazes, J.-P. 2014 'Le donjon du château de Saissac (Aude)' in Bourgeois and Rémy (eds), *Demeurer, défendre et paraître*, 153–8.

Champagne, Alain and Mandon, Fabrice 2014 'Le castrum de Pons (Charente-Maritime)' in Bourgeois and Rémy (eds), *Demeurer, défendre et paraître*, 159–67.

Châtelain, André 1973 *Donjons romans des Pays d'Ouest*. Paris.

— 1983 *Châteaux forts et féodalité en Île de France, du XIème au XIIIème siècle*. Paris.

— 1991 'Recherche sur les châteaux de Philippe Auguste', *AM* 21, 115–61.

Chauveau, Céline, Litoux, Emmanuel and Prigent, Daniel 2013 'Angers. Premiers résultats du suivi archéologique des travaux de restauration du front sud du château (XIIIe siècle), *BM* 171, 3, 249–54.

Chédeville, André and Tonnerre, Noël-Yves 1987 *La Bretagne féodale, XIe–XIIIe siècle*. Rennes.

Chibnall, Majorie (ed. and trans.) 1968 *The ecclesiastical history of Orderic Vitalis*, vol. 2. London.

— 1989 'Orderic Vitalis on castles' in C. Harper-Bill, C.J. Holdsworth and J. Nelson (eds), *Studies in medieval history presented to R. Allen Brown*, 43–56. Woodbridge.

Chiesa, Françoise 1998 'Les donjons normands d'Italie. Une comparaison', *Mélanges de l'École française de Rome. Moyen-Age* 110, 1, 317–39.

Clarke, Howard B. 2002 *Dublin, Part I, to 1610*. Irish Historic Towns Atlas (IHTA), no. 11, Royal Irish Academy. Dublin.

Clarke, Howard B., Prunty, Jacinta and Hennessy, Mark (eds) 2014 *Surveying Ireland's past: multi-disciplinary essays in honour of Anngret Simms*. Dublin.

Cohen, Meredith 2015 *The Sainte-Chapelle and the construction of sacral monarchy: royal architecture in thirteenth-century Paris*. Cambridge.

Coldstream, Nicola 2010 'James of St George' in Williams and Kenyon (eds), *The impact of the Edwardian castles in Wales*, 37–45.

Comber, Michelle and Hull, Graham 2010 'Excavations at Caherconnell Cashel, the Burren, Co. Clare: implications for cashel chronology and Gaelic settlement', *PRIA* 110, 133–71.

Cooper, Nicholas 1999 *Houses of the gentry, 1480–1680*. New Haven and London.

Corfield, Penelope J. 2007 *Time and the shape of history*. New Haven and London.

Corvisier, Christian 2001 'Château-Gaillard et son donjon. Une oeuvre expérimentale de Richard Cœur de lion' in Baudry (ed.), *Les fortifications dans les domaines Plantagenêt*, 41–54.

— 2001 'La grosse tour et le château du roi à Compiègne: premier donjon circulaire capétien at archetype des tour-maitresses de Philip Auguste', *Bulletin de la Société Historique de Compiègne* 37, 9–45.

— 2007 'La tour maîtresse du château de Beaugency, dite "Tour de César"', *BM* 165, 1, 3–30.

— 2010 'Le donjon de Châtillon-sur-Indre', *BM* 168, 1, 17–32.

Cotter, Eamonn 2013 (ed.), *Buttevant: a medieval Anglo-French town in Ireland*. Buttevant.

— 2013 'The archaeology of medieval Buttevant' in Cotter (ed.), *Buttevant*, 1–18.

Cotter, Eamonn, MacCotter, Paul and O'Keeffe, Tadhg 2015 'A blow to the temple: the "monastic castle" at Rincrew (Co. Waterford) reinterpreted', *JIA* 24, 163–78.

Coulson, Charles 1973 'Rendability and castellation in medieval France', *CG* 6, 59–67.

— 2003 *Castles in medieval society: fortresses in England, France, and Ireland in the Central Middle Ages*. Oxford.

Creighton, Oliver 2010 'Room with a view: framing castle landscapes', *CG* 24, 37–49.

— 2012 *Early European castles: aristocracy and authority, AD 800–1200*. London.

Crouch, David 2012 'Captives in the head of Montesquieu. Some recent work on medieval nobility', *Virtus: Jaarboek Voor Adelsgeschiedenis* 19, 185–9.

Cruden, Stewart 1999 *Castle Campbell*. Revised ed. Edinburgh.

Cunningham, George 1987 *The Anglo-Norman advance into the south-east Midlands*. Roscrea.

Curnow, Peter and Kenyon, John R. 2000 'Mortimer's Tower' in R. Shoesmith and A. Johnson (eds), *Ludlow Castle: its history & buildings*, 195–200. Almeley.

Curwen, John F. 1913 *The castles and fortified towers of Cumberland, Westmorland, and Lancashire North-of-the-Sands*. Cumberland and Westmorland Antiquarian and Archaeological Society Extra Series, vol. 13.

Davies, John A., Riley, Angela, Levesque, Jean-Marie and Lapiche Charlotte (eds) 2016 *Castles and the Anglo-Norman world*. Oxford.

Decaëns, Joseph 1997 'Le donjon de Chambois' in Baylé (ed.), *L'architecture normande au moyen âge*, 2, 320–2.

Davison, Brian K. 1967 'The origins of the castle in England: the Institute's research project', *AJ* 124, 202–11.

De Boüard, Michel 1973 'De l'*aula* au donjon. Les fouilles de la motte de La Chapelle, à Doué-la-Fontaine (Xᵉ-XIᵉ siècle)', *AM* 3–4, 5–110.

— 1981 'Thème I. La motte' in 'Les fortifications de terre en Europe occidentale du Xᵉ au XIIᵉ siècles (Colloque de Caen, 2–5 Octobre 1980)', *AM* 11, 5–19.

Debord, André 1979 '*Castrum* et *castellum* chez Adémar de Chabannes', *AM* 9, 97–113.

— 1988 'Châteaux et société dans le Rouergue médiévale (Xᵉ-XIIIᵉ siècles)', *CG* 14, 7–27.

Dempsey, Karen 2016a 'Rectangular chamber-towers and their medieval halls: a recent look at the buildings formerly described as "hall-houses"', *CG* 27, 113–19.

— 2106b 'Lea Castle: the story so far', *CSGJ* 30, 237–52.

— 2017 'Understanding "hall-houses": debating seigneurial buildings in Ireland in the 13th century', *MA* 61, 2, 372–99.

Desisle, Leopold (ed.) 1864 *Recueil de jugements de l'Echiquier de Normandie au XIIIe siècle (1207–1270)*. Paris.

Devane, Caitríona 2013 '"The Black Castle of Adare": a history of Adare Castle' in L. Dunne and J. Kiely, 'Archaeological excavation report Adare Castle, Co. Limerick', *Eachtra Journal* 16, 1–27.

Deyres, Marcel 1974 'Les châteaux de Foulque Nerra', *BM* 132, 1, 7–28.

Dhaeze, Wouter and Fairon, Guy 2014 *Le Burgknapp à Heinstert (Attert): la transformation d'une fortification a petite enceinte circulaire en motte castrale (Xe–XIIe s.)*. Attert.

Dimock, James F. (ed.) 1867 *Giraldi Cambrensis Opera V*. London.

Dixon, Philip 1992 'From hall to tower: the change in seigneurial houses on the Anglo-Scottish border after *c*.1250', *Thirteenth Century England IV*, 85–107.

— 2002 'The myth of the keep' in Meirion-Jones et al., *The seigneurial residence in western Europe*, 9–13.

— 2008 'The influence of the White Tower on the great towers of the twelfth century' in Impey (ed.), *The White Tower*, 243–75.

— 2018 'Patron and builder' in Guy (ed.), *Castles: history, archaeology, landscape, architecture and symbolism*, 376–92.

Dixon, Philip and Marshall, Pamela 1992 'The great tower at Hedingham Castle: a reassessment', *Fortress* 18, 16–23.

Dixon, Philip and Lott, Beryl 1993 'The courtyard and the tower: contexts and symbols in the development of late medieval great houses', *Journal of the British Archaeological Association* 146, 93–101.

Dobat, Andras 2009 'The state and the strangers: the role of external forces in a process of state formation in Viking-age south Scandinavia (*c*.AD 900–1050)', *Viking and Medieval Scandinavia* 5, 65–104.

Doherty, Charles 1998 'The Vikings in Ireland: a review' in H.B. Clarke, M. Ní Mhaonaigh and R. Ó Floinn (eds), *Ireland and Scandinavia in the early Viking Age*, 288–330. Dublin.

Donnelly, Colm 1999 'A typological study of the tower houses of County Limerick', *JRSAI* 129, 19–39.

Donnelly, Colm, O'Neill, John, McNeill, Tom, McCooey, Paul 2005 'De Courcy's castle: new insights into the first phase of Anglo-Norman building activity at Carrickfergus Castle, Co. Antrim', *MA* 49, 1, 311–17.

Donovan, Tom 2009 (ed.) *The Knights of Glin: seven centuries of change*. Glin.

Draper, Peter 2006 *The formation of English Gothic*. New Haven.

Duby, Georges 1953 *La société aux XIe et XIIe siècles dans la région mâconnaise*. Paris.

Duffy, Paul 2011 '*Ung sage et valent home*: Hugh de Lacy and the Albigensian Crusade', *JRSAI* 141, 66–90.

— 2015 'The architecture of defiance', *AI* 29, 1, 20–3.

— 2018 'From Carcassonne to Carrickfergus: the legacy of de Lacy's crusade experience in Britain and Ireland' in Duffy et al. (ed.), *From Carrickfergus to Carcassonne*, 295–328.

Duffy, Paul, Picard, Jean-Michel and O'Keeffe, Tadhg (eds) 2018 *From Carrickfergus to Carcassonne: the epic deeds of Hugh de Lacy during the Albigensian Crusade*. Turnhout.

Duffy, Seán 1995 'The first Ulster plantation: John de Courcy and the men of Cumbria' in Barry et al. (eds), *Colony and frontier in medieval Ireland*, 1–27

— 2011 '"The key of the Pale": a history of Trim Castle' in Hayden (ed.), *Trim Castle*, 6–28.

Dunbabin, Jean 2002 *Captivity and imprisonment in medieval Europe*. Basingstoke.

Dunbar, John G. 2002 'Scottish royal residences of the later Middle Ages: some aspects of domestic planning' in Meirion-Jones et al. (eds), *The seigneurial residence in western Europe*, 51–62.

Dunne, Laurence and Kiely, Jacinta 2013 *Archaeological excavation report: Adare Castle, Co. Limerick*. Innishannon.

Durand, Philip 1996 'Les conséquences de la datation dendrochronologique du donjon de Loches pour la castellologie', *BM* 154, 3, 224–8.

— 1999 *Le château fort*. Bordeaux.

Durkin, Philip 2014 *Borrowed words: a history of loanwords in English*. Oxford.

Eadie, Gillian 2010 'Detecting privacy and private space in the Irish tower house', *CG* 24, 69–73.

— 2015a 'Identifying functions in castles: a study of tower houses in Ireland' in Oram, *'A house that thieves might knock at'*, 2–18.

— 2015b '"Know you that serving folk be of three kinds": Irish towers and the *familia*' in Oram, *'A house that thieves might knock at'*, 174–88.

Early, Robert 1998 *Mayenne, le château* 1: *Synthèse globale du projet*. Nantes.

Emery, Anthony 1996a *Greater medieval houses of England and Wales*. Vol. 1. *Northern England*. Cambridge.

— 1996b *Greater medieval houses of England and Wales, 1300–1500*. Vol. 2. *East Anglia, Central England and Wales*. Cambridge.

— 2016 *Seats of power in Europe during the Hundred Years War. An architectural study from 1330 to 1480*. Oxford.

Empey, Adrian 1981 'The settlement of the kingdom of Limerick' in J. Lydon (ed.), *England and Ireland in the later Middle Ages: essays in honour of Jocelyn Otway-Ruthven*, 1–25. Dublin.

Ettel, Peter 2012a 'Ungarnburgen in Süddeutschland im 10. Jahrhundert', *CG* 26, 159–65.

— 2012b '"Ungarnburgen – Ungarnrefugien – Ungarnwälle". Zum Stand der Forschung', in T. Bitterli-Waldvogel (ed.), *Zwischen Kreuz und Zinne: Festschrift für Barbara Schock-Werner zum 65*, 46–66. Braubach.

Faith, Rosamond 1997 *The English peasantry and the growth of lordship*. London.

— 2020 *The moral economy of the countryside: Anglo-Saxon to Anglo-Norman England*. Cambridge.

Faravel, Sylvie 2014 'Le lexique de la résidence aristocratique et des fortifications en Entre-deux-Mers bazadais entre le XIe et la XVe siècle' in Bourgeois and Rémy (eds), *Demeurer, défendre et paraître*, 617–26.

Fenlon, Jane 2011 'Moving towards the formal house: room usage in early modern Ireland', *PRIA* 111C, 141–68.

Fernie, Eric 2000 *The architecture of Norman England*. Oxford.

Fichet de Clairfontaine, François, Mastrolorenzo, Joseph and Brown, Richard 2016 'Le château de Falaise (Calvados): état des connaissances sur l'évolution du site castral du dixième au treizième siècles' in Davies et al., *Castles and the Anglo-Norman world*, 231–56.

Finan, Thomas 2015 'Hall houses, church and state in thirteenth-century Roscommon: the origins of the Irish tower house' in Oram (ed.), *'A house that thieves might knock at'*, 19–27.

Finan, Thomas 2016 *Landscape and history on the medieval Irish frontier: the king's cantreds in the thirteenth century*. Turnhout.

Flambard Héricher, Anne-Marie 2002 'Quelques réflexions sur le mode de construction des mottes en Normandie et sur ses marges', *Cahier des Annales de Normandie* 32, 123–32.

Flanagan, Marie-Therese 1996 'Irish and Anglo-Norman warfare in twelfth-century Ireland' in T. Bartlett and K. Jeffrey (eds), *A military history of Ireland*, 52–75. Cambridge.

Forester, Thomas (trans.) 2000 *Giraldus Cambrensis: the topography of Ireland*. Cambridge, Ontario.

Francovich, Riccardo 1998 'L'incastellamento e prima dell' incastellamento', *'L'incastellamento'.* Actes des rencontres de Gérone (26–27 novembre 1992) et de Rome (5–7 mai 1994), 13–20. Rome.

Gardelles, Jacques 1970 'Le château d'Herrebouc', *Congrès archéologique de France* 128, 117–23

Garner, Lori A. 2010 *Structuring spaces: oral poetics and architecture in early medieval England.* Notre Dame.

Genet, Jean-Philippe 2010 'Identité, espace, langue', *Cahiers de recherches médiévales et humanistes* 19, 1–10.

Gilbert, John, T. 1889 *Register of the Abbey of St Thomas, Dublin.* London.

Gleeson, D.F. and Leask, Harold G. 1936 'The castle and manor of Nenagh', *JRSAI* 66, 247–69.

Goodall, John 2011 *The English castle, 1066–1650.* New Haven and London.

Gormley, Sarah and McNeill, Tom 2016–17 'Recent research on Carrickfergus Castle, Co. Antrim', *CSGJ* 30, 218–36.

Graham, Brian J. 1988 'Medieval timber and earthwork fortifications in western Ireland', *MA* 32, 110–129.

Grattan Flood, W.H. 1916 *History of the diocese of Ferns.* Waterford.

Grant, Lindy 1994 'Le patronage architectural de Henri II et de son entourage', *Cahiers de Civilisation Médiévale* 37, 73–84.

Grose, Francis 1791 *The antiquities of Ireland*, vol. 1. London.

Grove, Doreen 1996 *Cardoness Castle and Carsluith Castle.* Edinburgh.

Guerout, Jean 1953 *Le Palais de la Cité à Paris, des origines à 1417: essai topographique et archéologique.* Paris.

— 1966 'Les origines du château et de la seigneurie de Montaiguillon', *Bulletin de la Société d'histoire et d'archéologie de l'arrondissement de Provins* 120, 57–80.

Guillot, Florence 2014 'Aperçus terminologiques des fortifications dans la documentation ariégeoise, XIe-XVe siècle' in Bourgeois and Rémy (eds), *Demeurer, défendre et paraître,* 609–15.

Guy, Neil et al. 2011–12 'Castles of Essex and Suffolk (with the Tower of London)', *CSGJ* 25, 4–100,

Guy, Neil 2015–16 'The *portcullis* – design and development – 1080–1260', *CSGJ* 29, 132–201.

— 2016–17, 'CSG annual conference – Hereford – April 2016', *CSGJ* 30, 95–107.

— 2018–19 'CSG annual conference – Cork – April 2018', *CSGJ* 32, 4–91.

— (ed.) 2018 *Castles: history, archaeology, landscape, architecture and symbolism: essays in honour of Derek Renn.* Daventry.

Hagger, Mark S. 2001 *The fortunes of a Norman family: the de Verduns in England, Ireland and Wales, 1066–1316.* Dublin.

Harfield, C.G. 1991 'A hand-list of castles recorded in the Domesday Book', *English Historical Review* 106, 371–92.

Hartnett, P. J. 1945 'Some Imokilly castles', *JCHAS* 50, 42–53.

Harvey, John 1978 *The prependicular style, 1330–1485.* London.

Hautefeuille, F. 2006 *La Truque de Maurélis, donjon emmotté, Commune de Castelnau Montratier (46),* rapport intermédiaire n° 2, *Service Régional de l'Archéologie de Midi-Pyrénées.*

Hayden, Alan 2011 *Trim Castle, Co. Meath: excavations 1995–8.* Dublin.

— n.d. 'Archaeological excavations in Maynooth castle, Co. Kildare' (unpublished: https://independent.academia,edu/AlanHayden).

Hayot, Denis 2013 'Une nouvelle vision du rapport entre le Louvre et l'enceinte de Philippe Auguste à Paris', *BM* 171, 1, 3–10.

Héliot, Pierre 1965–6 'La genèse des châteaux de plan quadrangulaire en France et en Angleterre', *Bulletin de la Société Nationale des Antiquaires de France*, 238–57.

— 1969 'L'évolution des donjons dans le nord-ouest de la France et l'Angleterre au XIIe siècle', *Bulletin archéologique du Comité des travaux historiques et scientifiques* 5, 141–94.

Herity, Michael 1993 'Motes and mounds at royal sites in Ireland', *JRSAI* 123, 127–51.

Herlihy, David 1985 *Medieval households*, Harvard.

Herrnbrodt, Adolf 1958 *Der Husterknupp. Eine niederrheinische Burganlage des frühen Mittelalters.* Köln.

Heslop, T.A. 1991 'Orford Castle, nostalgia and sophisticated living', *Architectural History* 34, 36–58.

Hicks, Leonie V. 2009 'Magnificent entrances and undignified exits: chronicling the symbolism of castle space in Normandy', 35, 52–69.

Higham, Robert 2015 *Shell-keeps revisited: the bailey on the motte?* Castle Studies Group, Daventry.

Higham, Robert and Barker, Philip 1992 *Timber castles*. London.

Hill, Nick and Gardiner, Mark 2018 'The English medieval first-floor hall: Part 2 – the evidence from the eleventh to early thirteenth century', *AJ* 175:2, 315–61.

Hinz, Hermann 1981 *Motte und Donjon. Zur frühgeschichte der mittelalterlichen Adelsburg.* Zeitschrift für Archäologie des Mittelalters 17, Köln.

Hislop, Malcolm 2016 *Castle builders: approaches to castle design and construction in the Middle Ages.* Barnsley.

Hodkinson, Brian 1999 'Excavations in the gatehouse of Nenagh Castle, 1996–97', *Tipperary Historical Journal*, 162–82.

— 2003 'A summary of recent work on the Rock of Dunamase, Co. Laois' in Kenyon and O'Conor (eds), *The medieval castle in Ireland and Wales*, 32–49.

— 2004 'Was Quin Castle completed?', *NMAJ* 44, 53–8.

— 2005 'Thom Cor Castle: a 14th-century tower house in Limerick city?', *JRSAI*, 135, 119–29.

Hoek, C. 1981 'Discussion du Rapport I (La motte)' in 'Les fortifications de terre en Europe occidentale du Xe au XIIe siècles (Colloque de Caen, 2–5 Octobre 1980)', *AM* 11, 20–38.

Holland, Patrick 1987–8 'The Anglo-Normans in Co. Galway: the process of colonization', *JGAHS* 41, 73–89.

— 1997 'The Anglo-Norman landscape in County Galway; land-holdings, castles and settlements' *JGAHS* 49, 159–93.

Hollis, Edward 2009 *The secret lives of buildings*. London.

Hubert, Ètienne 2000 'L'*incastellamento* dans le Latium. Remarques à propos de fouilles récentes', *Annales. Histoire, Sciences Sociales* 55, 3, 583–99.

Hulme, Richard 2007–8 'Twelfth century great towers: the case for the defence', *CSGJ* 21, 209–29.

— 2013–14 'The impact of Château Gaillard and crusading on English castle architecture', *CSGJ* 27, 203–33.

Impey, Edward 1997 'La demeure seigneuriale en Normandie entre 1125 et 1225 et la tradition Anglo-Normande' in Baylé (ed.), *L'architecture normande au moyen âge*, 1, 219–41.

— 1999 'The seigneurial residence in Normandy, 1125–1225: an Anglo-Norman tradition?', *MA* 43, 45–73.

— 2002 'The *turris famosa* at Ivry-la-Bataille, Normandy' in Meirion-Jones et al. (eds), *The seigneurial residence in western Europe*, 189–210.

— 2002 'The donjon at Avranches (Normandy)', *AJ* 159, 1, 249–57.

— 2008 'The ancestry of the White Tower, in Impey, *The White Tower*, 227–41.

— (ed.) 2008 *The White Tower*. New Haven and London.

Impey, Edward and Harris, Roland 2002 'Boothby Pagnell revisited' in Meirion-Jones et al. (eds), *The seigneurial residence in western Europe*, 245–69.

Impey, Edward and Lorans, Elizabeth 1998 'Le donjon de Langeais (Indre-et-Loire) et son environnement. Étude historique et archéologique', *BM* 156, 1, 9–63.

Ingham, Richard 2010 'Anglo-Norman: new themes, new contexts' in R. Ingham (ed.), *The Anglo-Norman language and its contexts*, 1–7. Woodbridge.

Joanne, Paul 1992 *Dictionnaire géographique et administratif de la France*, 3. Paris.

Johnson, Matthew 2002 *Behind the castle gate: from medieval to Reniassance*. London.

Jope, Martyn (ed.) 1966 *Archaeological survey of County Down*. Belfast.

Jope, Martyn and Threlfall, R. 1959 'The twelfth-century castle at Ascot Doilly, Oxfordshire: its history and excavation', *AJ* 39, 219–70

Jones, Michael 2001 '*The naming of parts*: remarques sur le vocabulaire des residences seigneuriales et princières en Bretagne au Moyen Âge' in Renoux (ed.), *Aux marches du palais*, 45–54.

Kavaler, Ethan Matt 2012 *Renaissance Gothic*. London and New York.

Kenyon, John R. 2015 *Middleham Castle*. London.

— 2017 *Helmsley Castle*. London.

Kenyon, John R. and O'Conor, Kieran (eds) 2003 *The medieval castle in Ireland and Wales*. Dublin.

King, Andy 2007 'Fortresses and fashion statements: gentry castles in fourteenth-century Northumberland', *JMH* 33, 4, 372–97.

Knight, Jeremy K. 1987 'The road to Harlech: some aspects of early thirteenth-century Welsh castles' in J.R. Kenyon and R. Avent (eds), *Castles in Wales and the Marches*, 75–88. Cardiff.

— 2008 'Welsh space and the Norman invaders: Usk Castle, 1136–1245' in J.K. Knight and A. Johnson (eds), *Usk Castle, priory and town*', 55–68. Almeley.

— 2018 'Fog in the Channel? Influences in Anglo-French building' in Guy (ed.), *Castles: history, archaeology, landscape, architecture and symbolism*, 155–73.

Knox, H.T. 1911 'Mannin Castle. In the parish of Aghamore, barony of Costello and county of Mayo', *JGAHS* 7, 2, 115–20.

Kraus, Matthew A. 2017 'Rabbinic traditions in Jerome's translation of the Book of Numbers', *Journal of Biblical Literature* 136, 3, 539–63.

Kubach, Hans Erich 1975 *Romanesque architecture*. New York.

Labbé, Alain 1987 *L'architecture des palais et des jardins dans les chansons de geste. Essai sur le thème du roi en majesté*. Paris.

Lacy, Brian 1983 *Archaeological survey of County Donegal*. Lifford.

Laffont, Pierre-Yves 2009 *Châteaux du Vivarais. Pouvoirs et peuplement en France méridionale du haut Moyen Âge au XIIIe siècle*. Rennes.

Lambert, Tom 2017 *Law and order in Anglo-Saxon England*. Oxford.

Langeuin, Pascal 2002 'Les campagnes de construction du château d'Arques-la-Bataille (XIe-XVe siècles)', *BM* 160, 4, 345–78.

Latham, R.E. 1965 *Revised medieval Latin word-list*. London.

Le Maho, Jacques 1984 *La motte seigneuriale de Mirville (XIe- XIIe siècles). Recherches historiques et archéologiques*. Rouen.

Le Moing, Jean-Yves 1990 *Les noms de lieux bretons de Haute-Bretagne*. Spézet.

Leask, Harold G. 1951 *Irish castles and castellated houses*. Revised edition. Dundalk.

— 1943 'Terryglass Castle', *JRSAI* 73, 141–4.

Leblanc, Olivier 2005 'Aux origines de la seigneurie de Coucy, la lignée des Boves-Coucy', *Revue archéologique de Picardie* 1–2, 145–54.

Lett, Didier 2016 'Les voix du peuple à la fin du Moyen Âge', *Médiévales* 71, 159–76.

Loveluck, Christopher 2013 *Northwest Europe in the early Middle Ages, c.650–1150: a comparative archaeology*. Cambridge.

Lucken, Christopher 2015 'Le beau français d'Angleterre. Altérité de l'anglo-normand et invention du bon usage', *Médiévales* 68, 35–56.

Ludlow, Neil 2018–19 'William Marshal, Pembroke Castle and Angevin design', *CSGJ* 32, 209–92.

Lynn, C.J. 1981–2 'The excavation of Rathmullan, a raised rath and motte in County Down', *UJA* 3rd ser., 44/45, 65–171.

MacCotter, P. 1987 'The sub-infeudation and descent of the Fitz Stephen/Carew moiety of Desmond, part ii', *JCHAS* 102, 89–106.

— 2008 *Medieval Ireland: territorial, political and economic divisions*. Dublin.

— 2009 'Medieval history' in Manning (ed.), *The history and archaeology of Glanworth Castle*, 1–3.

— 2009 'Gleann Corbraighe before the Normans' in Donovan (ed.), *The knights of Glin*, 38–45.

MacDonald, Philip 2014–15 'CSG annual conference – Belfast – April 2014 – Dundrum Castle', *CSGJ* 28, 38–52.

Maguire, J.B. 1974 'Seventeenth-century plans of Dublin Castle', *JRSAI* 104, 5–14.

Manning, Conleth 1998 'Dublin Castle: the building of a royal castle in Ireland', *CG* 18, 119–22.

— 2002 'Low-level roofs in Irish great towers', *CG* 20, 137–40.

— 2003 'The Record Tower, Dublin Castle' in Kenyon and O'Conor (eds), *The medieval castle in Ireland and Wales*, 72–95.

— 2009 *The history and archaeology of Glanworth Castle, Co. Cork: excavations 1982–4*. Dublin.

— 2013 *Clogh Oughter Castle, County Cavan: archaeology, history and architecture*. Dublin.

— 2017–18 '"But you are first to build a tower" – the Bermingham Tower, Dublin Castle', *UJA* 74, 145–54.

Maréchal, Jean-François 1979 'Colonisation et fortifications vikings et normandes: un problème', *Flaren 1: Châteaux et peuplements en Europe occidentale du Xe au XVIIIe siècle*, 181–9. Auch.

— 1984 'La question du rattachement des mottes féodales aux Terpen ou Wurten frisons du haut Moyen Age et de l'Antiquité', *Caesarodunum* 19, 191–200.

— 1991 'Les enceintes circulaires et les mottes ecclésiales médiévales', *Bulletin de la Société Nationale des Antiquaires de France*, 264–76.

Marshall, Pamela 2002 'The great tower as residence' in Meirion-Jones et al. (eds), *The seigneurial residence in western Europe*, 27–44.

— 2012 'Making an appearance: some thoughts on the phenomenon of multiple doorways and large upper openings in Romanesque donjons in western France and Britain', *CG* 25, 233–41.

— 2015 'The Angevin donjon and its legacy in post-Conquest England' in Oram (ed.), *'A house that thieves might knock at'*, 198–213.

Martin, David and Martin, Barbara 2013 'A reinterpretation of the gatehouse at Tonbridge Castle', *Archaeologia Cantiana* 133, 235–76.

Matasovic, Ranko 2009 *Etymological dictionary of Proto-Celtic*. Leiden.

McAlister, Vicky and Barry, Terry (eds) 2015 *Space and settlement in medieval Ireland*. Dublin.

McAlister, Victoria L. 2019 *The Irish tower house: society, economy and environment c.1300–1650*. Manchester.

McGarry, James 1980 *Collooney*. Collooney.

McManama-Kearin, Lisa Karen 2012 'Forced focus: a room with viewshed', *CG* 25, 233–41.

McManus, Damian 1983 'A chronology of the Latin loan-words in Early Irish', *Ériu* 34, 21–71.

McNeill, Tom 1980 *Anglo-Norman Ulster: the history and archaeology of an Irish barony, 1177–1400*. Edinburgh.

— 1981 *Carrickfergus Castle*. Belfast.

— 1985–6 'Church building in 14th century Ireland and the "Gaelic revival"', *JIA* 3, 61–4.

— 1992 'The origins of tower houses', *AI* 6, 1, 13–14.

— 1993 'The outer gate at Dunamase Castle, Co. Laois', *MA* 37, 236–9.

— 1997 *Castles in Ireland: feudal power in a Gaelic world*. London.

— 2002 'The gap below the castle in Ireland' in Meirion-Jones et al. (eds), *The seigneurial residence in western Europe*, 45–50.

— 2003 'Squaring circles: flooring round towers in Wales and Ireland' in Kenyon and O'Conor (eds), *The medieval castle in Ireland and Wales*, 96–106.

— 2007 'Where should we place the boundary between the medieval and post-medieval periods in Ireland?' in A. Horning, R. Ó Baoill, C. Donnelly and P. Logue (eds), *The post-medieval archaeology of Ireland, 1550–1850*, 7–13. Dublin.

— 2011 'Mountains or molehills? Different uses for mottes in the lordships of eastern Ireland', *AJ* 168, 227–71.

— 2014–14 'Carrickfergus Castle', *CSGJ* 28, 9–32.

McNeill, Tom and Scott, Gillian 2018 'Langley Castle, Northumberland' in Guy (ed.), *Castles: history, archaeology, landscape, architecture and symbolism*, 315–49.

Meirion-Jones, Gwyn, Impey, Edward and Jones, Michael (eds) 2002 *The seigneurial residence in western Europe AD c.800–1600*. Oxford.

Meirion-Jones, Gwyn, and Jones, Michael (eds) 1993 *Manorial domestic buildings in England and northern France*. London.

Meirion-Jones, Gwyn, Jones, Michael and Pilcher, Jon 1993 'The seigneurial domestic buildings of Brittany, 1000–1700' in Meirion-Jones et al. (eds), *Manorial domestic buildings in England and northern France*, 158–91.

Mercer, David 2019–20 'Bowes castle: a revised interpretation', *CSGJ* 33, 265–76.

Mesqui, Jean 1977 'La fortification dans le Valois du XIe au XVe siècle et le rôle de Louis d'Orléans', *BM* 135, 2, 109–49.

— 1980 'Joseph Délivré, Grande, petite et véridique histoire du château fort de Montaiguillon-en-Brie (Monuments historiques de Seine-et-Marne, n° 5)', *BM* 138, 2, 241–2.

— 1981 'La fortification des portes avant la Guerre de Cent Ans. Essai de typologie des défenses des ouvrages d'entrée avant 1350', *AM* 11, 203–29.

— 1987 'Le château de Romefort à Ciron', *Congrès archéologique de France, 1984, Bas-Berry*, 81–8.

— 1991 *Châteaux et enceintes de la France médiévale, 1: Les organes de la défense*. Paris.

— 1993 *Châteaux et enceintes de la France Médiévale, 2: De la défense à la résidence*. Paris.

— 1998 'La tour maîtresse du *donjon* de Loches', *BM* 156, 1, 65–128.

— 2008 'Le château de Pierrefonds. Une nouvelle vision du monument', *BM* 166, 3, 197–245.

— 2010 'La tour maîtresse d'Avranches', *BM* 168, 1, 106–7.

— 2011 'La tour des Archives et le fort des Tourelles de Vernon (Eure). Deux édifices royaux exceptionnels édifiés vers 1200', *BM* 169, 4, 291–318.

— 2014 'L'église Saint-Liphard et la tour Manassès de Garlande à Meung-sur-Loire', *BM* 172, 1, 3–46.

— 2016 'Guainville, le vieux-château', *BM* 174, 4, 497–9.

— 2018 'Philippe Auguste "tours"' in Guy, *Castles: history, archaeology, landscape, architecture and symbolism*, 129–39.

Mesqui, Jean and Toussaint, Patrick 1990 'Le château de Gisors aux XIIᵉ et XIIIᵉ siècles', *AM* 20, 253–317.

Meuret, Jean-Claude 1998 'Construction et habitat aux confins Anjou-Bretagne du XIe au XVe siècle: des textes au terrain' in D. Prigent et N.-Y. Tonnerre (eds), *La Construction en Anjou au Moyen Âge*, 141–76. Angers.

Meyer, Kuno 1910 'Brian Borumha', *Ériu* 4, 68–73.

Miller, Maureen 2009 '*Incastellamento*. Two texts from Verona (906, 923)' in K.L. Jansen et al. (eds), *Medieval Italy: texts in translation*, 25–9. Philadelphia.

Monk, Judith and Tobin, Red 1991 *Barryscourt Castle: an architectural survey*. Carrigtwohill.

Mortet, Victor and Deschamps, Paul 1929 *Recueil des textes relatifs à l'histoire de l'architecture et à la condition des architects en France au moyenâge, XIe–XIIe siècles*, vol. 2. Paris.

Mostert, A.H.E. 2013 *Werven en voorhoven. Een interdisciplinair onderzoek naar de mottekastelen op Walcheren*, Walcherse Archeologische Rapporten 37, 13–14. Middelburg.

Müller-Wille, Michael 1966 *Mittelalterliche Burghügel im nördlichen Rheinland*. Graz/Köln.

Morris, Marc 2016 'Rochester Castle' in Davies et al. (eds), *Castles and the Anglo-Norman world*, 69–74.

Moss, Rachel (ed.) 2014 *Art and architecture of Ireland* I: *medieval c.400–c.1600*. Dublin.

Mouton, Daniel 1997 'Le fort et l'éminent. La rocca en Provence depuis le début du Moyen Age', *Le Monde alpin et rhodanien. Revue régionale d'ethnologie* 2–4, 179–86.

Mullally, Evelyn (ed.) 2002 *The Deeds of the Normans in Ireland. La Geste des Engleis en Yrlande*. Dublin.

Murphy, Margaret and O'Conor, Kieran 2008 *Roscommon Castle – a visitor's guide*. Roscommon.

Murtagh, Ben 2016 'The medieval tower of Hook: a review of its dating and history' in I.W. Doyle and B. Browne (eds), *Medieval Wexford: essays in memory of Billy Colfer*, 124–80. Dublin.

— 2017 'William Marshal's great tower at Pembroke: a view from Ireland' in J. Bradley, C. Ó Driseoil and M. Potterton (eds), *William Marshal and Ireland*, 111–82. Dublin.

Murtagh, Harman 1994 *Athlone*. Irish Historic Towns Atlas (IHTA), no. 6, Royal Irish Academy. Dublin.

Nelson, Ian S. 1998 *Etal Castle*. London.

Nelson, Janet L. 1992 *Charles the Bald*. London.

Ní Mhaonaigh, M. 2007 *Brian Boru: Ireland's greatest king?* Stroud.

Nicholls, Kenneth and MacCotter, Paul 2009 'Feudal warlords: the knights of Glencorbry' in Donovan (ed.), *The Knights of Glin*, 48–79.

O'Conor, Kieran 1997 'The origins of Carlow Castle', *AI* 11, 3, 13–16

— 1999 'Anglo-Norman castles in Co. Laois' in P. Lane (ed.), *Laois: history and society*, 183–211. Dublin.

— 2014a 'Castles' in Moss (ed.), *Art and architecture of Ireland*, I, 341–5.

— 2014b 'Roscommon Castle' in Moss (ed.), *Art and architecture of Ireland,* I, 350–1.

O'Conor, Kieran and Manning, Conleth 2000 'Clonmacnoise Castle' in H. King (ed.), *Clonmacnoise Studies 2*, 137–65.

O'Conor, Kieran and Naessens, Paul 2012 'Pre-Norman fortification in eleventh- and twelfth-century Ireland', *CG* 25, 259–68.

Ó Corráin, Donnchadh 1972 *Ireland before the Normans*. Dublin.

O'Kelly, Michael J. 1962 'Beal Boru, Co. Clare', *JCHAS* 27, 1–27.

O'Keeffe, T. 1984 'An early Anglo-Norman castle at Ballyderown, County Cork', *JRSAI* 114, 48–56.

— 1990 'The archaeology of Anglo-Norman castles in Ireland. Part 2: stone castles', *AI* 4, 4, 20–2.

— 1996 'Rural settlement and cultural identity in Gaelic Ireland, 1000–1500', *Ruralia* 1 (1996), 142–53.

— 1997a 'Diarmair Mac Murchada and Romanesque Leinster: four twelfth-century churches in context', *JRSAI* 127, 52–79.
— 1997b *Barryscourt Castle and the Irish tower-house*. Kinsale.
— 1998 'The fortifications of western Ireland, AD 1100–1300, and their interpretation', *JGAHS* 50, 184–200.
— 2001a 'Concepts of "castle" and the construction of identity in medieval and post-medieval Ireland', *Irish Geography* 34, 1, 69–88.
— 2001b 'Ballyloughan, Ballymoon and Clonmore: three castles of *c.*1300 in County Carlow', *Anglo-Norman Studies* 23, 167–97.
— 2003 *Romanesque Ireland: architecture and ideology in the twelfth century*. Dublin.
— 2004a *Ireland's round towers: buildings, rituals and landscapes of the early Irish Church*. Stroud.
— 2004b 'Space, place, habitus: geographies of practice in an Anglo-Norman landscape' in Clarke et al. (eds), *Surveying Ireland's past*, 73–98.
— 2007a *Archaeology and the Pan-European Romanesque*. London.
— 2007b 'Angevin lordship and colonial Romanesque in Ireland' in M. Costen (ed.), *People and places: essays in honour of Michael Aston*, 117–29. Oxford.
— 2009 'Dublin Castle's donjon in context' in John Bradley, Alan Fletcher & Anngret Simms (eds) *Dublin in the medieval world: studies in honour of Howard B. Clarke*, 277–94. Dublin.
— 2011a 'Building lordship in thirteenth-century Ireland: the donjon of Coonagh Castle, Co. Limerick', *JRSAI* 141, 91–127.
— 2011b 'Landscapes, castles and towns of Edward I in Wales and Ireland: some comparisons and connections', *Landscapes* 11, 2, 60–72.
— 2013a 'What did Tara mean to the Anglo-Normans?' in M. O'Sullivan, C. Scarre and M. Doyle (eds) *Tara from the past to the present*, 121–4. Dublin.
— 2013b 'Trim Castle uncovered: some thoughts', *Ríocht na Midhe* 24, 1–9.
— 2013c 'Trim's first cousin: the twelfth-century donjon of Maynooth Castle', *AI* 27, 2, 26–31.
— 2013d 'Liscarroll Castle: a note on its context, function and date' in E. Cotter (ed.), *Buttevant: a medieval Anglo-French town in Ireland*, 51–66. Cork.
— 2013–14 'Halls, "hall-houses" and tower-houses: disentangling the needlessly entangled', *CSGJ* 27, 298–307.
— 2014a 'The pre-Norman "castle" in Connacht: a note on terminology', *JGAHS* 66, 26–32.
— 2104b 'Roesia de Verdon and the building of Castleroche, Co. Louth', *CSGJ* 28, 123–34.
— 2014c '*Aula* and *camera*: the architecture of public and private lives in medieval Irish castles', *Virtus: Jaarboek Voor Adelsgeschiedenis* 20, 39–69.
— 2015 *Medieval Irish buildings, 1100–1600*. Dublin.
— 2017a 'Trim before 1224: new thoughts on the caput of the de Lacy lordship in Ireland' in Duffy et al. (eds), *From Carrickfergus to Carcassonne*, 31–56.
— 2017b 'Kilcolman Castle, Co. Cork: a new interpretation of Edmund Spenser's residence in Plantation Munster', *International Journal of Historical Archaeology* 21, 223–39.
— 2018a 'Theory and medieval archaeology in Ireland and beyond: the narrative tradition and the archaeological imagination', *JIA* 26, 99–116.
— 2018b 'Archaeologies of a medieval Irish castle: thinking about Trim' in S.W. Silliman (ed.), *Engaging archaeology: 25 case studies in research practice*, 169–78. New Jersey.
— 2018c 'Frontiers of the archaeological imagination: rethinking landscape and identity in thirteenth-century Roscommon', *Landscapes* 19, 1, 66–79.
— 2018d 'Roscommon Castle, the Otherworld, and the True Cross' in Guy (ed.), *Castles: history, archaeology, landscape, architecture and symbolism*, 194–208.

— 2019a 'Feudal power in a Gaelic world? Contextualizing the encastellation of pre-Norman Ireland', *JIA* 28 (2019), 119–38.

— 2019b 'The archaeology of Ireland's long Middle Ages: retrospective and prospective', *European Journal of Post-Classical Archaeologies* 9, 299–332.

— 2019c 'Invasion hypotheses', *AI* 33, 2, 36–39.

— 2019d 'Meelick friary's hidden history', *AI* 33, 3, 38–41.

O'Keeffe, Tadhg and Coughlan, Margaret 2003 'The chronology and formal affinities of the Ferns donjon, Co. Wexford' in Kenyon and O'Conor (eds), *The medieval castle in Ireland and Wales*, 133–48.

O'Keeffe, Tadhg and Liddiard, Rob 2016 'King John (d.1216), castle-builder', *AI* 31, 3 (2016), 32–5.

O'Keeffe, Tadhg and MacCotter, Paul 2020 'Ireland's oldest stone castle', *AI* 34, 1 (2020), 14–18.

O'Keeffe, Tadhg and Virtuani, Paolo 2020 'Reconstructing Kilmainham: the topography and architecture of the chief priory of the Knights Hospitaller in Ireland, c.1170–1349', *JMH* https://doi.org/10.1080/03044181.2020.1788626.

O'Keeffe, Tadhg and Whelan, David 2019–20 'Ireland's Pembroke? The cylindrical great tower of Mocollop Castle', *CSGJ* 33 (2019–20), 269–79.

O'Sullivan, Aidan, McCormick, Finbar, Kerr, Thomas, Harney, Lorcan 2014 *Early medieval Ireland, AD 400–1100: the evidence from archaeological excavation*. Dublin.

Oram, Richard 2008 'Royal and lordly residence in Scotland c.1050 to c.1250: an historiographical review and critical revision', *Antiquaries Journal* 88, 165–89.

— 2012 'Dundonald, Doune and the development of the tower and hall in late medieval Scottish lordly residences', *CG* 25, 269–79.

— 2015a 'The incomplete exemplar: Doune Castle and the great tower in later medieval Scottish castles' in Oram (ed.), *'A house that thieves might knock at'*, 129–51.

— 2015b 'Towers and households in later medieval Scotland' in Oram (ed.), *'A house that thieves might knock at'*, 231–57.

— (ed.) 2015 *'A house that thieves might knock at'*, *Proceedings of the 2010 Stirling and 2011 Dundee Conferences on 'The Tower as Lordly Residence' and 'The Tower and the Household'*. Donington.

— 2019 'Introduction' in R. Oram (ed.), *'Urbs Turrita': urban towers in medieval and Renaissance Europe*, vii–xx. Donington.

Orpen, Goddard H. 1906 'Mote and bretasche building in Ireland', *English Historical Review* 21, 417–44.

— 1907a 'Motes and Norman castles in Ireland', *JRSAI* 37, 123–52

— 1907b 'Athlone Castle: its early history, with notes on some neighbouring castles', *JRSAI* 37, 257–76.

— 1911 *Ireland under the Normans*, vol. 1. Oxford.

O'Sullivan, Harold, 2006 *Dundalk*. Irish Historic Towns Atlas 16, Royal Irish Academy, Dublin.

Platt, Colin 1982 *The castle in medieval England and Wales*. London.

Poisson, Jean-Michel 1994 'Église et château sur le site de Villars' in P. Guichard et al. (eds), *Papauté, monachisme et théories politiques*, vol. 2, 763–75. Lyon.

Pollock, Dave and Manning, Conleth 2017 'Description of the castle and thoughts on its building history' in Pollock, *Barryscourt Castle*, 29–54.

Pollock, Dave 2017 *Barryscourt Castle, Co. Cork: archaeology, history and architecture*. Dublin.

Pounds, Norman 1990 *The medieval castle in England and Wales*. Cambridge.

Pringle, Denys 1996 *Craigmillar Castle*. Revised ed. Edinburgh.

Prodéo, Frédéric, Marembert, Fabrice, and Massan, Patrick 2006 'Pineuilh, La Mothe (Gironde): une résidence aristocratique à la charnière de l'An Mill', *Archéologie du Midi médiéval. Supplément* 4, 419–24.

Proust, Raymond 1981 'Discussion du Rapport I (La motte)' in 'Les fortifications de terre en Europe occidentale du Xe au XIIe siècles (Colloque de Caen, 2–5 Octobre 1980)', *AM* 11, 32.

Quiney, Anthony 1999 'Hall or chamber? That is the question. The use of rooms in post-conquest houses', *Architectural History* 42, 24–46

Racinet, Philippe 2008 'Phase 1: la construction de la motte (début Xe siècle)' in 'Le site castral de Boves (Somme) du Xe au XVIIe siècle. Bilan des recherches archéologiques 2001–2006', *Revue archéologique de Picardie* 1–2, 17–24.

Remfry, Paul, 2005 *Montgomery Castle, a royal fortress of Henry III.* Worcester.

Renn, Derek 1993 'Burhgeat and gonfanon: two sidelights from the Bayeux Tapestry', *Anglo-Norman Studies* 16, 178–98.

Renoux, Anne (ed.) 1987 *Aux marches du palais: qu'est-ce qu'un palais médiéval? Données historiques et archéologique.* Caen.

— 1991 *Fécamp. Du palais ducal au palais de Dieu.* Paris.

— 1997 'Palais et souveraineté en Francie occidentale (fin IXe-début XIII siècle)' in É. Magnou-Nortier (ed.), *Aux sources de la gestion publique III, Hommes de pouvoir, ressources et lieux de pouvoir (Ve–XIIIe siècles)*, 227–62. Lille.

— 2002 '*Palatium* et *castrum* en France du Nord (fin IXe – début XIIIe siècle)' in Meirion-Jones et al., *The seigneurial residence in western Europe*, 15–25.

— 2018 *Château et pouvoirs en Champagne: Montfélix, un castrum comtal aux portes d'Épernay.* Turnhout.

Reuter, Timothy 1997 'The "feudal revolution"', *Past and Present* 155, 177–95.

Reynolds, Susan 1994 *Fiefs and vassals: the medieval evidence reinterpreted.* Oxford.

Riou, S. and Marteaux, F. 2012 'Une motte castrale dans le contexte des recompositions politiques au tournant de l'an mil (Région Centre, Indre-et-Loire)', *Revue archéologique du Centre de la France* 51, 189–216.

Robinson, David M. 2010 *Tretower Court and Castle.* Cardiff.

Rolland Denis 1984 'Le château et les chatelains de Vic-sur-Aisne', *Mémoires de la Fédération des Sociétés d'histoire et d'archéologie de l'Aisne* 29, 139–76.

Ronnes, Hanneke 2012 'An archaeology of the noble house: the spatial organization of fifteenth- and sixteenth-century castles and country houses in the Low Countries and the privacy debate', *Medieval and Modern Matters* 3, 135–63.

St John Brooks, Eric 1946 'The grant of Castleknock to Hugh Tyrel', *JRSAI* 63 (1933), 206–20.

— 1950 *Knights' fees in counties Wexford, Carlow and Kilkenny, 13th–15th century.* Dublin.

Salamagne, Alain 2012 'La distribution des espaces dans le château français XIIe-XIVe siècle' in G. Danet, J. Kerhervé and A. Salamagne (eds), *Châteaux et modes de vie au temps des Ducs de Bretagne*, 177–96. Tours.

Salch, Charles-Laurent 1979 *Dictionnaire des châteaux et des fortifications du moyen âge en France.* Strasbourg.

Salter, Mike 2000 *The castles of Kent.* Malvern.

— 2004a *The castles of Connacht.* Malvern.

— 2004b *The castles of north Munster.* Malvern.

— 2004c *The castles of south Munster.* Malvern.

Samson, Ross 1987 'The Merovingian nobleman's home: castle or villa?', *JMH* 13, 4, 287–315.

Saunders, Andrew D. 1980 'Lydford Castle, Devon', *MA* 24, 123–86.

— 2017 'Castles and fortification' in P.E. Szarmach et al. (eds), *Routledge revivals: medieval England (1998): an encyclopedia*, 163–5. London.

Scott, A.B. and Martin, F.X. (eds) 1978 *Expugnatia Hibernica: the Conquest of Ireland by Giraldus Cambrensis*. Dublin.

Séraphin, Gilles 1999 'Salles et châteaux gascons, un modèle de maisons fortes', *BM* 157, 1, 11–42.

— 2006 'Les tours féodales du Quercy' *Archéologie du Midi médiéval*. Supplement 4, 127–38.

Shapland, Michael G. 2019 *Anglo-Saxon towers of lordship*. Oxford.

Sherlock, Rory 2006 'Cross-cultural occurrences of mutations in tower house architecture: evidence for cultural homogeneity in late medieval Ireland?', *JIA* 15, 73–91

— 2011a 'The evolution of the Irish tower-house as a domestic space', *PRIA* 111C, 115–40.

— 2011b 'An introduction to the history and architecture of Bunratty Castle' in R.A. Stalley (ed.), *Limerick and south-west Ireland: medieval art and architecture*. Transactions of the British Archaeological Association XXXIV, 202–18.

— 2013 'Using new techniques to date old castles', *AI* 27, 2 (2013), 19–23.

— 2014a 'Hall-houses' in Moss (ed.), *Art and architecture of Ireland*, I, 352–4.

— 2014b 'Tower houses' in Moss (ed.), *Art and architecture of Ireland*, I, 35–56.

— 2015 'The spatial dynamic of the Irish tower house hall' in McAlister and Barry (eds), *Space and settlement in medieval Ireland*, 86–109.

— 2017 'Barryscourt castle: chronology and context', in Pollock (eds), *Barryscourt Castle, Co. Cork*, 286–92.

Shopkow, Leah (ed.) 2010 *The history of the hounts of Guines and lords of Ardres*. Philadelphia, 2010.

Spiegel, Gabrielle M. 1990 'History, historicism, and the social logic of the text in the Middle Ages', *Speculum* 65, 1, 59–86.

Stalley, Roger 1971 *Architecture and sculpture in Ireland, 1150–1350*. Dublin.

— 1992 'The Anglo-Norman keep at Trim: its architectural implications', *AI* 6, 4, 16–19.

Stell, Geoffrey 2011 'Foundations of a castle culture' in A. Dakin, M. Glendinning and A. MacKechnie (eds), *Scotland's castle culture*, 3–34. Edinburgh.

— 2014–15 'Scottish "hall-houses": the origins and development of a modern castellological concept', *CSGJ* 28, 134–9.

Swallow, Rachel E. 2019 'Living the dream: the legend, lady and landscape of Caernarfon Castle, Gwynedd, north Wales', *Archaeologia Cambrensis* 219, 153–95.

Sweetman, David 1979 'Archæological excavations at Ferns Castle, Co. Wexford', *PRIA* 79C, 217–45.

— 1992 'Aspects of early thirteenth-century castles in Leinster', *CG* 15, 325–34.

— 1998 'The hall-house in Ireland', *AI* 12, 3, 13–16.

— 1999 *Medieval castles of Ireland*. Cork.

— 2003 'The hall-house in Ireland' in Kenyon and O'Conor (eds), *The medieval castle in Ireland and Wales*, 121–32.

Tabraham, Chris 1988 'The Scottish tower-house as lordly residence', *Proceedings of the Society of Antiquaries of Scotland* 118, 267–76.

— 1993a *Threave Castle*. Revised ed. Edinburgh.

— 1993b *Smailholm Tower*. Edinburgh.

— 1994 *Lochleven Castle*. Edinburgh.

Thompson, Michael W. 1960 'Recent excavations in the keep of Farnham Castle, Surrey', *MA* 4, 81–94.

— 1995 *The medieval hall: the basis of secular domestic life, 600–1600 AD*. Aldershot.

Tietzsch-Tyler, Daniel 2011 'Reconstructing the earl of Desmond's Castle, Newcastle West, Co. Limerick', *NMAJ* 51, 1–25.

— 2013 'King John's Castle: staged development, imperfect realization', *NMAJ* 53, 135–71.

— 2018a 'Carrickfergus and the revolution in castle design, *c.*1200' in Duffy et al. (eds), *From Carrickfergus to Carcassonne*, 77–106.

— 2018b 'Innovative castle design on the western fringe of the Angevin empire' in Guy (ed.), *Castles: history, archaeology, landscape, archaeology and symbolism*, 105–28.

Tock, B.-M. 1998 'Remarques sur le vocabulaire du château dans les textes diplomatiques français et belges antérieurs à 1200' in F.-X. Cuche (ed.), *La vie de château*, 13–31. Strasbourg.

Todd, James H. 1867 *Cogadh Gáedhel re Gallaibh. The war of the Gáedhel with the Gaill*. London.

Toubert, Pierre 1973 *Les structures du Latium médiéval: Le Latium méridional et la Sabine du IXe siecle a la fin du XIIe siècle*. 2 vols. Rome.

Trachtenberg, Marvin 2001 'Desedimenting time: Gothic column/paradigm shifter', *Res: Anthropology & Aesthetics* 40, 5–27.

Trotter, David 2001 'The ups and downs of the dongeon', *Castle Studies Group Newsletter* 15, 15.

Ua Cróinín, Risteárd and Breen, Martin 1986 'Daingean Ui Bhigin Castle, Quin, Co. Clare', *The Other Clare*, 10, 52–3.

Valente, Mary E. 2015 'Fleets, forts and the geography of Toirdelbach Ua Conchobair's bid for the high-kingship' in McAlister and Barry (eds), *Space and settlement in medieval Ireland*, 48–63.

Vallery-Radot, Jean 1929 'Note sur les chapelles hautes dédiées à Saint Michel' *BM* 88, 453–78.

Van Strydonck, M. and Vanthournout, C. 1996 'Dating the "Hoge Andjoen" motte at Werken (Prov. W. Fl.)' in M. Lodewijckx (ed.), *Archaeological and historical aspects of west-European societies*, 441–52. Leuven.

Vendryes, Joseph 1987 *Lexique étymologique de l'irlandais ancient: Lettre C*. Paris.

Verbruggen, J.F. 1950 'Note sur le sens des mots castrum, castellum, et quelques autres expressions qui désignent des fortifications', *Revue belge de philologie et d'histoire* 28, 147–55.

Waterman, D.M. 1956 'Moylough Castle, Co. Galway', *JRSAI* 86, 73–6.

— 1959 'Excavations at Lismahon, Co. Down', *MA* 3, 139–76.

— 1963 'Excavations at Duneight, Co. Down', *UJA* 26, 55–78.

— 1968 'Rectangular keeps of the thirteenth century at Grenan (Kilkenny) and Glanworth (Cork)', *JRSAI* 98, 67–73.

Waterman, D.M. and Collins, A.E.P. 1952 'Excavations at Greencastle, Co. Down, 1951', *UJA* 15, 87–102.

Westropp, Thomas J. 1898–1900 'Notes on the lesser castles or "peel towers" of the County Clare', *PRIA*, 5, 348–65.

— 1916–17 'On certain typical earthworks and ring-walls in the County Limerick. Part II: the royal forts in Coshlea (continued)', *PRIA* 33, 444–92.

Wheatley, Abigail 2004 *The idea of the castle in medieval England*. York.

White, Hayden 1973 *Metahistory: the historical imagination in nineteenth-century Europe*. Baltimore and London.

Whitehead, Christiania 2003 *Castles of the mind*. Cardiff.

Wiggins, Ken 2016 *A place of great consequence: archaeological excavations at King John's Castle, Limerick, 1990–8*. Dublin.

Williams, Ann 1986 '"A bell-house and a *burhgeat*": lordly residence in England before the Norman conquest' in C. Harper-Bill and R. Harvey (eds), *The ideals and practice of medieval knighthood*, 221–40. Woodbridge.

Williams, Diane M. and Kenyon, John R. (eds) 2010 *The impact of the Edwardian castles in Wales*. Oxford.

Wilson, Christopher 1990 *The Gothic cathedral: the architecture of the great church, 1130–1530*. London.

Wood, Margaret 1935 'Norman domestic architecture', *Archaeological Journal* 92, 167–242.

Wood-Martin, William G. 1886 *The lake dwellings of Ireland*. Dublin.

Woolgar, Christopher 1999 *The great household in late medieval England*. London.

Index